Inclusive Education for Social Change

Inclusive Education for Social Change
NEP 2020
Key Transforming Agent

Editors

Jasim Ahmad
Aerum Khan
Ansar Ahmad

SHIPRA

And the project is funded by ICSSR, New Delhi

₹ 595; US$ 16
ISBN: 978-93-91978-60-0

2024
First Published in India

Inclusive Education for Social Change: NEP 2020
Key Transforming Agent

Published by:
SHIPRA PUBLICATIONS
LG 18-19, Pankaj Central Market
I.P. Ext., Patparganj, Delhi 110092, India
+91 11 47322068; 96500 28065, 9810522367
info@shiprapublication.com
www.shiprapublication.com

Foreword

Inclusive education represents a source of optimism and advancement in our continually evolving society, embodying the notion that each person, irrespective of their background, capabilities, or circumstances, is entitled to receive quality education and equal chances for personal development. In the face of the intricacies of the contemporary world, it is crucial to endeavour towards establishing inclusive educational settings that nurture societal transformation and empower disadvantaged groups.

In line with this vision, we take pride in introducing '*Inclusive Education for Social Change: NEP 2020 - Key Transforming Agents*' a compiled publication delving into the transformative influence of inclusive education in shaping a more fair and all-encompassing society. This compilation amalgamates a varied array of viewpoints, perspectives, and research discoveries from prominent academics, practitioners, and proponents within the realm of education.

The sections contained in this publication explore diverse facets of inclusive education, spanning from theoretical frameworks and policy standpoints to pragmatic approaches and illustrative case studies. Through meticulous scrutiny and empirical substantiation, the contributors illuminate the obstacles and openings inherent in the quest for inclusive education geared towards societal transformation.

At the core of this publication lies a profound dedication to advocating for social justice and fairness in education. We are staunch believers that inclusive education serves not just as a vehicle for academic accomplishments but as an inherent human entitlement with the capacity to revolutionize lives and societies. By embracing diversification, fostering empathy, and dismantling hindrances to learning, inclusive education possesses the potential to bridge gaps, challenge preconceptions, and cultivate a more inclusive and empathetic society.

The voyage towards inclusive education is fraught with challenges. From addressing structural disparities to surmounting ingrained attitudes and prejudices, there exist numerous hurdles that necessitate confrontation along the path. Nevertheless, the sections in this publication provide invaluable perceptions and practical methodologies for navigating these challenges and furthering the advocacy for inclusive education.

An essential theme explored within this publication is the function of inclusive education in propelling social transformation. Through case studies and practical instances, the contributors showcase how inclusive education can embolden marginalized individuals and communities, champion diversification and inclusivity, and nurture a culture of empathy and comprehension.

This book underscores the significance of cooperation and collaboration in propelling the agenda of inclusive education forward. By uniting stakeholders from various sectors – encompassing educators, policymakers, researchers, and community influencers – we can collaboratively work towards constructing inclusive educational frameworks that cater to the requirements of all learners.

I extend profound appreciation to the individuals who have graciously imparted their knowledge and perspectives within this compilation. My appreciation is also extended to the editors, and publishing personnel whose contributions have been integral to the growth and dissemination of this publication.

I believe that the book '*Inclusive Education for Social Change: NEP 2020 – Key Transforming Agents*' will function as a valuable asset for educators, policymakers, scholars, and proponents dedicated to advancing inclusive education and fostering positive societal transformations. May this publication stimulate fresh concepts, initiate significant dialogues, and propel initiatives towards a future that is more inclusive and just for all.

Prof. Mohammad Shakeel
Officiating Vice Chancellor
Jamia Millia Islamia

Acknowledgements

It gives us immense pleasure to recall all the university officers, faculty members, and the funding agency who helped at all stages of Jamia International Conference on Education (JICE-2024), whose final published book is now in hand.

We first and foremost thank Prof. Eqbal Hussain, Vice Chancellor, Jamia Millia Islamia for guiding us at all stages of the conference. Prof. Nazim Husain Jafri, Registrar, Jamia Millia Islamia has been very supportive during the conference preparation and organisation.

We are indebted to Prof. H.C.S. Rathore, Chairperson, NRC, NCTE & former Vice Chancellor, Central University of South Bihar, and Prof. Dhananjay Joshi, Vice Chancellor, Delhi Teachers University for gracing the occasions of Inaugural and Valedictory sessions respectively as chief guests. We thank Prof. Jyotsna Pattnaik, California State University, Long Beach, USA, Prof. Theodoros Karakasidis, University of Thessaly, Greece, for delivering the keynote address during inaugural and valedictory functions and Prof. Joey Martinez Dela Cruz, University of Abra, Philippines, for his plenary talk in the valedictory session of the conference.

The Dean, Faculty of Education, Prof. Sara Begum and Head, Department of Teacher Training and Non-formal Education, Prof. Jessy Abraham have extended all kinds of support throughout the conference planning and execution. Without their support, it could not have materialised in the grand way it went on.

We acknowledge and thank our superannuated faculty members Prof. Mohammad Akhtar Siddiqui, former Chairman, NCTE, for delivering the keynote address, Prof. Najma Amin, Prof. Shoeb Abdullah, Prof. Ahrar Hussain, and Prof. Ilyas Husain for chairing the technical sessions and guiding us whenever we approached them for their support and guidance. We also thank Prof. Mohd. Miyan, former Vice Chancellor, MANUU, and Prof. Talat Aziz, former Dean, Faculty of Education, JMI for their benign presence in the inaugural session and the moral support they provided throughout the preparation of the conference.

We acknowledge and thank the key members of the conference organising team - Prof. Sara Begum, Prof. Jessy Abraham, Prof. Naheed Zahoor, Prof. Kartar Singh, Prof. Kaushal Kishore, Prof. Savita Kaushal, Prof. Roohi Fatima, Dr. Dori Lal, Dr. Ajit Kumar Bohet, Dr. Sameer Babu M, Dr. Raisa Khan, Dr. Sajjad Ahmad, Dr. Andleeb, Dr. Sarita Kumari, Dr. Ali Haider, Dr. Shadma Yasmeen, Dr. Aysha, Dr Saman Zaki and Ms. Nazneen for their constant support and contributions towards the organisation of JICE-2024.

Thanks are due to all faculty members from both departments, Department of Teacher Training and Non-formal Education (IASE) and Department of Educational Studies for their cooperation in reviewing papers, convening/ chairing/ co-chairing technical sessions and doing all the associated works during the entire process of JICE-2024.

We must thank the Indian Council of Social Science Research (ICSSR), the agency which funded the organisation of the international conference JICE-2024. Without the financial support of ICSSR, it would not be possible to organise the conference on such a big scale.

It is important to mention that we decided to publish ISBN books instead of publishing papers in the form of proceedings with a vision to make the researchers' work wider dissemination. It is generally observed that proceedings are read by a fewer number of people, but books are more read as they reach in the form of course material for certain programmes and are useful for teachers as well as students. This book will be very useful for teachers and students of Education in the specified area of study. We thank and acknowledge the worthwhile and important piece of work contributed by researchers and faculty members for their presentation in the conference and allowing us to publish it in the form of a chapter in an edited book with an ISBN Number. We thank them all and wish to have the same support, motivation, and encouragement in our future conferences.

We acknowledge the utmost efforts and untiring day and night work of our scholars - Mr. Md. Ashique Husain, Ms. Zahra Kazmi, Ms. Soumya Panigrahi, Ms. Ambrin Khanam, Ms. Aditi Tiwari, Ms. Sehar Nigar, Ms. Shahla Khanam, Mr. Sajuddin Saifi, Mr. Haroon Salmani, Mr. Mohd. Noor Alam, Ms Sania Noor, Mr. Dhananjay Kumar, Ms. Humaira Khatoon, Mr. Dheeraj Kumar, Ms. Maria Waseem, Ms. Samra Jamal, Ms. Shaista Tanweer, Mr. Mohammad Haider Raza, Mr. Nisar Ahmad, Ms. Khushnuda Bano, Dr. Noor Alam, and Mr. Taj Mohammad in the timely completion of all necessary preparations of the conference and its publication work including this book. We wish them all great success in their future endeavours.

Special appreciation is due to Mr. Sajuddin Saifi, research scholar, IASE for his sincere, dedicated, and rigorous efforts towards the content management and proofing of the manuscript.

We would like to extend our sincere thanks to all the contributors for their insightful work in the area. We would also like to convey our gratitude to those who have put great efforts and supported us during the publication of this book.

Editors

Contents

1
Introduction

In this edited volume, titled "Inclusive Education for Social Change," we have assembled a diverse ensemble of scholars, researchers, educators, and practitioners. They generously share their expertise and insights, shedding light on the intricate and rapidly evolving dynamics within the realm of inclusive education.

Gagana Bihari Suar, in his research "Implicit Gender Bias in Educational Materials: A Call for Inclusivity" addresses implicit gender bias in educational materials, focusing on aligning with NEP 2020 principles for inclusive and diverse content. It highlights the impact of biases on students' perceptions and values and emphasises the need to challenge traditional gender norms. The study methodically analysed a Class 9 English textbook, "The Priceless Gift," revealing instances of gender bias through character portrayals, dialogues, and language usage. The analysis showcases how the text reinforces conventional gender stereotypes, affecting students' perceptions and aligning with prior research findings on gender biases in educational content globally. The inter-rater reliability process confirmed high agreement among raters, validating the research findings. The analysis reveals how the male character is depicted as a soldier, emphasising strength and courage, while the female character is portrayed as a caregiver, aligning with traditional gender expectations. The study compares instances of bias with NEP 2020 objectives, highlighting misalignments with principles of holistic education, inclusivity, critical thinking, and diverse exploration. Implications for NEP 2020 include the necessity to challenge traditional gender norms, diversify perspectives, and promote critical thinking in educational materials. Recommendations to combat implicit bias involve revising content to represent diverse roles, implementing gender sensitivity training, introducing diverse role models, and promoting gender-neutral language. Additionally, diversifying literature selections with stories known for cultural richness and gender neutrality is suggested to create a more inclusive and equitable educational environment aligned with NEP 2020's goals.

Jamshed Ahmad in his study "Modern Education through Madrasas: Prospects and Challenges—A Study of the Selected Madrasas in Uttar Pradesh" delves into the integration of modern education into Madrasas in Uttar Pradesh, exploring prospects and challenges. It highlights the historical significance of Madrasas and the evolving need to incorporate modern subjects into their curriculum. Factors influencing modernisation efforts include religious education, modernisation initiatives, government support, and community perception. Challenges faced by Madrasas encompass infrastructure, teacher qualifications, financial constraints, and curriculum diversification. Recommendations for effective modern education through Madrasas include teacher training programmes, infrastructure development, curricular integration, digital integration, government collaboration, community engagement, and inclusive education policies. These measures aim to bridge the gap between traditional religious teachings and contemporary knowledge, ensuring a well-rounded education for students. The study emphasises the importance of collaborative efforts to address challenges and leverage opportunities for positive change in Madrasa education. Strategic initiatives focusing on curriculum diversification, teacher training, and infrastructure improvement are key to unlocking the full potential of Madrasas in Uttar Pradesh. The findings underscore the dynamic nature of modernising Madrasa education and advocate for a continued dialogue to enhance educational practices and promote inclusivity in the educational landscape.

Lalrochami Ralte and Prof. Lalbiakdiki Hnamte in the study "Paradigm Shift in Education of Children with Special Needs: With Special Reference to Mizoram" delve into the paradigm shift towards inclusive education, emphasising the integration of students with special needs into mainstream classrooms. It highlights the importance of technology, educator training, community involvement, and government support in fostering a more inclusive educational environment. The study explores the impact of the Rights of Persons with Disabilities Act of 1995 and its amendments in 2016, focusing on policies for children with special needs and their implementation in Mizoram state. Findings include initiatives such as resource rooms, special educators, accessible infrastructure, aids and appliances, teacher training, and community orientation programs aimed at supporting children with special needs. The evolution of policies under the RPWD Acts of 1995 and 2016 showcases enhancements in disability definitions, job reservations, and educational initiatives for persons with disabilities. The study in Mizoram evaluates the state's compliance with the RPWD Act, emphasising education, employment, accessibility, healthcare, social security, and legal aid for individuals with disabilities. The research underscores the ongoing efforts towards inclusive education for children with special needs, emphasising the need for comprehensive policy implementation, technology integration, educator empowerment, community engagement, and government support. By analysing the schemes, policies, and frameworks, the study aims to enhance inclusivity, empower individuals with disabilities, and foster a more equitable and supportive educational landscape.

Ali Asgar, Shabir Ahmed Wani and Parvesh Kumari in their study "National Education Policy 2020: Empowering the Socio-economically Disadvantaged Groups through Open Distance and Online Education" focus on the educational empowerment of disadvantaged groups in India, particularly through the

National Education Policy (NEP) 2020 and Open Distance Learning (ODL) initiatives. The study aims to analyse NEP 2020 provisions for disadvantaged groups, explore ODL's role in achieving policy objectives, and discuss prospects, challenges, and suggestions for effective NEP 2020 implementation by ODL institutions to benefit disadvantaged groups optimally. NEP 2020 emphasises inclusive education, aiming to achieve Sustainable Development Goal 4.3 for universal access to higher education. It addresses the educational condition of disadvantaged groups, highlighting enrolment disparities and dropout rates. The policy underscores equity and inclusion in higher education through constitutional provisions, government initiatives, funding, scholarships, and support systems for transparency and equality. NEP 2020's focus on gender-inclusive education, representation of minorities, and addressing illiteracy among women reflects a commitment to social justice and equality. ODL emerges as a cost-effective, innovative, and flexible mode of educational delivery, especially beneficial for disadvantaged groups facing socio-economic barriers. It provides opportunities for higher education on a large scale, offering flexibility, autonomy, and access to diverse learner groups. NEP 2020 recognises ODL's potential and recommends its effective use for participative and inclusive education, particularly for disadvantaged groups. The implementation of NEP 2020 poses challenges, including inadequate infrastructure, high costs, language barriers, unfavourable home environments, technical glitches, and teachers' attitudes. Addressing these challenges requires monitoring, funding for infrastructure, awareness campaigns, financial assistance, gender-inclusive initiatives, and creating an inclusive environment in higher education institutions. To enhance NEP 2020 implementation and benefit disadvantaged groups optimally, suggestions include maintaining transparency, removing barriers, increasing awareness, offering programmes in local languages, empowering women and transgenders, earmarking funds, creating inclusive environments, conducting teacher training, utilising technology effectively, collaboration, and continuous professional development. These measures aim to ensure equitable access to quality education, promote inclusion, and overcome barriers to educational empowerment for disadvantaged groups.

Dr Anil Manjhi and Rahul Tiwari explore "Transformative Pathways: Education of Transgender in the Post-NEP 2020 Framework – Addressing Issues, Concerns and Best Practices". Address the educational obstacles encountered by the Khwaja Siras (Transgender) community in India within the confines of the NEP 2020. Notwithstanding the NEP's stress on inclusivity, the Khwaja Siras community persists in facing exclusion in the realm of education. Attempts were initiated after the NALSA ruling of 2014, yet they have not yielded full efficacy owing to the absence of a comprehensive dissemination strategy and appropriate pedagogical approaches. The investigation strives to advance parity and fair admission to education for the Khwaja Siras community through the cultivation of a pedagogy that is welcoming to transgender individuals. This is underpinned by interviews conducted with twenty Khwaja Siras individuals representing diverse educational and professional spheres. The discoveries underscore the significance of cultural and social proficiency, gender awareness, and the employment of affirming language by educators. It underscores the necessity for an encompassing syllabus, secure environments, supportive services, and the formulation of policies to establish a nurturing and anxiety-free setting for the Khwaja Siras community within educational establishments.

Dr Madhu Singh and Sana Fatima in their study "Psychosocial Well-being of Children with Learning Disabilities: Impact of Parental Support" investigate the relationship between children with learning difficulties' psychosocial well-being and the degree of parental support. The study contrasts groups with high and low levels of parental support across five important psychosocial variables: behaviour patterns, social interaction, self-concept, parental support, and home environment. Data from 52 participants are used, and t-tests are used in the analysis. The study's objectives are to evaluate mean variances and find patterns and distinctions within these categories. The findings shed light on the intricate interactions between psychosocial factors and parental support, which can be helpful for educators, parents, and other professionals working with children who have learning issues. The study also emphasises how critical it is to comprehend these dynamics in order to successfully meet the needs of kids with learning impairments.

Dr. Shiney Vashisht in her research focuses on the "Denotified Communities: Educational Status, Aspirations and Access – A Study of Sansi and Sapera Communities of Delhi". Historically labelled as Criminal Tribes under the Criminal Tribes Act of 1871 during colonial rule, these communities were subjected to geographical and social restrictions due to perceived associations with criminality. Despite the removal of this act in 1949, denotified communities like Sansi and Sapera continue to face socio-economic marginalisation and stigma. The study, conducted as part of a PhD research, examines the impact of societal and constitutional injustices on these communities and investigates their educational status, access to government support, and aspirations, particularly in the context of the additional challenges posed by the COVID-19 pandemic. The findings shed light on the enduring stigma and socio-economic challenges faced by these communities, highlighting the need for targeted interventions and support measures to address their needs effectively.

Fariha Siddiqui and Dr. Sajjad Ahmad in the study "As it Unfolds: Schooling, Aspirations and Muslim Children's lived Experiences in the Walled City of Delhi" investigate the unique childhood experiences of young Muslim children aged 5-7 years in Shahjahanabad (or 'Purani Dilli'), focusing on how their schooling and engagement with their densely populated and culturally rich environment shape their perceptions and aspirations. Utilising ethnographic methods and children's drawings, the study explores the notion of schools as 'leisure spaces' amidst the crowded living conditions, and how such environments impact the children's sense of space, aspirations, and life outside school. The findings suggest that the high-density residential areas, coupled with the area's economic activities, offer these children a distinct set of experiences and perceptions, markedly different from those in less congested environments.

Mahvish Bano, Dr. Vidyapati and Dr. J.P. Sahae in their research delve into the current landscape of Madrasa education within the framework of the National Education Policy emphasis on inclusivity and addressing the educational disparities among minority communities in their paper "Inclusion and Minorities: A Special View on Madrasa Education System". It recognises the historical significance of Madrasas in providing education to marginalised segments of Muslim society and aims to analyse their present role, shortcomings, and policy concerns. Through data collection via open-ended questionnaires and subsequent numerical and theoretical coding, the study sheds light on key features, importance, pedagogical approaches, and attitudes of stakeholders towards Madrasa education. It underscores the necessity of collaborative efforts to ensure full inclusion and proposes remedial measures to enhance the quality and effectiveness of Madrasa education, thereby aligning with the NEP's overarching objectives.

Mohammad Haider Raza's study addresses the issues and concerns encountered by madrasas and other minority educational institutions in India in his paper "Madrasas and Other Minority Educational Institutions: Issues and Concerns", notwithstanding their pivotal role in dispensing religious instruction and contributing to personal and national progress. Challenges from within encompass inflexible curricula and teaching methods, absence of steady financial resources, and inadequately trained educators. External challenges arise from governmental intervention masked as modernisation efforts and accusations of promoting terrorism directed at madrasas. The primary objective of the study is to bring to light these issues and suggest remedies to tackle the distinct challenges confronted by these establishments, ensuring the effective realisation of their intended objectives.

Mohd Farhan and Dr. Aerum Khan's paper "Educational Status of Muslims in India: The AISHE Report 2020-21" examines the educational status of Muslims in India using data from the AISHE report 2020-21. Despite India's diversity, with various cultures, religions, castes, and communities, educational attainment varies across these groups. Muslims, as the largest minority community and the second-largest religious group, face challenges in education despite government initiatives aimed at their development. The AISHE survey, initiated in 2011, provides comprehensive data on various educational parameters such as teacher numbers, student enrolment, infrastructure, and financial aspects, aiding policy decisions. The 2020-21 AISHE was conducted online for the first time, allowing Higher Education Institutions (HEIs) to submit data through the Web Data Capture Format. The paper finds the following issues using this latest AISHE data Enrolment Decline: The AISHE Report indicates a concerning 8% decline in Muslim community enrolment in higher education, contrasting with improvements seen in other marginalised groups like SCs, STs, and OBCs. Gender Disparities: Despite challenges, a positive trend emerges with more female Muslim students enrolled in higher education compared to their male counterparts, signalling progress in breaking societal barriers. Representation in Teaching Staff: The report reflects a lower representation of teachers from the Muslim community, accounting for 5.6% of total teachers, with a higher percentage of female teachers compared to male ones. State-wise Disparities: State-wise data in the report can provide insights into the educational landscape for Muslims, PWDs, and other minority communities, shedding light on regional variations and challenges.

Mohd Zuber and Dr. Eram Nasir in the manuscript concentrate on exploring the perspectives of educators concerning students with dysgraphia in inclusive educational settings. It underscores the significance of favourable teacher outlooks in establishing inclusive learning environments for individuals with dysgraphia. Dysgraphia, which impacts writing abilities, exhibits a prevalence rate between 5% and 20%, with a growing incidence. Despite the extensive examination of various learning disabilities, dysgraphia remains a comparatively under-researched area. The objective of the investigation is to scrutinise the experiences, obstacles, and instructional approaches of teachers in Delhi government schools when educating students with dysgraphia in inclusive environments. The aim is to determine how educators assist dysgraphia learners, analyse the challenges encountered, and propose methods to enhance professional growth and inclusive instructional strategies. The study will evaluate writing difficulties among primary school students to gain insight into the obstacles teachers face when instructing individuals with writing difficulties, thereby offering suggestions for future research endeavours. The manuscript emphasises the inadequacy of teachers' awareness, training, resources, and collaborative efforts, impeding the provision of effective assistance to individuals with dysgraphia.

Tanvi Pahwa and Dr Faijullah Khan in their study entitled "Sustainable Development through Inclusive Education: A Focus on Twice-Exceptional Learners in Inclusive Schools" focus on twice-exceptional (2E) learners, who are both gifted and have disabilities, within inclusive education frameworks aligned with Sustainable Development Goal 4 (SDG 4) - Quality Education. It explores challenges, impact on learning, and proposes innovative strategies based on a systematic literature review. Inclusive education is crucial for empowering twice-exceptional learners, providing tailored support, fostering acceptance, and enabling meaningful contributions. Recognising their dual exceptionalities and accommodating their needs creates a positive educational experience, promoting equity and sustainable development. Identification of 2E learners is complex due to masking effects where strengths may obscure weaknesses and vice versa. Addressing challenges in learning and development requires understanding asynchronous growth rates, social and emotional impacts, and accommodating unique needs within educational settings. Differentiated instruction, strengths-based approaches, Universal Design for Learning (UDL), personalised learning, social-emotional learning, IEPs, peer support, and continuous professional development are key strategies to support 2E learners, promoting inclusive and equitable quality education as per SDG 4. Combining differentiation, IEPs, and supportive environments offers a comprehensive framework for meeting the unique needs of 2E learners, enhancing academic and social-emotional development. These practices align with inclusive education principles, promote universal design of learning, and contribute to achieving SDG 4 goals.

Nayab Parveen in her research addresses the issues and challenges faced by students with disabilities in accessing higher education in India. It emphasises the role of accessibility in enabling equitable access to higher education for students with disabilities, allowing them to participate fully and perform well. While global statistics suggest that about 15% of the world's population has disabilities; in India, based on 2011 census data, 2.21% of the population is disabled. Despite being the third-largest higher education system globally, only 0.24% of students with disabilities are enrolled in higher education institutions. The study aims to examine the physical accessibility of higher education facilities for students with disabilities, focusing on infrastructure and learning-related facilities. It discusses regulations and resources available for students with disabilities and highlights the challenges they encounter in accessing higher education, including institutional, environmental, and attitudinal barriers.

Sana Mukhtar Khan and Dr. Eram Nasir in the paper entitled "Employment Challenges and Support Strategies for Dyslexic Adults: A Literature Review." explore the employment challenges faced by dyslexic adults and propose support strategies to address these issues. It emphasises that while dyslexic individuals may encounter obstacles in the workplace, they also possess strengths that contribute to their success. Through a comprehensive literature review spanning from 2002 to 2022, the study identifies various challenges such as difficulties in recruitment, limited access to accommodations, and societal stigma. However, it highlights the potential for dyslexic adults to excel in their careers with the implementation of supportive interventions. The paper calls for employers, policymakers, and educators to create inclusive environments by offering tailored accommodations, promoting awareness, implementing supportive policies, and providing targeted training programs. These efforts aim to unlock the full potential of dyslexic adults and enhance their professional success.

Shahla Khanam and Dr. Md Abu Tarique explore the consequences of communal riots on the discontinuation of studies among primary school students, specifically examining those affected by the Muzaffarnagar riots in 2013 in their paper "Impact of Communal Violence on the Dropout Rates: A Case Study of Victim Children in Muzaffarnagar Riots". It emphasises that societal and political elements, such as violence, play a substantial role in the decision of children to cease their education in impacted regions. The importance of education in the growth of a child and advancement of a community is significant; however, communal turmoil hinders the ability of many children to attain education. By conducting on-site surveys in areas affected by the riots, the analysis scrutinises information from a sample of 100 children between the ages of 6 and 14 who encountered communal violence in 2013. The results demonstrate that 70% of these children terminated their schooling that year, with a higher rate of discontinuation observed among girls (62%) in comparison to boys (36%). This emphasises the adverse consequences of communal unrest on the educational pursuits of children and their future opportunities.

Sheikh Mohammed Farhan and Dr. Sarika Tomar examine the role of women in addressing educational and socioeconomic disparities within socioeconomically disadvantaged communities in their paper "Role of Gender in Education of Socio-economically Disadvantaged Groups". It emphasises that despite facing gender inequality and socioeconomic challenges, women can be pivotal in promoting education and economic empowerment, especially for girls. The study discusses the impact of the National Education Policy (NEP) 2020 on gender-based education and explores women's roles as mentors, advocates, and educators in fostering ambition, questioning societal norms, and providing quality learning opportunities. Additionally, it discusses how entrepreneurship, economic empowerment, and capacity-building programmes can contribute to community development through women's involvement. Recognising the link between socioeconomic well-being and education, the research underscores women's contributions to health, parental involvement, and community support networks. It advocates for policy changes to benefit socioeconomically disadvantaged populations and emphasises women's empowerment as a strategic approach for holistic development and gender equality. Policymakers, educators, and practitioners seeking to address disparities in education and socioeconomic growth in marginalised areas can benefit from the insights provided in this study.

2

Implicit Gender Bias in Educational Materials

A Call for Inclusivity

Gagana Bihari Suar

Introduction

The imperative for aligning educational materials with the principles of NEP 2020 becomes all the more apparent in light of the profound influence that textbooks and reading materials wield over students' educational journeys. NEP 2020 advocates, "Any biases and stereotypes in school curriculum will be removed, and more material will be included that is relevant and relatable to all communities (p. 28)".

Educational materials wield substantial influence on young learners' perceptions and values, either reinforcing or challenging biases. NEP 2020's emphasis on holistic development and inclusivity underscores the necessity for diverse and bias-free content. However, materials with implicit gender bias limit students to traditional roles, hindering their growth and critical thinking. This research, exemplified by "The Priceless Gift," aims to address and rectify gender bias in educational materials, aligning with NEP 2020's principles to empower students as critical thinkers in an inclusive, diverse educational environment, fostering a society that acknowledges and celebrates all voices.

Literature Review

Extensive research both in India and internationally has revealed a persistent issue of gender bias in educational materials, inadvertently reinforcing traditional gender norms (Dhiman, 2023; Stewart et al., 2021). This literature review offers a comprehensive overview of significant studies on this topic, with a central focus on addressing implicit bias in line with the principles of the NEP 2020. For example, Kumar et al. (2022) identified implicit bias in Hollywood movies, where male characters are associated with diverse themes, while female characters are often confined to romance. Similarly, Singh & Bammi's 2013 analysis of Indian (Bhopal city) textbooks revealed a glaring lack of female representation, perpetuating stereotypes.

Islam and Asadullah's 2018 study in Malaysia, Indonesia, Pakistan, and Bangladesh exposed a pro-male bias in English language textbooks. According to UNESCO (2008), gender bias in textbooks acts as a hidden obstacle to gender equality. Additionally, Aina and Cameron's 2011 research in Nigeria underscored the urgent need to challenge traditional gender norms in educational content.

In contrast, NCERT's "Position Paper on Gender Issues in Education" in 2006 advocated for gender-sensitive pedagogy and inclusive curricula, significantly contributing to discussions on gender equality in Indian education. Also, Aydınoglu's 2014 research in Turkey highlighted the scholarly interest in addressing gender bias in English Language Teaching coursebooks at various educational levels, from primary schools to universities.

Foundational gender theories, such as Connell's "hegemonic masculinity" and Swain's insights on "masculinity in education," offer broader perspectives on how gender biases shape educational materials in diverse cultural contexts.

These reviewed literatures emphasise that gender bias in educational materials is a global concern, not limited to Odisha, and underline the necessity of challenging implicit gender bias in educational materials to align with the goals of holistic development and inclusivity outlined in NEP 2020. Eliminating gender bias is crucial for creating equitable and diverse educational content. This review advocates for gender-neutral and inclusive materials to support these objectives.

The Study

Methodology

This research applied a rigorous methodology to analyse implicit gender bias in the Class 9 English textbook, "The Priceless Gift," used in secondary schools in Odisha. The objective was to systematically identify instances of gender bias in the text, guided by predefined criteria and a structured analysis process. The selection of this educational material was pivotal due to its significance within the curriculum, allowing for a comprehensive examination of subtle gender biases. The assessment criteria included character portrayal, dialogues and interactions, occupations and activities, and language usage. These criteria helped uncover how traditional gender roles and stereotypes were reinforced in the text, such as the portrayal of the male character as a soldier and the female characters as vulnerable caregivers. The research process was thorough and systematic, aiming to shed light on implicit gender bias in educational content.

Analysis Process

The analysis process followed a systematic approach, commencing with an in-depth examination of "The Priceless Gift" to understand its narrative and context, identifying instances of gender bias like the portrayal of the male character as a soldier and female characters' roles in the kitchen. These instances were documented with context and concrete evidence, including quotes and excerpts. Thematic categorisation revealed patterns of gender bias, such as male dominance and female vulnerability, supported by both quantitative and qualitative analyses.

Inter-rater Reliability

The inter-rater reliability process involved three raters independently assessing "The Priceless Gift" for gender bias, followed by collaborative discussions to resolve discrepancies. Rater 1, trained in gender bias criteria and NEP 2020 objectives, identified instances such as the portrayal of a male character as a soldier and actively participated in discussions with other raters. Raters 2 and 3, also trained, identified examples such as male-dominated dialogues and worked collaboratively to resolve discrepancies and analyse the portrayal of female characters. The results showed a high level of agreement among the raters, validating the research findings. This collaborative and systematic approach minimised subjectivity, enhancing research credibility.

Analysis

The analysis of "The Priceless Gift" unveils implicit gender bias that conforms to traditional gender norms, specifically in the portrayal of male and female characters and their roles within the narrative, thus perpetuating conventional gender stereotypes. The male character, Franky, is depicted as a soldier, emphasising attributes associated with strength and courage, aligning with the traditional view of men as protectors and warriors. This portrayal aligns with prior research on gender biases in educational materials that often-cast male characters in strong, heroic roles.

Conversely, the female character, Maggie, is subtly characterised as a caregiver, displaying emotional connections to her brother, Franky, and her mother, Mrs. Bethy. This caregiving role aligns with longstanding gender expectations that relegate women to nurturing and domestic roles, indirectly endorsing the idea that women should primarily engage in caregiving responsibilities.

The implicit gender bias in "The Priceless Gift" is not unique but mirrors patterns found in previous research on gender biases within educational materials. These studies have consistently highlighted how conventional gender roles and stereotypes persist in various forms of content, such as textbooks and narratives. In this context, "The Priceless Gift" perpetuates traditional gender norms that could shape students' perceptions of gender roles.

The above analysis highlights the importance of addressing implicit gender bias in educational materials to promote inclusivity and equitable education, aligning with the objectives outlined in the National Education Policy (NEP) 2020. This methodical process ensured a comprehensive evaluation of gender bias within the text, as depicted in Table 1.

Table 1: Frequency of Male Dominance in Dialogues extracted from *The Priceless Gift* (2019)

Aspect	*Number of Instances*	*Certain Examples*
Male Character Portrayal	6	"As she was going out, she asked the cashier in a low voice, 'Is that gentleman an Indian?'" "My son is in Punjab. He is a soldier." • The male character in 'The Priceless Gift' is depicted as a soldier, implying strength. The male character is referred to as a 'gentleman' and a 'soldier,' emphasising honour and strength. "I chose the corner table, seated myself, and started skimming through the newspaper." "'No, Sir, I notice she has lunch here on Saturdays. She comes on payday only. Perhaps she does not earn much.'" "Maggie's face filled with gratitude. As she thanked me her voice choked." • The male character takes the lead in the conversation, which is evident when he initiates the interaction with Maggie. The use of "gentleman"- a sense of decorum and respect; men are seen as breadwinners; men are expected to be chivalrous and women to be grateful.
Female Character Portrayal	4	"At that moment I noticed a very young girl looking at me. Her eyes were large and they had a sad expression." "As she was going out, she asked the cashier in a low voice, 'Is that gentleman an Indian?' " 'Are you leaving today?' she asked. 'Yes,' I replied, 'today is the day of my departure.' " "'How can I ever thank you,' she said. 'Goodbye. Remember to write.'" Female characters like Maggie and her mother are shown as vulnerability and innocence, with Maggie's shy and hesitant demeanour, a sense of dependence or curiosity, traditional expectations of women being polite and grateful, which are the common stereotype associated with female characters.
Male-dominated Dialogues and Interactions	8	"I went up to her and took the chair opposite hers." "'May I know your name?" The male character initiates and leads the conversation, showcasing a power dynamic. Male character leading and initiating conversations.
Female-submissive Dialogues and Interactions	6	"The girl looked at me once more, and went out for now." "She was eating. I went up to her and took the chair opposite hers." "'Mother, 'said Maggie from the doorway, 'an Indian gentleman has come to see you.' "

Aspect	*Number of Instances*	*Certain Examples*
Male Character's Profession (Soldier)	3	"My brother is in India. He is a soldier." The male character's role as a soldier emphasizes strength, associated with bravery.
Female Characters' Domestic Activities	3	"The old woman asked eagerly. With a smile I stepped into the kitchen behind Maggie." "I am making cakes. People will come to buy them this evening. This is the way we make our living - lots of trouble."
Biased Language and Terminology	5	"gentleman" and "soldier;" "young girl" with "large, sad eyes." Can reflect societal stereotypes and expectations about gender roles and attributes.

Comparison with NEP 2020 Objectives

The analysis considered NEP 2020's holistic education, critical thinking, and inclusivity objectives when assessing gender bias instances in 'The Priceless Gift.' Table 2 compares gender bias with NEP 2020 goals, revealing misalignment with principles of holistic education, inclusivity, equitable education, critical thinking, and diverse field exploration.

Table 2: Comparing Gender Bias with NEP 2020 Objectives

Aspect	*NEP 2020 Objectives*	*Alignment with NEP 2020 Objectives*
Male Character Portrayal	Promotes holistic education.	Misalignment: Reinforces traditional gender norms, limiting the holistic portrayal of characters.
Female Character Portrayal	Fosters inclusivity and equitable education.	Misalignment: Portrays female characters as vulnerable, not aligned with inclusivity and equity principles.
Male-dominated Dialogues and Interactions	Encourages critical thinking and communication skills.	Misalignment: Fails to encourage diverse and balanced dialogues, impacting critical thinking.
Female-submissive Dialogues and Interactions	Fosters inclusivity and equitable education.	Misalignment: Promotes submissive interactions, not aligned with inclusivity and equity principles.
Male Character's Profession (Soldier)	Encourages cross-disciplinary learning and exploration.	Misalignment: Assigns traditional gender roles, limiting exploration of diverse professions.

Aspect	*NEP 2020 Objectives*	*Alignment with NEP 2020 Objectives*
Female Characters' Domestic Activities	Fosters inclusivity and equitable education.	Misalignment: Reinforces gender stereotypes in domestic roles, not aligned with inclusivity and equity principles.
Biased Language and Terminology	Promotes holistic education.	Misalignment: Uses language that emphasises traditional gender roles, affecting holistic portrayal.

Implications for NEP 2020

The analysis of "The Priceless Gift" reveals significant implications for NEP 2020, which aims to transform education by promoting inclusivity, holistic development, critical thinking, and equity. The presence of implicit gender bias in the text contradicts NEP 2020's objectives and highlights the need to challenge traditional gender norms, diversify perspectives, and foster critical thinking. It underscores the importance of teacher training, curriculum development, and creating inclusive learning materials to align with NEP 2020's principles and create an equitable and balanced learning environment.

Recommendations

To combat implicit gender bias in educational materials and align with the objectives of NEP 2020, comprehensive recommendations are proposed. These include revising educational materials to represent diverse roles for male and female characters, implementing teacher training programmes on gender sensitivity, introducing diverse role models, fostering critical analysis, involving diverse authors, engaging parents, and the community, establishing regular assessment, and promoting gender-neutral language. These measures aim to create a more inclusive and equitable educational environment in line with NEP 2020's principles. Furthermore, curriculum developers should actively seek gender balance in portrayals and diversify literature selections, like the stories in Indian literature in English mentioned, known for their cultural richness and absence of implicit gender bias. Selections, such as, Manoj Das's "The Crocodile and the Monkey", Ruskin Bond's "The Secret Garden", Sudha Murty's "The Dream Catcher", Chitra Banerjee Divakaruni's "Mrs. Dutta Writes a Letter", Fakir Mohan Senapati's "Rebati", Prativa Ray's "Yajnaseni", "The Churning of the Ocean (Samudra Manthan)", Parable: "The Story of the Salt Doll", R. K. Narayan's "A Horse and Two Goats", Kamala Das's "An Introduction", Rabindranath Tagore's "The Kabuliwala", Jhumpa Lahiri's "Interpreter of Maladies", and from the Upanishads: "The Two Birds" etc., are known for their diverse themes, cultural richness, and the absence of implicit gender bias, making them valuable for educational purposes.

These recommendations collectively offer a strategic roadmap for creating a more inclusive and equitable education system aligned with NEP 2020's objectives.

Conclusion

The analysis of "The Priceless Gift" underscores the pervasive issue of implicit gender bias in educational materials, with profound implications for the principles and goals set forth in NEP 2020. Several instances of implicit gender bias, particularly in the portrayal of male and female characters, were identified within the text, perpetuating traditional gender norms and reinforcing associated stereotypes. To fully realise the objectives of NEP 2020, addressing and rectifying this gender bias is imperative. The policy emphasises holistic education, inclusivity, equitable opportunities, and critical thinking, all of which are adversely affected by the presence of such biases in educational materials. Aligning with the policy's objectives necessitates active efforts to promote inclusivity and gender neutrality in educational content through challenging traditional gender norms, introducing diverse role models, providing teacher training, and revising materials to incorporate a broader spectrum of gender-neutral roles. This is a critical step toward fostering a more equitable and balanced education system thus contributing valuable insights for educators and policymakers in seeking a holistic and contemporary approach to inclusivity in educational materials.

References

Aina, O. E., & Cameron, P. A. (2011). Why Does Gender Matter? Counteracting Stereotypes with Young Children. Dimensions of Early Childhood, 39, 11-19

Aydınoğlu, N. (2014). Gender in English language teaching coursebooks. *Procedia - Social and Behavioral Sciences*, *158*, 233–239. https://doi.org/10.1016/j.sbspro.2014.12.081

Connell, R. W., & Messerschmidt, J. W. (2005). Hegemonic masculinity. *Gender & Society*, *19*(6), 829–859. https://doi.org/10.1177/0891243205278639

Dhiman, Dr. B. (2023). *Education's Role in Empowering Women and Promoting Gender Inequality: A Critical Review*. https://doi.org/10.36227/techrxiv.24329284

Islam, K. Md. M., & Asadullah, M. N. (2018, January 19). *Gender stereotypes and education: A comparative content analysis of Malaysian, Indonesian, Pakistani and Bangladeshi school textbooks*. PLOS ONE. https://journals.plos.org/plosone/article?id=10.1371%2Fjournal.pone.0190807

Kumar, A. M., Goh, J. Y., Tan, T. H., & Siew, C. S. (2022). Gender stereotypes in Hollywood movies and their evolution over time: Insights from network analysis. *Big Data and Cognitive Computing*, *6*(2), 50. https://doi.org/10.3390/bdcc6020050

MHRD (2019). National Education Policy 2020. Ministry of Human Resource Development, Government of India. https://www.mhrd.gov.in/sites/upload_files/mhrd/files/NEP_Final_English_0.pdf

NCERT-National focus group on Gender Issues in Education. (2006). https://ncert.nic.in/pdf/focus-group/gender_issues_in_education.pdf

Singh, P., & Bammi, R. (2013). Gender portrayal in school textbooks: A study in Bhopal City. *Prabandhan: Indian Journal of Management*, *6*(8), 32. https://doi.org/10.17010/pijom/2013/v6i8/60023

Stewart, R., Wright, B., Smith, L., Roberts, S., & Russell, N. (2021). Gendered stereotypes and norms: A systematic review of interventions designed to shift attitudes and behaviour. *Heliyon*, *7*(4). https://doi.org/10.1016/j.heliyon.2021.e06660

Swain, J. (n.d.). Masculinities in education. *Handbook of Studies on Men & Masculinities*, 213–229. https://doi.org/10.4135/9781452233833.n13

The Priceless Gift. (2019). Excerpt from Class 9 English Textbook - Skills of Communicative English. Ed. Board of Secondary Education, Odisha https://textbookbureauodisha.in/book/odisha-class-1-to-10-books-pdf/

Unesdoc.unesco.org. (2008). https://unesdoc.unesco.org/ark:/48223/pf0000155509

3

Modern Education through Madrasas: Prospects and Challenges

A Study of the Selected Madrasas in Uttar Pradesh

Jamshed Ahmad

Introduction

In the diverse educational landscape of India, Madrasas, or Islamic religious schools, stand as unique institutions that have traditionally focused on imparting religious teachings. Madrasas were never restricted to only providing religious instructions because Madrasa education is not a new concept in today's world because it was used to educate people when there were no formal schools. In the meantime, many non-Muslims, such as Raja Ram Mohun Roy, Dr. Rajendra Prasad, and Munshi Prem Chand began their early schooling in the village Madrasa under the instruction and supervision of maulvis due to the absence of primary education systems in India's villages. Over a period, this notion has shifted, and Madrasas have become the epicentre of religious education (Ahmad, 2022).

However, in the ever-evolving global context, there is an increasing recognition of the need to integrate modern education within the framework of Madrasa pedagogy. This study delves into the dynamic intersection of traditional religious education and contemporary learning by examining the prospects and challenges of implementing modern education within selected Madrasas in the state of Uttar Pradesh.

Uttar Pradesh, with its rich cultural tapestry and significant Muslim population, serves as an intriguing backdrop for this investigation. The study aims to shed light on the ongoing efforts and initiatives taken by Madrasas in Uttar Pradesh to embrace a more comprehensive educational approach, encompassing not only religious studies but also a broader spectrum of subjects such as science, mathematics, and languages.

Basically, the notion of modern education is rooted in the concept of modernisation, which is about socio-cultural transformation within society.

Modern education is a sub-component of modernisation. Modern education refers to introducing modern subjects such as English, Hindi, Mathematics, Social Studies, Science, and Computer etc. into the curriculum.

As we navigate through the pages of this research, we will explore the factors influencing the modernisation of Madrasa education, and the challenges encountered in striking a balance between traditional religious teachings and contemporary knowledge. By focusing on selected Madrasas in Uttar Pradesh, this study seeks to provide valuable insights into the intricate dynamics shaping the future of Madrasa education in the context of a rapidly changing educational landscape.

The Study

Objectives

1. To find out the nature and extent of coverage of modern education imparted through Madrasas along with the prospects and challenges of Madrasa education.
2. To suggest suitable measures for effective modern education through Madrasas.

Questions

1. What are the prospects of providing modern education in Madrasas?
2. What obstacles do Madrasas encounter in delivering modern education?

Methodology

The research strategy of this study was based on both the qualitative and the quantitative in nature. Primary and secondary data were used. Primary sources were largely employed to find out existing research in the area. The secondary sources were taken from several journals, books, online databases, and reports from the field of education and are multidisciplinary in nature.

Area and Sampling

The present study was conducted in the Meerut district of Uttar Pradesh, and focuses on four Madrasas, but two Madrasas were unable to co-operate properly due to paucity of time. This study focuses on two different Madrasas namely: Johar Islamiyah Arabia Madrasa (Lakhipura) and Danish Islamic Madrasa (Ahmad Nagar).

Sampling is a crucial part of any research, especially in social sciences. Bryman (2008, P.414), explained that "most sampling in qualitative research entails purposive sampling of some kind."

For this study, purposive as well as snowball sampling was used for collecting data from different stakeholders. In purposive sampling, you decide the purpose you want informants (or communities) to serve, and you go out to find some.

This is somewhat like quota sampling, except that there is no overall sampling design that tells you how many of each type of informant you need for a study. You take what you can get (Bernard 2006, p.189).

A sample size of 40 students from different classes was taken by purposive sampling.

Students' Profile

12-16 years of age group students were chosen for the interviews, there were 20 boys and 20 girls in the sample. All the students belonged to different socio-economic backgrounds as informed by the Madrasa Head.

Table 1: Sampling details

S. No.	*Name of the Madrasa*	*Classes*	*Area*	*Types*	*Student*	*Teacher*	*Madrasa Head*	*Parents*
1.	Danish Islamic Madrasa (Ahmad Nagar)	I-VIII	Urban	Co-ed	20	2	1	10
2.	Johar Islamiyah Arabia Madrasa (Lakhipura)	I-VIII	Urban	Co-ed	20	2	1	10

Source: Author, 2022.

Research Methods and Tools

A brief census of the study area (information schedule), documentation, observation, semi-structured interviews, photographs, and visual data collection are some of the different methodological approaches used as tools for gathering verbal and non-verbal data. The current study is based on both qualitative and quantitative approaches.

Development and Prospects of Modern Education through Madrasa -- Uttar Pradesh

Uttar Pradesh is the largest state in India in terms of population with the largest Muslim population in the state as well as the largest number of Madrasas functioning in the state of Uttar Pradesh. P. Nair (2008) mentioned that as of December 2006, 557 Madrasas have received temporary recognition on the other hand 930 Madrasas have been given permanent recognition by the Uttar Pradesh Arabi Farsi Board (UPAFB)[1]. Out of these, only 359 Madrasas were receiving grant-in-aid through the state government (MW&WD and

[1] Before Uttar Pradesh of Madrasa Education Board, UPAFB was looking all matters related to registration and recognition.

SSA). 132 girls' Madrasas are recognised and only 35 of these Madrasas were receiving grant-in-aid. A large number of Madrasas were unrecognised in the state of Uttar Pradesh.

Table 2: Recognised and aided Madrasas in Uttar Pradesh

Types of Madrasas	*Recognised (Permanent)*		*Recognised (Temporary)*	*Aided (From amongst the recognised)*		*Unrecognised*
	Boys	*Girls*		*Boys*	*Girls*	
Numbers	798 (135 Girls' Madrasas)	132 Madrasas	557	324 Madrasas	35 Madrasas	9000 (Estimated)

Source: P. Nair, 2008.

The domain of the latest scheme, The Scheme to Provide Quality Education in Madrasas (SPQEM) of MHRD now known as the Ministry of Education emphasised qualitative improvement in the realm of Madrasas education to connect Muslim children with the national education system. In the domain of SPQEM, a large number of Madrasas have been covered, including student enrolment and teacher appointments under this centrally sponsored scheme in the state of Uttar Pradesh. Under the SPQEM there are approximately 8,584 Madrasas in the state, out of which 560 Madrasas come under Grant-in-aid by the state Government (NIEPA, 2018).

Table 3: Coverage of Madrasas, Students, and Teachers under SPQEM in Uttar Pradesh

S. No.	*State*	*Number of Madrasas Covered Under SPQEM*	*Number of Students Covered Under SPQEM*	*Number of Teachers Appointed Under SPQEM*
1.	Uttar Pradesh	8,584	18,27,566	25,500
S. No.	*Name of the State*	*District*	*Total Madrasas*	*Adhunikrit Madrasas*
1.	Uttar Pradesh	Meerut	273	110

Source: SPQEM, 2018. UP Board of Madrasa Education, 2022.

On the basis of the above two tables and discussion that the developments of Madrasa education has extended on a large scale in the state of Uttar Pradesh. In the state of Uttar Pradesh different types of Madrasas are functioning including recognised aided, private unaided, and community-based Madrasas. Madrasa education in India has both challenges and potential for growth. Madrasas, or Islamic religious schools, play a significant role in providing education to a considerable number of students, primarily focusing on religious studies.

Factors Influencing Prospects of Madrasa Education in India

Religious Education: Madrasas primarily focus on Islamic studies, including Quranic teachings, theology, and the Arabic language. While this caters to the religious needs of the Muslim population, there is a growing recognition of the importance of integrating modern subjects such as science, mathematics, and language skills.

Modernisation Efforts: There have been efforts to modernise Madrasa education by incorporating mainstream curriculum components. Some Madrasas have started including subjects like English, mathematics, and science to provide a more well-rounded education to their students.

Government Initiatives: The Indian government has initiated various schemes and programmes to support and improve Madrasa education. Financial aid and infrastructure development projects aim to enhance the quality of education provided in these institutions.

Challenges: Madrasas face challenges related to curriculum diversification, infrastructure, and qualified teachers for non-religious subjects. There is a need for a balance between religious and modern education to ensure that students are equipped with skills relevant to contemporary society.

Community Perception: Changing the perception of Madrasa education within the broader community is crucial. Recognising the value of religious education while emphasising the importance of a well-rounded, modern education can contribute to the acceptance and growth of Madrasa education.

Employability: A focus on skill development and vocational training within Madrasas can enhance the employability of students. This could help bridge the gap between traditional religious education and the practical skills needed for various professions.

In conclusion, the prospects of Madrasa education in India are evolving. With concerted efforts from the government, communities, and educational institutions, there is potential for Madrasas to play a more significant role in shaping well-rounded individuals who are both religiously literate and equipped with skills for the modern world.

Problems and Constraints Faced by Madrasas in Providing Modern Education

Madrasas are important institutions that provide basic education to the country's marginalised Muslim population. Future generations of the Muslim community should be educated in both religious and modern subjects. Imparting modern education to children is a challenging task for all Madrasa because there are several challenges that exist in the domain of modern education through Madrasas.

Major Issues Concerning the Quality of Education

1. A lack of basic amenities in terms of infrastructure development like proper buildings, classrooms, and furniture- benches, blackboards, whiteboards, and washroom facilities in some of the Madrasas. In addition to that, there were some Madrasas where obsolete methods and techniques of teaching and learning were used by the teachers and students.
2. Education planning, administration, and management of some of the Madrasas were below the standard. There were brittle financial conditions as far as management is concerned.
3. There were limited teachers for limited subjects and somehow these things compromise with choosing the subjects of students' choices.
4. Lack of awareness about government initiatives in the form of scholarships, schemes, etc. in the realm of introducing modern subjects, and for the betterment of the minority community.
5. In terms of modern education, the availability of professional teachers meaning those who have degrees in the education sector like -- B.Ed, M.Ed, etc. were absent in most of the Madrasas. Mostly, they were simply graduates or postgraduates in the concerned subjects.
6. Another challenge of imparting modern education through Madrasas is the absence of computer labs, science labs and library facilities in most of the Madrasas as far as the quality of education is concerned.
7. Apart from that, the salary of teachers was very low. Besides, they do not receive their salary on a regular basis, in most cases, teachers' salaries are pending for the last six months. Perhaps, these things make teachers reluctant to give their hundred percent in the profession.
8. Inspection and supervision were not up to the mark and in some of the cases were absent.
9. There were lacunae in the examination and evaluation.
10. Distribution of scholarships was another challenge in the pathways of Modern education through Madrasas because most of the famlies' financial status was brittle in nature, they were unable to pay the fee. Besides, most of the children pay their fees by getting scholarships. Hence, Scholarship should be distributed on time.
11. Most of the students' scholarship amount is spent to meet their educational expenses. Like Fees, Exam Fees, Lab fees, Computer fees etc. Therefore, there should be an ideal fee structure for private unaided Madrasas. So that justified fee can be obtained from the children and at the same time, Madrasa education should not be allowed to become a commercialisation of education.
12. Recognition and registration of Madrasas by state Madrasa boards is another concern because, in most cases, Madrasas who are willing to start modern

education in their Madrasas are facing difficulties in getting recognition by the authority. There is a need to take positive steps for its redressal.

The above problems and challenges have been found in the field of modern education in Madrasas, whose redress is the need of the hour. There is a need to take positive steps to strengthen the modern education system through Madrasas.

Recommendations

Suggesting suitable measures for effective modern education through Madrasas involves considering various aspects to ensure a comprehensive and successful integration of contemporary educational practices. Here are some key points to consider:

Teacher Training Programmes: Implement teacher training programmes that equip Madrasa educators with the skills and knowledge required to teach modern subjects. Training should focus on effective pedagogical methods, the use of technology in education, and fostering a learner-centric approach.

Infrastructure Development: Invest in improving infrastructure to create conducive learning environments. This includes upgrading classrooms, providing modern teaching aids, and ensuring access to relevant educational resources, including libraries and laboratories.

Curricular Integration: Advocate for a balanced curriculum that includes both religious studies and modern subjects such as science, mathematics, language, and social sciences. This ensures that students receive a well-rounded education that prepares them for diverse academic and professional pursuits.

Digital Integration: Promote the integration of digital technology in the teaching and learning process. Provide Madrasas with access to online resources, e-learning platforms, and educational apps to enhance the educational experience and keep pace with technological advancements

Government Collaboration: Encourage collaboration between Madrasas and government bodies to facilitate the implementation of modern education initiatives. Seek government support in terms of funding, policy advocacy, and alignment with national educational standards.

Community Engagement: Foster community awareness and support for modern education initiatives in Madrasas. Engage with parents, religious leaders, and community members to address concerns, build understanding, and garner support for the positive changes being introduced

Inclusive Education Policies: Advocate for inclusive education policies that recognise and validate the achievements of Madrasa students. Ensure that qualifications obtained from modernised Madrasas are recognised by mainstream educational institutions, opening avenues for higher education and employment.

Skill Development and Vocational Training: Introduce skill development and vocational training programs within Madrasas to enhance students' practical skills and increase employability. This can include training in areas such as computer literacy, communication skills, and vocational trades.

Cultural Sensitivity and Identity Preservation: Implement measures that respect and preserve the cultural and religious identity of Madrasas. Ensure that modernisation efforts are culturally sensitive, and that traditional values are maintained alongside the incorporation of contemporary educational practices.

Regular Monitoring and Evaluation: Establish a system for regular monitoring and evaluation to assess the effectiveness of modern education initiatives. This involves gathering feedback from students, teachers, and stakeholders to identify areas of improvement and refine strategies accordingly.

Teacher related Issues: Teachers should be given pre-service training so that they can perform their duties in the education profession well and at the same time, their salary should be increased and the salary should be received on time.

Simplified Procedures and Timely Approvals for Madrasas Embracing Modern Education: The provisions related to registration and recognition should be made easy and systematic and should not be delayed for those Madrasas who want to propose modern education within their Madrasas.

Establishment of Madrasa Board (National Level): At the national level, a National Board of Madrasa Education should be established with the objective of facilitating the states in various dimensions to strengthen the Madrasa education system.

By implementing these measures, Madrasas can embark on a successful journey towards providing effective modern education, ensuring that students are well-prepared for the challenges and opportunities of the contemporary world.

Conclusion

In conclusion, the study on "Modern Education Through Madrasas: A Study of the Prospects and Challenges of Madrasa Education in Selected Madrasas in Uttar Pradesh" has illuminated the intricate dynamics at play in the realm of Madrasa education. The exploration of prospects revealed promising avenues for the integration of modern education within these traditional Islamic institutions. The acknowledgment of historical significance and the potential to diversify curricula signify a positive shift towards a more comprehensive educational approach.

However, the study also unveiled a spectrum of challenges that Madrasas face in their endeavour to modernise. These challenges range from infrastructural deficiencies to teacher related concerns especially low salary and delayed distribution of salary etc. The delicate task of navigating between tradition and modernity requires strategic measures to ensure a harmonious coexistence that respects cultural identities while meeting contemporary educational standards.

The prospects and challenges identified underscore the need for nuanced and context-specific solutions. The potential lies in collaborative efforts involving government bodies, educators, communities, and stakeholders to address these challenges and harness the opportunities for positive change. Initiatives such as curriculum diversification, teacher training, and infrastructure improvement hold the key to unlocking the full potential of Madrasa education in Uttar Pradesh.

As we reflect on the study, it becomes evident that the journey towards modernising Madrasa education is a dynamic and ongoing process. The findings provide valuable insights that can inform policy decisions, guide future research endeavours, and foster a more inclusive educational landscape in Uttar Pradesh and beyond. The study encourages a continued dialogue on the role of traditional institutions in adapting to contemporary needs, ultimately contributing to the holistic development of students and the enrichment of India's diverse educational tapestry.

Refrences

Ahmad, J. (2022). *Modern Education Through Madrasas: A Study Of The Selected Madrasas In Uttar Pradesh.* New Delhi.

Ahmad, J. (2022, April). Retrieved from http://www.niepa.ac.in/scholar/Batch/2020/11_Jamshed%20Ahmad%20(20201023).

Bryman, J. (2008). *Social Research Method.* New York: Oxford University.

Bernard. Russel, H. (2006). *"Research methods in Anthropology, Qualitative and Quantitative approaches".*

Nair, P. (2008). *The state and Madrasas in India." International Development Department (IDD).".*

Singh, A.K. et.al. (2018). *The Scheme for providing Quality Education in Madrasa Evaluation Report.* New Delhi.

Websites

https://www.livehistoryindia.com/story/monuments/decoding-Madarsas. https://www.madarsaboard.upsdc.gov.in/ https://censusindia.gov.in/

4

Paradigm Shift in Education of Children with Special Needs

With Special Reference to Mizoram

Lalrochami Ralte
Lalbiakdiki Hnamte

Introduction

The global education landscape has experienced a paradigm shift towards inclusive practices, emphasising the integration of students with special needs into mainstream classrooms. These plans empower each learner on their educational journey and acknowledge the diversity within the student body. Technology has also become integral to inclusive education, offering tools like educational apps, assistive technologies, and adaptive learning platforms that cater to the learning needs of children with special requirements. These tools supplement traditional teaching methods and provide interactive and engaging learning opportunities. Educator training and professional development are crucial components in ensuring that educators are well-prepared to implement inclusive practices. Special education training and professional development programs help create a cadre of skilled and empathetic educators, making the educational landscape more adept at meeting the varied requirements of all learners.

Community involvement is also essential in inclusive education, as successful programmes often hinge on active community participation. Building awareness, reducing stigma, and encouraging community involvement contribute significantly to the overall success of inclusive education initiatives. Governments play a pivotal role in shaping the educational landscape for children with special needs, providing funding, infrastructure development, and legal frameworks that promote inclusivity.

In conclusion, the paradigm shift towards inclusive education is a multifaceted process that includes individualized planning, technological integration, teacher empowerment, community engagement, and governmental support. This comprehensive approach reflects a commitment to creating an educational environment where every child can thrive and contribute meaningfully to society.

Paradigm Shift

A paradigm shift is a fundamental change in a particular domain or field's basic concepts, practices, and beliefs. It represents a shift in how people perceive, understand, and approach a particular subject. The term "paradigm" was popularized by Thomas Kuhn, in his book "The Structure of Scientific Revolutions."

In the context of science and philosophy, a paradigm shift occurs when the dominant framework or model used to explain phenomena is replaced by a new and different framework. A change in the underlying assumptions, methodologies, and perspectives within a scientific community or a broader societal context often accompanies this shift. Paradigm shifts can occur in various fields, including science, technology, business, culture, and the social sciences. They often lead to significant advancements, breakthroughs, or changes in the way people approach problems and understand the world.

For example, in the late twentieth century, the broad use of the internet and digital technology resulted in a paradigm shift in communication, commerce, and daily living. Similarly, advances in medical knowledge or alterations in society's views towards certain situations can cause paradigm shifts in healthcare or social dynamics.

A paradigm shift represents a profound transformation in the foundational concepts and practices that shape a particular discipline or area of human knowledge.

The Study

Rationale

This study aims to examine the paradigm shift in the education of children with special needs, focusing specifically on the context of Mizoram State. The research aims to investigate the changes that have taken place for children with special needs and assess the government's interventions and initiatives in response to these shifts. With the enactment of the RPWD Act in 2016 and the introduction of the latest policies, this paper will explore and analyse the paradigm shift in education for children with special needs, considering the evolving legal and policy frameworks.

Research Questions

1. What is the scheme/policy made for children with special needs (CWSN)?
2. What is the paradigm shift of the RPWD Act 1995 and 2016 policies and framework?

Statement of the Problem

The statement of the problem has been stated as "Paradigm Shift in Education of Children with Special Needs with Special Reference to Mizoram State." The primary objective is to investigate the educational landscape for children with special needs (CWSN) and explore the interventions implemented to support their learning. It is essential to recognise that changes in government often bring about new policies, and the current context involves the Rights of Persons with Disabilities Act (RPWD Act) of 2016. This study aims to elucidate the initiatives and strategies employed for CWSN before enacting the RPWD Act in 2016.

Objective

1. To analyse the scheme/policy made for CWSN
2. To analyse the RPWD Act 1995 and 2016
3. To examine the changes observed in the various policies for PWD (Persons with Disabilities)
4. To study the implementation of these policies in the state of Mizoram

Methodology

Source of data: The findings and analysis of the study presented in the study are based on secondary data, specifically sourced for this research study. The researcher personally engaged with employees from SCERT, SAMAGRA, and Disability Commissioner to gather the necessary information for this research.

Findings

Objective 1 – Findings

Objective One conducted a thorough investigation into the programs and policies affecting children with special needs. The study delves into the intricacies of existing programs to acquire a thorough grasp of their effectiveness and opportunities for development. Objective One aimed to provide significant insights that might drive future policy development, creating a more inclusive and supportive environment for children with special needs. The study's emphasis on policy analysis indicates a dedication to improving the overall well-being and possibilities accessible to this vulnerable group, promoting a society that values diversity and inclusion in education and support services.

Table 1: Scheme/ Policy for Children with Special Needs (CWSN)

Sl. No.	*Scheme/ Policy for Children with Special Needs (CWSN)*
1.	Resource room
2.	Special Educator and Resource Person
3.	Accessible infrastructure (Ramp with railings, special toilets, etc)
4.	Aids and appliances (Glasses, crutch, wheelchair, large print textbook, hearing aids, braille paper, physical therapy, home base education, and teaching learning materials)
5.	Teacher training
6.	Orientation for Principals, Educational Administrators, Teachers, and Guardians.
7.	Survey and Assessment

Table 2: State Wise Progress in Inclusive Education in 2021-2022

State Wise Progress in Inclusive Education in 2021-2022								
Sl. No.	*State*	*No. of CWSN Identified*	*No. of CWSN enrolled in schools Only as Per UDISE*	*No. of CWSN provides aids and appliances*	*No. of Schools made Barrier Free (with Ramps, Handrails)*	*% of Schools made Barrier-free (with Ramps, Handrails)*	*No. of Schools with Disabled Friendly Toilets*	*% of Schools with Disabled Friendly Toilets*
1.	Mizoram	2623	2623	525	1310	59.00%	205	9%

Source: UDISE 2021-2022

Objective 2 – Findings

Objective Two conducted a comprehensive study on the Rights of Persons with Disabilities Act of 1995 and its subsequent amendments in 2016. The aim was to understand the complexities of these legal frameworks, their impact, history, and effectiveness in safeguarding the rights and well-being of disabled individuals. The study aimed to inspire policy changes, foster a more inclusive and empowered legal environment for disabled individuals, and demonstrate a commitment to social justice.

Table No: 3

Sl. No.	*RPWD Policies and Framework*	*RPWD Act 1995*	*RPWD Act 2016*
1.	Definition of Disabilities	The 1995 Act primarily addressed seven disabilities: blindness, low vision, leprosy-cured, hearing impairment, locomotor disability, mental retardation, and mental illness.	The 2016 Act expanded the list of disabilities to 21, including intellectual disabilities, mental illnesses, acid attack victims, and specific learning disabilities.
2.	Reservation in Government job	1995 Act reserved 3% of government jobs for persons with disabilities.	2016 Act increased the reservation to 4%.
3.	Accessibility	The 1995 Act did not explicitly address issues related to accessibility.	The 2016 Act mandated that all public buildings, information, communication technologies, and transportation be accessible to persons with disabilities.

Sl. No.	RPWD Policies and Framework	RPWD Act 1995	RPWD Act 2016
4.	Education	The PWD Act 1995 prohibits disability discrimination in education, requiring institutions to reserve seats, provide facilities, and appoint special educators, but it lacks the comprehensiveness of the Rights of Persons with Disabilities Act, 2016.	The 2016 Act emphasised inclusive education and mandated that all government and private educational institutions must provide inclusive education up to the age of 18.
5.	Legal Capacity	The 1995 Act did not explicitly address the legal capacity of persons with disabilities.	The 2016 Act granted the right to all persons with disabilities to live in the community and possess legal capacity.
6.	Complaint Mechanism	The 1995 Act did not have a dedicated mechanism for addressing complaints related to the rights of persons with disabilities.	The 2016 Act established the Chief Commissioner for Persons with Disabilities and State Commissioners for Persons with Disabilities, providing a formal mechanism for the redressal of grievances.

Objective 3 – Findings

Objective three is to study the changing policies related to Persons with Disabilities (PWD) to understand their transformations. The aim is to provide insights into initiatives that enhance their well-being and inclusivity and contribute valuable knowledge for future efforts to create more effective and responsive support systems for PWDs.

1. *Introduction of Policies for Persons with Disabilities (PWD):*
   There have been significant changes in policies affecting people with disabilities (PWD) over time. A collaborative partnership between the Social Welfare Department and significant education-focused projects like SSA, Rashtriya Madhyamik Shiksha Abhiyan (RMSA), and Samagra Shiksha Abhiyan (SSA) characterises the historical story.
2. *Development of Educational initiatives:*
   SCERT initiated the Education of Disabled Children in 1985, which later transformed into a Resource Centre for Inclusive Education. This marked the beginning of educational efforts. At first, SCERT took a proactive role in running evaluation camps and giving help. Nevertheless, there was a noticeable change in emphasis with a focus on B.Ed. Special Education under Sarva Shiksha Abhiyan (SSA).

3. *Collaboration Dynamics Unveiled:*
   Following the incorporation of Samagra Shiksha Abhiyan, collaborative efforts saw a downturn. Collaborative endeavours encountered a downturn initially defined by beneficial cooperation between SSA and the Social Welfare Department, notably during identification camps and joint medical assessments. This decrease in collaboration might be related to possible financial constraints.
4. *Financial Support and Resource Dynamics:*
   SSA served as a Nodal Department, providing financial assistance, and utilising human resources from the SCERT for community awareness. However, due to funding restrictions, the SSA obtained medical assessments from SCERT and the National Institute for the Empowerment of Persons with Intellectual Disabilities (NILD).
5. *Operational Shifts Post Integration:*
   There was a considerable decline in cooperative activities with the Social Welfare Department following the merger of Samagra Shiksha Abhiyan. When such measures were launched, however, they proceeded smoothly. During this time, efforts were unified under the Samagra Shiksha Abhiyan, effectively combining Sarva Shiksha Abhiyan (SSA), RMSA, and the SCERT.
6. *Programmes and Assessment:*
   SSA carried out district-wide student profiles and frequent evaluations, with an emphasis on home-based education for selected pupils. The RMSA programme included environmental construction, community programmes, awareness campaigns, and teacher training. SCERT's policies were aligned with those of SSA and RMSA, and it provided critical assistance.
7. *Transition and Consolidation under Samagra Shiksha Abhiyan:*
   Samagra Shiksha Abhiyan included new elements such as specialised physical therapy facilities for CWSN while maintaining consistency with the policies of its predecessors. Even while joint efforts fluctuated, maybe due to budgetary limitations, the overall goal remained the same—improving educational possibilities for every child.

In conclusion, the evolution of policies for persons with disabilities, particularly those addressing the requirements of children with special needs, exemplifies a continuous process characterised by modest modifications. The move from SSA to Rashtriya Madhyamik Shiksha Abhiyan (RMSA) and, eventually, Samagra Shiksha Abhiyan (SSAA) demonstrates a commitment to creating inclusive education and complete support structures. Despite changes in cooperation efforts, the primary goal remains constant: to improve educational opportunities and holistic development for all children, regardless of ability.

Objective 4 – Findings

Objective Four undertook a comprehensive study in Mizoram, focusing on the execution of policies outlined in the Rights of Persons with Disabilities (RPWD) Act. On April 17, 2018, this investigation delved into the state's adherence to the Mizoram Rights of Persons with Disabilities Rules, 2017. The publication of these rules was a mandatory step as per Section 101 of the Rights of Persons with Disabilities Act, 2016 (49 of 2016). The study scrutinized the extent to which the state of Mizoram had incorporated and operationalised the provisions mandated by the RPWD Act. This initiative aimed to assess the effectiveness of the policy implementation, identifying areas of success and areas requiring improvement. By examining the Mizoram Rights of Persons with Disabilities Rules, 2017, the study sought to contribute valuable insights into the state's compliance with the broader national framework for ensuring the rights and well-being of individuals with disabilities. This research served as a vital step in promoting inclusivity and enhancing the quality of life for persons with disabilities in Mizoram.

Key Aspects of the Policies Implemented in Mizoram

1. *Education:* The RPWD Act emphasises inclusive education, ensuring that persons with disabilities have equal access to educational opportunities. Implementation may involve the creation of accessible infrastructure in schools, the provision of special educators, and the adaptation of teaching methods and materials to accommodate diverse learning needs.
2. *Employment:* The act aims to promote equal opportunities in employment. The implementation may involve affirmative action measures to ensure a certain percentage of jobs for persons with disabilities, reasonable accommodations in the workplace, and awareness programs to reduce discrimination.
3. *Accessibility:* The act mandates that public places and government buildings be made accessible. Implementation may involve the construction of ramps, accessible bathrooms, and the removal of architectural barriers to facilitate the easy movement of persons with disabilities.
4. *Healthcare:* Access to healthcare services is a key focus. Implementation may include measures to make healthcare facilities and information accessible, training healthcare professionals to cater to the needs of persons with disabilities, and providing assistive devices as needed.
5. *Social Security:* The act outlines provisions for social security persons with disabilities. Implementation may involve the development and execution of schemes that provide financial assistance, pensions, or other forms of support to individuals with disabilities.
6. *Legal Aid and Redressal:* The act includes provisions for legal support and mechanisms for grievance redressal. Implementation may involve setting up legal aid services and establishing bodies to address *complaints* related to rights violations.

Conclusion

This research examined the transformation in the education of children with special needs in Mizoram State, focusing on the state's unique context. The Education for Disabled Children in Mizoram (ECD) initiative was initially led by the State Council of Educational Research and Training (SCERT) within the Integrated Education for Disabled Children scheme. However, the introduction of the Samagra Shiksha Abhiyan (SSA) scheme in 2013 consolidated efforts under the umbrella of Samagra Shiksha.

Successful initiatives include establishing 26 resource rooms, deploying special educators, enhancing accessibility infrastructure, providing adaptive facilities, and offering assistive devices. Technology has also become integral to inclusive education, offering tools like educational apps, assistive technologies, and adaptive learning platforms.

Recognising the pivotal role of educator training and professional development, this research underscores their significance in ensuring educators are well-prepared to implement inclusive practices. The involvement of the community emerges as an essential element in the realm of inclusive education, with successful programs often reliant on active community participation. *Governments* are recognised as playing a central role in shaping the situation of children with special needs, providing essential support through funding, infrastructure development, and the establishment of legal frameworks that foster inclusivity.

References

Authority., (2018) *The Mizoram Rights of Persons with Disabilities Rules, 2017*, Published and Issued by Controller, Printing and Stationery Department of Mizoram Printed at the Mizoram Government Press, Aizawl. C/100

Bhatnagar, N., & Das, A. (2013). Nearly Two Decades after the Implementation of Persons with Disabilities Act: Concerns of Indian Teachers to Implement Inclusive Education. *International Journal of Special Education*, *28*(2), 104-113. https://files.eric.ed.gov/fulltext/EJ1023312.pdf

Class. M., (2022) *Paradigm shift definitions: 6 examples of paradigm shifts.* https://www.masterclass.com/articles/paradigm-shift-explained

Diago. G.G., (2019) *Paradigm shift* https://www.researchgate.net/publication/338177526_Paradigm_Shift

Dr. Ruata. V.L., et al., (2014) *Naupang Mamawh Bik Neite Kaihruaina*, Special Education Cell SCERT Mizoram, Aizawl

The Right of Persons with Disabilities Act, 2016., (2016). https://www.iitg.ac.in/eo/sites/default/files/RPwDAct2016.pdf

The Persons with Disabilities (Equal opportunities, protection of rights and full participation) Act, 1996 (1995). https://www.indiacode.nic.in/bitstream/123456789/8866/1/ind51207_%282%29disableact1995.pdf

5

National Education Policy 2020 and Empowering Socio-economically Disadvantaged Groups through Open Distance and Online Education

Ali Asgar
Shabir Ahmed Wani
Parvesh Kumari

Introduction

Teaching and learning are continuous processes that play a crucial role in the progress and development of a nation by empowering individuals equally in contemporary society. Looking back at constitutional provisions and policies, education has always been considered a major tool to ensure the welfare of the common masses, irrespective of factors such as colour, caste, creed, or gender. The National Education Policy 2020 sets ambitious targets, aiming for a 100% literacy rate by 2030 and a 50% Gross Enrolment Ratio (GER) in higher education by 2035 (NEP, 2020). Furthermore the policy aims to reform higher education to achieve Sustainable Development Goal (SDG) 4.3, targeting universal access to higher education which could not be possible without the educational empowerment of disadvantaged groups in India. Further, achieving these goals requires dedicated efforts beyond traditional modes of education and thus Open Distance Learning (ODL) by default emerges as the best alternative and efficient mode of educational delivery in a cost-effective, innovative, and flexible way. Despite a few challenges, this system may be helpful for governments in achieving the ambitious educational targets by spreading literacy among all segments of society and implementing provisions for inclusive education.

The Study

Rationale

After independence, the government took various steps in the form of policies and educational reform agendas and a good number of studies have been conducted in these areas. However, despite these efforts over a period of time,

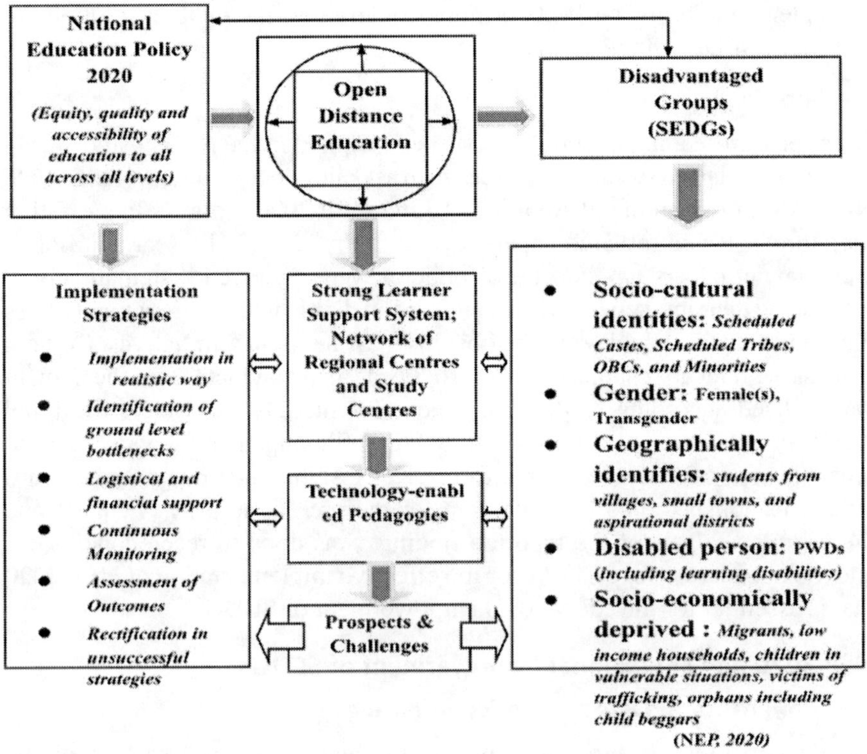

Figure 1. Conceptual Framework: NEP 2020, ODL and SEDGs

there remains a notable gap in the literature regarding studies specifically focused on disadvantaged groups and the deprived sections of society. In the context of distance education, limited attention has been paid to understanding the implications of NEP 2020 and the ODL system on educational equity and access for individuals from SEDGs and this poses a significant obstacle to achieving the policy goals of ensuring equity and equal educational opportunities for all. Therefore, a critical gap exists in our understanding of how government policies, specifically the NEP 2020, intersect with the ODL, and this research shall surely be helpful in understanding the nuances of emerging challenges and developing targeted implementation strategies for the inclusion and empowerment of these communities with unique requirements.

Objective

1. To examine and analyse the provisions of NEP 2020 for the disadvantaged groups and policy implications for SEDGs.
2. To describe open distance education role and related issues in achieving policy objectives.

3. To discuss prospects and challenges and propose suggestions to make implementation of NEP 2020 more effective by the ODL institutions to benefit SEDGs at the optimal level.

Methodology

Descriptive.research methodology has been applied in the present study. Data were collected from secondary sources such as policy documents like, NPE 1968, NPE 1986, Programme of Action 1992 and NEP 2020. Sources like existing literature, selected research papers related to the identified research problem and relevant papers on educational policies were reviewed systematically to understand their implementation and impact on disadvantaged groups and assess the role of ODL in achieving the objectives of the policy initiatives. Content analysis of relevant chapters of NEP 2020 was also conducted and the content was utilised according to the study requirements. Data available in digital formats were retrieved from Google Scholar, Shodhganga, e-GyanKosh and other educational and research platforms. Key insights and findings of previous studies established a solid foundation for the present study. Systematic and meticulous analysis of the reported findings was done to reach conclusions and make concrete suggestions for the effective implementation of NEP 2020 that is essential for the educational empowerment of SEDGs.

NEP 2020 and Educational Empowerment of SEDGs

Components of SEDGs and policy initiatives

Besides constitutional provisions, previous policy documents like the National Policy on Education (NPE) of 1986 had categorically recognised the importance of providing education to all sections of society, with a focus on addressing the needs of disadvantaged groups through inclusive and equitable education to create a more egalitarian society. Similarly, the NEP 2020 which has come after 35 years presses upon major reforms so that "India has an education system by 2040 that is second to none, with equitable access to the highest-quality education for all regardless of social or economic background." The policy leads to a comprehensive approach to break down barriers to education, to ensure that all individuals, regardless of their socio-economic background or geographic location, have equal access to quality education. Identified Socio-Economically Disadvantaged Groups (SEDGs) as per NEP (2020) include Scheduled Castes, Scheduled Tribes, Other Backward Classes (OBCs), minorities, students from rural areas, girls, transgender individuals, children with disabilities, and those from vulnerable socio-economic conditions, whose needs require policy redressal. Furthermore, the policy recognises the educational needs and empowerment of migrant communities, low-income households, children in vulnerable situations, victims of trafficking, orphans, child beggars and the urban poor through access to education, According to Batra (2020), the SEDGs as described in the policy cover 80% of the population of India constituting a major chunk of our society.

New Policy Provisions and Inclusive Education

Higher education is positioned as an indispensable component in achieving inclusive growth by ensuring access, equality, quality, and the expansion of educational opportunities. Realising this fact, the Indian government adopted the 2030 agenda for Sustainable Development Goal 4 in 2015 to "ensure inclusive and equitable quality education and promote lifelong learning opportunities for all by 2030 (NEP 2020). In Chapter 6: Equitable and Inclusive Education: Learning for All and Chapter 14: Equity and Inclusion in Higher Education of the NEP 2020 the issue of low educational penetration and higher dropout rates among SEDGs and strategies to resolve these problems have been deliberated upon in detail. The NEP 2020 describes the educational condition of SEDGs as follows: "According to U-DISE 2016-17 data, about 19.6% of students belong to SCs at the primary level, but this fraction falls to 17.3% at the higher secondary level. These enrolment drop-offs are more severe for ST students (10.6% to 6.8%), and differently-abled children (1.1% to 0.25%), with even greater declines for female students within each of these categories. The decline in enrolment in higher education is even steeper." According to the new education policy, full equity and inclusion are the cornerstones of all educational decisions to ensure that all students are able to thrive in the education system. Therefore, the government aims to strengthen the Indian culture of inclusion, innovation, and institution-building through various measures. Thus, education policy is emphasising upon equity and inclusion in higher education through existing constitutional provisions, government initiatives, funding, targeted schemes, scholarship programmes for SCs, STs, OBCs, and other members of SEDGs and a strong support and monitoring system to guarantee transparency and equality. It also recognises many socio-economic barriers, and restrictions faced by women in some communities, therefore targeted initiatives for girls within SEDGs are proposed. Bordoloi (2018) highlights the urgency to address illiteracy among women for achieving SDG4 goals. The new education policy also focuses on the creation of a Gender-Inclusion Fund to promote gender-inclusive education. The policy also categorically admits that the representation of minorities in school and higher education is relatively low and calls for interventions to increase the presence of underrepresented minority communities in education.

According to Mandal (2021) policy recognises and tries to address the multifaceted needs of disadvantaged groups having multifaceted socio-economic and cultural backgrounds and facing impediments to education due to various other factors Bordoloi (2018) also agrees with the provisions that inclusive growth encompasses equal access to education, health services, economic opportunities, and many more aspects. "*Education is the single greatest tool for achieving social justice and equality*" (NEP 2020 pp. 24 -50). Therefore the NEP is designed with the overarching goal of promoting equitable access to quality education for all, with a particular focus on SEDGS. This approach actually empowers every citizen to lead a meaningful life and attain a decent standard of living free from social injustice and all forms of exploitation. This transformative initiative has the potential to reshape the country's education system by addressing myriad social, economic, and environmental challenges (Kaur & Sharma, 2023).

ODL: Educational Opportunities for All

Open distance learning (ODL) provides opportunities to all for higher education on a large scale. Various limitations of traditional education institutions such as limited infrastructure and inadequate funding are overcome by open distance education creating opportunities and alternative avenues for higher education especially to the disadvantaged groups facing numerous socio-economic barriers. ODL is considered open for all where teaching-learning happens from distance. "Distance education is a concept that covers the teaching-learning activities in the cognitive and/or psycho-motor and affective domains of a learner that is characterised by non-contiguous communication and can be carried out anywhere and at any time, which makes it attractive to adults with professional and social commitments" (Holmberg, 2005). Due to flexibilities in teaching-learning methods and autonomy to learners a big chunk of disadvantaged groups gets enrolled in distance education programmes. It has a strong support system, management and administration network managed by different cadre of officials. These characteristics of this system make it like an industry where there is clear division of labour (Keegan, 2014). This broad-based system has been successful in addressing educational aspirations of a diverse groups coming from backward regions burdened with different responsibilities, and special needs groups who may be able to access materials from home (Khokhar, 2007) in a safe environment and cost-effective way and the advent of technology has made these tasks more effective for ODL institutions. NEP 2020 too has rightly recognised the potentiality of this system and recommended the effective and large-scale use of ODL system for participative and inclusive education, especially for SEDGs.

IGNOU, NIOS and other DEIs

Education is the most critical aspect of the holistic development of every human being and educational institutions whether single-mode or dual-mode, play a significant role in the uplift and development of students irrespective of their level of education. ODL institutions especially IGNOU and NIOS have contributed significantly to achieving the targets of equitable and inclusive education as envisaged in NEP 2020. In the realm of online and digital education, IGNOU has made notable strides through the creation of online platforms and TEL such as the e-GyanKosh portal, e-content development, MOOCs, and SWAYAM Prabha channels and the ing of online programmes. These efforts have significantly increased accessibility, equity, and inclusion. According to IGNOU (2023) "the university is ensuring access, equity, and inclusion through 69 regional centres (RCs) and 2063 learners' support centres (LSCs) and tries to reach out to students, including those from SEDGs, and learners from inaccessible remote areas. It also operates exclusive LSCs for jail inmates, women and disabled groups.

To address the digital divide in education NIOS has adopted a multifaceted approach including collaboration with the Postal Department, *Gram Panchayats*, NGOs, and others to ensure accessibility to devices, power, and internet connectivity. It has adopted a comprehensive approach to make its delivery mechanism more inclusive and accessible by creating additional support centres, particularly in rural and remote areas, which are crucial for disseminating information about admissions, courses, online classes, and examinations (NIOS, 2022). The new policy also emphasises providing equal opportunities for Children with Special Needs (CWSN) and recommends the implementation of assistive devices and suitable technologies to guarantee barrier-free access to education for all. NIOS has taken major initiatives in this direction by creating Sign Language videos, talking books, and e-Pub formats, a Learners Support Cell equipped with IVRS, video chat facilities, and an accessible web portal. Moreover, it has accommodated need-based technologies in examinations, especially for learners with disabilities, such as voice recorders, video recorders, scanners, OCR, and speech-to-text software. Admitting the important role of open schooling, NEP 2020 recommends, "ODL programmes offered by the NIOS and State Open Schools (SIOS) will be expanded and strengthened for meeting the learning needs of young people who are not able to attend a physical school.... states will be encouraged to develop these offerings in regional languages."

Other state open universities and open schools are also making continuous strides towards the integration of technology in their delivery methods; however, these institutions need to establish dedicated units focused on developing and maintaining thc technological infrastructure. Providing comprehensive training to teachers in Learning Management Systems (LMSs) and making their use mandatory for all educational purposes can elevate the institution, teachers, and students to a new level of proficiency in the digital realm as advocated by Joshi et al. (2021). Bordoloi (2018) highlights the research review concludes by shedding light on the potential role of Open and Distance Learning (ODL) in strengthening India's higher education system. ODL is recognised as a transformative force, capable of providing quality education to large segments of society at a lower cost and facilitating global learning. Bordoloi's work advocates for ODL institutions to align their vision with local needs, design need-based and skill-based courses, and contribute to elevating living standards. The effective implementation of these strategies is anticipated to empower and transform the higher education landscape in India.

Online Digital Education: Innovative Strategy

In the field of education, innovation and technology are considered very important to make teaching-learning more liberal and convenient for all. Technology has transformed the education system, especially distance education by introducing emerging and innovative modes like online education, digital education, e-learning, m-learning and blended learning approaches etc. Finch and Jacobs (2012) mention the advantages of these innovative modes of teaching-learning- they reduce the time and costs for travel; increase opportunities to access and collaborate with expert professionals on a global range; provide students with the flexibility to access courses at their convenience; and allow adjustments to subjects and content as needed. NEP 2020 also underscores the importance of online education in Chapter 14: Online Digital Education: Ensuring Equitable Use of Technology encouraging HEIs to allocate budgets for EdTech tools and advocating for the integration of advanced technological tools such as artificial intelligence (AI), big data, virtual reality, 3D printing, and robotics with instructional strategies and teaching-leaning curriculum. The policy provides a roadmap, and institutions can seize the opportunity to revolutionise education by leveraging technology for enhanced teaching and learning experiences.

Online Digital Education and SEDGs

Online distance education plays or could play a bigger and important role in educating all sections of society especially the disadvantaged and disabled groups who may not be able to move from one place to another due to reasons such as – old age, social barriers, financial issues, disability and many more. In this situation online education fulfils their dreams. Even though online education is more challenging compared to other modes of education because familiarity and use of technology are essential in this situation and may be expensive for learners if there is no support or funding system for SEDGs. A study conducted by ERSOY (2023) sheds light on the intricate challenges faced by SEDGs while going for online distance learning that include, limited digital literacy, socio-economic constraints, language and cultural disparities, lack of support and motivation, and all these collectively obstruct the attainment of equitable educational opportunities. Mehra *et al.*, (2004) therefore calls for active involvement of SEDGs in shaping various aspects of internet access, training, content development, and system design and evaluation to remove barriers and foster inclusivity for all users, irrespective of their backgrounds. However, Ching-Chiang et, al. (2022) in their study found that in the non-formal educational context, SEDGs facing digital disparities showcased greater adaptability, morecreativity and meaningful learning experiences. Therefore they emphasised setting up a rich framework of community-driven learning supported by innovative lessons, learner support mechanisms and initiatives to bridge gaps and promote equitable access to technology and education.

Implementation of NEP 2020: Prospects and Challenges

As the implementation strategies begin to unfold, the involvement of various stakeholders – state and central governments, private and government-run schools and HEIs, and international partners, will be crucial in realising the full potential of the new policy and ensuring its positive impact on India's education landscape and beyond. NEP 2020 will certainly help the country achieve SDG 4 and has the potential to act as a powerful agent of social change. Although it offers hope for a more inclusive and dynamic educational system in India, there are numerous hurdles to overcome for educational institutions and academic leadership.

Inadequate Infrastructure, high cost and language

There are some major challenges to implement these policies like limited infrastructure, shortage of teachers/faculties; institutions and funding that affect the planning and performance of any HEIs. In addition to these HEIs are required to be monitored regularly and outcomes are reported especially in the implementation are marked for the disadvantaged group. Hussain (2023) too stresses on monitoring and effective implementation and measures like funding for infrastructure, hostel for learner, healthy environment, increase accessibility and SEDGs participation without any harassment or discrimination and strong and quick decision to resolve this. Besides these lack of awareness among SEDGs regarding opportunities in higher education; higher cost involved in advanced/professional courses; financial constraints faced by SEDGs, geographical and language barriers, and a dearth of adequate guidance and support services mechanisms are another challenges to be addresses by universities and colleges, To address these problems, NEP 202 proposes fostering a more inclusive and accessible higher education landscape and creation of an environment where tailored solutions are provided to the members of SEDGs. So that they can overcome from barriers (NEP, 2020). In essence, the new education policy considers the HEIs as agent of social change that must shoulder responsibility of promotion of inclusion and elimination of exclusion in the Indian society.

Unfavourable Home-environment, Technical Glitches, and Teachers' Attitude

As witnessed during COVID 19, online digital education has shown good results and future of educational delivery appears to be increasingly technology-driven. However, Joshi et, al. (2021) and Asgar and Ratra (2020) identify significant barriers and challenges in four main areas Table 1.

Table 1: Major Challenges in Online Education

S. No.	*Major Barriers*	*Examples*	*Steps to be taken*
1.	Unfavourable home environment settings	lack of basic facilities at home; external distractions; and family interruptions	• Allocate EdTech budget • Invest in infrastructure • Conduct training for teachers; • Provide technical support to faculty; • Foster a positive attitude towards online education and use of technology; • Create policies that prioritize the well-being and motivation of teachers
2.	Lack of institutional support	budget constraints for purchasing advanced technologies; insufficient training; lack of technical support; no clarity in vision and direction; professional development of teachers not a priority	
3.	Technical glitches	Inadequate technological infrastructure; limited awareness of online teaching platforms; security concerns	
4.	Personal problems	Techno-phobia; lack of technical knowledge; negative attitudes towards technology; challenges in integrating courses with technology; lack of motivation	

Joshi et al., (2021) & Asgar and Ratra (2020)

Factors reflected in the above table underscore the importance of creating conducive home environments and enhancing the overall support system for teachers engaged in online education for effective and smoother online teaching-learning. Moreover, HEIs should take a holistic and comprehensive approach to address these issues so that the full potential of TEL (technology-enabled learning) is realised (Joshi et, al., 2021). To address challenges, ERSOY (2023) also proposes potential solutions and strategies such as enhanced digital literacy training, financial aid, localised content as per linguistic backgrounds, cultural sensitivity in instructional design, creation of virtual support communities, collaboration among educational institutions, policymakers, instructors, and stakeholders to formulate multifaceted strategies to mitigate the barriers faced by distance learners from SEDGs. This shall further help in creating quality human capital (Bordoloi, 2018) leading towards a more resilient and effective education system. Mehra et.al., (2004) advocate a holistic approach that considers the specific needs, goals, and contexts of diverse marginalised groups to effectively empower them through online education, emphasising the need to understand the everyday life of these groups to harness the full potential of the internet and technology for social and personal empowerment.

Developing skills, creating of employment and teachers' training

Critically examining the NEP 2020, Sunny (2021) underscores "the dire need to reimagine an education system that upholds the voices and dreams of labouring and marginalised individuals. The vision for education should extend beyond deciphering the world; it should strive to change it in the pursuit of equality and justice." According to him education should become a transformative force that embraces inclusivity, empowers the marginalised, and fosters a sustainable relationship with the environment. Sunny's argument seems valid because, despite several initiatives' enrolment disparities among SEDGs still persist, especially at the secondary level. Therefore, the new education policy proposes targeted scholarships, cash transfers, providing bicycles, and other tailored interventions for specific SEDGs. Regions with large populations from SEDGs are recommended to be declared Special Education Zones (SEZs) for focused and concerted educational planning and strategies (NEP, section 6.6, p25). However, Batra (2020) finds the proposal divisive. According to her "by proposing the creation of SEZs, the NEP effectively proposes to establish a segregated national school and teacher education system: one educational system for the 20 per cent more privileged 'general' population and another for the majority (80 per cent) of SEDGs." Meanwhile, the policy also promotes targeted hiring of teachers and leaders from minorities and other SEDGs. This recommendation may create more space for jobs in educational sector for SCs, STs and other SEDGs (Nand, 2020). Pressing upon creating education and employment opportunities for SEDGs, Kumar & Singh (2022) suggest that there is a need to revamp HEIs, skill development and training institutions infrastructure to ensure equality of educational and employment opportunities to empower the local population of disadvantaged groups. Furthermore, Kumar & Singh (2022) emphasise the development of indigenous craft industries and the promotion of eco-tourism to preserve indigenous culture and sustainable livelihoods for the local population.

Understanding ground realities

According to Kaur & Sharma (2023), collective efforts and collaboration between Union-state governments, government and private HEIs and other stakeholders shall be crucial for the successful implementation of the policy. According to Batra (2020) the policy does little to address specific and endemic problems that plague India's education system. The proposed interventions are largely based on a shallow understanding of the ground realities of education in an unequal society, so they could suffer from deep infirmities in execution. While (Joshi et.al, 2021) acknowledge the policy's focus on equity and inclusivity, they underline that the true impact of the policy shall be evident when underrepresented, disadvantaged, rural and remote areas' students gain equal access to education. This shall be a key outcome in the coming years.

Conclusion and Suggestions

In India, every segment of society is entitled to access education at different levels according to their personal and professional needs. The state and central governments have consistently introduced various initiatives and framed policies from time to time that aim to provide holistic educational support to the common masses, with a special focus on SEDGs, women, transgender individuals, PWDs, CWSNs, minorities and other marginalised sections of society identified by the government. The NEP 2020 strives to bring comprehensive reforms in the present education system so that the issues of accessibility and equity are addressed and quality education is available for all, especially for the SEDGs. The policy recognises the diverse needs of various deprived sections and groups and endeavours to promote educational outreach and accessibility. In this context, ODL due to it flexible teaching-learning methods and cost-effectiveness becomes a viable alternative to educate a big chunk of society that is socially and economically deprived. There is no doubt that NEP 2020 is a visionary document and its recommendations will have a lasting impact on the Indian education system. However, there are a few bottlenecks such as inadequate infrastructure, a shortage of trained faculty and their unfamiliarity with technology, high costs of education, language barriers, and different social and ground realities that must be addressed if institutions seek to educate the SEDGs in a holistic and effective manner. To realise the vision of the policy in the direction of social and educational empowerment of disadvantaged groups, the distance higher education institutions shall have to consider following suggestions:

- Maintain transparency in the admission process and evaluation; conduct regular monitoring and reporting to ensure the effective implementation of NEP 2020 and guarantee quality education.
- Remove identified barriers, increase the awareness level of disadvantaged groups about opportunities in higher education.
- Offer programmes and courses in local/regional languages to attract learners from SEDGs.
- Maintain timely and regular communication with SEDGs to offer educational and financial benefits like fee exemption, scholarships, grants-in-aid and

financial assistance meant for them so that they may be motivated towards education.

- Empower women and transgender individuals by maintaining gender balance in admission, making special provisions, facilities for these groups and minorities.
- Earmark funds to achieve set targets for SEDGs.
- Create an inclusive environment and disabled-friendly infrastructure like setting up ramps, Braille systems, sign language labs.
- Build infrastructure; converge technology with pedagogy.
- Conduct continuous professional development of teachers, especially in the area of TEL and computer-mediated assessment & evaluation.
- Go for collaboration and partnerships to reach the doorstep of learners residing in remote areas.
- Conduct seminars, workshops and regular intervals to sensitise teachers on provisions made for SEDGs and implementation strategies.
- Regular reviews of technological interventions should prioritise digital inclusivity

References

Asgar, A., & Ratra, A. (2020). Continuous professional development of teachers in India amid Covid-19 crisis leveraging ICT tools in online environment. *Global Journal of Enterprise Information System, 12*(3), 56-65.

Batra, P. (2020). NEP 2020: Undermining the constitutional education agenda? *journals.sagepub.com/home/sch.* SAGE Publication. Accessed on 06/01/2024

Bordoloi, R. (2018). Transforming and Empowering Higher Education through Open and Distance Learning in India. *Asian Association of Open Universities Journal, 13*(1), 24-36.

Ching-Chiang, L.W.C., Fernández-Cárdenas, J. M., Lotz, N., González-Nieto, N. A., Gaved, M., Jones, D., ... & Machado, R. (2022). From Digital Divide to Digital Discovery: Re-thinking Online Learning and Interactions in Marginalised Communities. In *Innovation Practices for Digital Transformation in the Global South: IFIP WG 13.8, 9.4, Invited Selection* (pp. 34-58). Cham: Springer International Publishing.

ERSOY, N. Ş. (2023). Empowering Inclusion: Addressing Barriers in Distance Learning for Disadvantaged Groups. *TOJET: The Turkish Online Journal of Educational Technology, 22*(4).

Finch, D., & Jacobs, K. (2012). Online education: Best practices to promote learning. In *Proceedings of the human factors and ergonomics society annual meeting* (Vol. 56, No. 1, pp. 546-550). CA: SAGE Publications.

Holmberg, B. (2003). Distance education in essence. *Oldenburg: Bibliotheks-und Informations system der Universität Oldenburg.*

Hussain, A, 2023. National Education Policy 2020 and Inclusive Education: A Comprehensive Analysis. International Journal of Creative Research Thoughts- *IJCRT,* 11(7).

IGNOU (2023). Profile IGNOU-2023, available at http://www.ignou.ac.in/ accessed on 01/12/2023.

Joshi, A., Vinay, M., & Bhaskar, P. (2021). Impact of coronavirus pandemic on the Indian education sector: perspectives of teachers on online teaching and assessments. *Interactive technology and smart education, 18*(2), 205-226.

Kaur, P., & Sharma, A. (2023). The Challenges of New Education Policy 2020 of India and Sustainable Development Goal for Education: An Extensive Literature Review. *Phalanx,* 18(2) pp. 64-78.

Keegan, D. (2014). The Industrialization of Teaching and Learning, Routledge: London

Kumar, R., & Singh, A. K. (2022). A Geographical Study of Education and Empowerment of Weaker Section in Latehar District, Jharkhand. *Gyanshauryam, International Scientific* 5(1) 69-78.

Mandal, B. (2021). *An Appraisal of National Education Policy 2020 With Respect To Higher Education.* Available at: https://www.researchgate.net/publication/353923637 accessed 01/01/2024.

Mehra, B., Merkel, C., & Bishop, A. P. (2004). The internet for empowerment of minority and marginalized users. *New media & society,* 6(6), 781-802.

Nand, R, (2020). National Education Policy 2020 and Marginals: A Primer. Available at SSRN: https://ssrn.com/abstract=3947658 accessed on 02/01/2024.

NEP (2020): National Education Policy, Ministry of Human Resource Development, GOI, available at https://static.pib.gov.in/WriteReadData/user fi les/NEP_Final_English_0.pdf. accessed 01/12/2023

NIOS (2022). Inclusive Education Policy for Open Schooling, NIOS, Noida, available at: https://www.nios.ac.in/ accessed on 01/12/2023.

Sunny, Y. (2021). National Education Policy 2020: Realigning the *Bhadralok.* Economic and Political Weekly, 56(10), 17-20

6

Transformative Pathways: Education of Transgender in the Post-NEP 2020 Framework

Addressing Issues, Concerns and Best Practices

Anil Manjhi
Rahul Tiwari

Introduction

The term Khwaja Sira (Transgender) originated in medieval South Asian history as a title for the head eunuch of the Mughal court. Castrated male eunuchs worked as harem guards, army generals, and imperial advisors, among other positions of authority (Reddy, 2005). This name resurfaced in the first decade of the twenty-first century, when gender-ambiguous persons, who differed from their medieval counterparts in terms of sex, gender, and sexuality, repurposed it as an identity title to replace the derogatory term 'Hijra.' Despite the recent mainstreaming of the regal epithet Khwaja Sira, Hijra is still extensively used in the social networks of gender-ambiguous persons (F. A. Khan, 2019).

In the modern era, Khwaja Sira serves as an umbrella term for several overlapping sex and gender subcategories, which may include individuals with congenital genital irregularities (Khunsa), feminine males who situationally cross-dress (Zennana), and Zennanas who excise their male genitalia and assume a more permanent feminine presentation (hijra). Zennanas and hijras both believe that they were born with a feminine spirit. (F. Khan, 2016). They believe that this soul has formed not only their physical look and gender role but also their fondness for males. Khwaja Siras have a centuries-old social organisation system based on the guru-chela (master-disciple) connection, through which gender-ambiguous people form ceremonial relationships. Most are from lower-income families, have little or no formal education, and make a living via singing and dancing, begging, and sex work.

The Hon. Supreme Court of India explored the idea of "gender identity" in the case of *National Legal Service Authority v. Union of India in 2014. It designated* transgender as the 'third gender' in this historic ruling, Jerry-Peter 2021). It also urged authorities to treat the transgender minority as a "socially and educationally backward class," with restrictions in education and employment. Education is the only instrument in society that can make a person civilised, reasonable, and logical. The current state of education in transgender communities is deplorable, and as a result, the people of this group are lagging in terms of growth. There could be no forward-thinking endeavours in this community's education sphere. NEP 2020 has a provision for equitable and inclusive education for everyone. Such communities now have access to education, but the correct teaching method and appropriate teaching-learning environment are still the primary concerns in the current scenario.

Literature Review

A review of twenty relevant literature pieces, including theses, research articles, books, and news articles, was closely conducted. Through careful study, it is revealed that in the context of transgender people, only a little research has been conducted on the education of Khwaja Siras. None of this literature makes any direct provision for the education of this community, nor are there any specific education-related policies. Apart from this, in some literature, only the fact that Khwaja Siras are not educated has been highlighted. Further, the reasons for their inability to get an education have not been clarified. Also, the essential suggestions have not been talked about. There is no clear explanation of the figures in any literature as to what is the transgender population in India and how many transgender people are currently illiterate. Education for Transgender individuals can act as a boon in uplifting their status as they are also a part of the population, yet do not benefit from education due to the lack of appropriate measures. Therefore, the present study focuses on equality and inclusive education for the transgender community and creating transgender-friendly pedagogy for this community.

National Education Policy 2020

The National Policy for Education 2020 is the first update to the national education policy in decades and one of the most significant changes made to the system because policymakers have mentioned transgender people for the first time. "The policy recognises that education is a public benefit everyone deserves rather than a luxury. It appears to be an attempt to address various social groups that do not receive adequate policy attention, maybe owing to their numbers or past experiences. It focuses on equal, equitable and inclusive education. It will assist in providing the TGC with a voice for all of their societal aches and sorrows, as the bulk of societal problems can be remedied with enough knowledge (Balabantaray & Singh, 2020, p. 2)." However, the million-dollar question is whether NEP 2020 has taken shape as it was dreamt of or is merely an update in the policy for education. There are several hurdles to turning this dream into reality, and this study addresses those issues.

Issues and Concerns

The situation of Khwaja-Sira (transgender) people in Indian society has been quite pathetic, and this situation continues even today. The first educational institution of any child is their family. Still, in the families where they are born, that family, instead of educating them, does not accept them; they despise and insult them (Shaikh et al., 2016). Society considers them stigmatised and thinks that the family will get a bad name because of that child. Many atrocities are committed against such children, and they are asked to live in such a situation in which they cannot survive.

In the secondary educational institution where such children go for academic education, they become victims of teasing by their classmates. They need to be adequately treated and shown sensitivity by the teachers. They undergo maltreatment, misbehaviour, and insult and so on. Because of these reasons, they leave their educational institutions (Hafford-Letchfield et al., 2019). Further, it is evident that, at present, no appropriate policy has been made for education in this community.

Best Practices for Inclusive Education

To resolve the issues related to the education of the Khwaja-Siras and their concerns, some best practices are suggested for their inclusive education.

Inclusive Curriculum

The curriculum should be inclusive. A proposed curriculum could be "Navigating Gender: A Comprehensive Approach to Transgender Education." The target audience should be high school students, as high school is a critical time for personal development, and introducing students to diverse perspectives fosters inclusive attitudes early on. The views that shall be dealt with are age-appropriate discussions on gender identity, a historical overview of transgender figures and movements, and an exploration of the impact of stereotypes and discrimination (Shrivastava & Shrivastava, 2023). Another target audience could be the college students. The rationale is that the College students are in a phase of intellectual exploration, making it an ideal time for in-depth discussions and critical analysis. The contents should include an interdisciplinary exploration of transgender studies, case studies on legal, social, and health issues facing transgender individuals and opportunities for research and project-based learning. (Jecke & Zepf, 2023).

Further, the Community Groups must be targeted as they consist of diverse adults who can benefit from open dialogue and community building. The contents that should be addressed here are practical information on creating inclusive spaces, discussions on fostering acceptance and support within communities, and the invitation of guest speakers from diverse transgender backgrounds. The goals of the curriculum shall be

(i) Increasing awareness of transgender history, experiences, and contributions,
(ii) Fostering a deep understanding of gender identity, challenges faced by transgender individuals, and the societal context,
(iii) Developing empathy by connecting emotionally with transgender individuals and their experiences,
(iv) Promotion of inclusivity by challenging stereotypes and biases and encouraging respectful dialogue,
(v) Encouraging critical thinking about gender, identity, and societal norms and
(vi) Equiping of students with the skills to be allies and advocates for transgender individuals.

The Implementation Strategies that can be followed are Interactive Learning by incorporating group discussions, case studies, and hands-on activities, as well as utilising multimedia resources, inviting transgender individuals, activists, and experts to share their experiences and facilitating Q&A sessions for direct engagement with the audience, including assessments that measure understanding and empathy and collaboration with local Khwaja Sira organisations for support and additional resources. For Evaluation, pre-and post-assessments, Student Feedback, and Long-Term Impact can be conducted. So, by aligning the curriculum with the needs and developmental stages of the target audience and clearly defining the goals, educators can create an impactful and inclusive educational experience that promotes understanding and empathy towards transgender individuals (Lombardi et al., 2021).

Safe and Inclusive Spaces

Safe spaces and inclusive environments are essential for promoting Khawaja Siras education. This can be achieved by addressing bullying, harassment, and discrimination. Schools must actively promote a culture of acceptance and understanding. This involves implementing comprehensive anti-bullying policies, conducting regular diversity and inclusion training for staff and students, and promptly addressing incidents to ensure accountability (*Reimagining Our Futures Together: A New Social Contract for Education - UNESCO Digital Library*, n.d.). Providing gender-neutral restrooms and changing facilities is an essential step in acknowledging and respecting the diverse needs of transgender students.(Chappell et al., 2018). This inclusive infrastructure not only affirms their gender identity but also helps mitigate the anxiety and discomfort often associated with gender-specific facilities. Schools can further support transgender students by offering access to confidential counselling services, support groups, and designated safe spaces where they can express themselves without fear of judgment.

Professional Development

Training educators on transgender issues, terminology, and best practices is essential for creating an inclusive and supportive learning environment. Understanding these aspects enables educators to address the unique needs of transgender students and contribute to a more accepting school community. Training equips educators with the knowledge to navigate the complexities of gender identity, ensuring they use accurate and respectful terminology (McGuire et al., 2010). This proficiency helps create an environment where transgender students feel acknowledged and valued. Educators trained in best practices can foster a culture of respect, preventing unintentional microaggressions and promoting positive interactions among students.

Moreover, such training empowers educators to implement inclusive teaching methods, adapt curriculum materials, and advocate for transgender students within the school system. Awareness of the challenges transgender students may face, such as bullying or discrimination, allows educators to address these issues and provide necessary support proactively. By cultivating a diverse and knowledgeable teaching staff, schools can better meet the diverse needs of their student body, fostering a safe space where all students, including transgender individuals, can thrive academically and emotionally. Ongoing professional development ensures that educators stay current with evolving understandings of gender identity and continue to implement inclusive practices in their classrooms.

Affirmative Language

Language that respects and affirms diverse gender identities is crucial to creating a Khwaja Sira-friendly classroom culture. One key strategy is prioritising open communication and creating an inclusive environment where students feel comfortable expressing their gender identity. This can be implemented through several steps. Firstly, educators should introduce themselves with their pronouns, signalling a commitment to inclusivity, etc. (F. A. Khan, n.d.). They can then incorporate inclusive language into classroom discussions and materials, avoiding assumptions about gender. For instance, instead of saying "boys and girls," educators can use gender-neutral terms like "everyone" or "students." Additionally, educators can integrate activities that promote understanding and respect for diverse gender identities. For example, a lesson plan might include discussions about famous individuals who have challenged gender norms, allowing students to explore and appreciate different perspectives.

Crucially, educators should consistently use students' preferred names and pronouns, creating a safe and affirming space. This can be achieved through regular check-ins with students about their preferred pronouns, ensuring that any changes are seamlessly incorporated into classroom interactions. By proactively cultivating a culture of respect for diverse gender identities, educators empower students to express themselves authentically. This approach contributes to a positive and supportive learning environment where every student, regardless of gender identity, feels acknowledged and valued.

Intersectionality

In transgender education within the classroom, it is essential to recognise and address the intersectionality of identities. Educators should acknowledge that individuals may face discrimination based on both their gender identity and other factors such as race, ethnicity, socioeconomic status, and sexual orientation. This recognition is vital for creating a comprehensive and inclusive educational experience (*Harris, A., & Leonardo, Z. 2018).* To achieve this, educators should integrate diverse perspectives that illuminate the unique challenges faced by transgender individuals with intersecting identities. This involves incorporating content that explores the complex interplay of gender identity with race, ethnicity, socioeconomic status, and sexual orientation. For instance, classroom discussions, readings, or case studies can delve into the experiences of transgender individuals from different racial or ethnic backgrounds, emphasising the significance of understanding these multifaceted identities. Educators must also be mindful of the potential for compounded discrimination and privilege. Recognising the intersectionality of identities enables the challenging of stereotypes and avoids oversimplified narratives. Activities and discussions can focus on how systemic inequalities impact transgender individuals differently based on their intersecting identities (*Gender: A Four-Lesson Unit Plan for High School Psychology Teachers*, n.d.). Creating a safe space for dialogue is crucial in this context. Encouraging students to share their unique experiences and perspectives fosters an environment where everyone feels heard and validated. By addressing the intersectionality of identities in transgender education, educators contribute to a more nuanced understanding of the challenges faced by transgender individuals and promote a more inclusive and empathetic classroom culture.

Case Studies

Some exemplary excerpts from the interviews with Khwaja-Siras are stated to understand their need for education. For instance, Kapil alias Zara, age 32 years, on being about her life, replied with great enthusiasm:

> *I also wanted to do something in life, wanted to become something, but I am not very educated, so what will I be able to become? When I went to school, the teachers there did not behave properly with me. They did not know how to talk*

> *to a transgender person. The rest of my classmates used to tease me by calling me Chhakka Hijda because of my feminine behaviour. They would harass me, sometimes try to touch my private parts, and sometimes touch my backside; because of all this, I stopped going to school. Even the government does not do anything for us. I wish the government would have made a separate school/ college for us in which the teachers who taught us would have known about us. It would have been better if we could have studied too, and would not have done things like begging and would have got a job at a good place."*

Parmeshwar alias Pari (age 25 years)
When she talks about her life, she says –

> *I could only study until 6th class because after seeing my expressions, people did not come near me or talk to me; they used to say 'Mamu'. My studies in school were good, and I also wanted to study, but the teasing in the classroom hurt me a lot, and even while going to the bathroom, I did not know where or how to go. That is why I stopped going to school, I am done, now I earn money by dancing and singing."*

These excerpts and many more Khwaja Sira interactions state their love for education. Initially, they try to cope with the adverse situation in the classes but finally give up when things go beyond the bearable limits in the schools.

Conclusion and Recommendations

In Indian society, the situation of the transgender community in the field of education remains very lamentable, mainly due to a lack of access to education and society's ignorance of their educational needs. One of the biggest reasons is the need for more practical experience for teachers and classmates towards this community. Similarly, the absence of an inclusive form of education and transgender-friendly pedagogy is pushing this community away from education and into darkness. Therefore, several best practices can be followed so that the Khwaja-Sira community can emerge as leaders in the field of education by providing completely equal and equitable inclusive education and by preparing a community-friendly curriculum and pedagogy. Only when education is accessible to this community will society undergo a new change. The sun of NEP 2020 will rise and diminish the darkness of ignorance for them.

Recommendations

Legal action: For this community to be included in education, first of all, a special provision should be made in the country's supreme law, which is the Indian Constitution, so that all the states and educational institutions of the country can work according to it. No provision has been made for this community in the Right of Children to Free and Compulsory Education (RTE) Act 2009. (*Right to Education Ministry of Education, GoI*, n.d.) Therefore, both the Central and State Governments should make a provision in this Act to make the education of the transgender community inclusive.

Community Engagement: A national committee should be formed by the government which includes academicians from higher educational institutions, policymakers, psychologists, eminent personalities from the transgender community, etc. and through which the community can be informed about how to ensure their participation in the field of education (Kaplin et al., 2019). Think and consider how to bring the community into the mainstream of education. How can education be provided to this community using current technical methods? A policy should be formulated considering how to increase their reach through the new education system.

Policy Development: Work towards developing and implementing policies that protect the rights and well-being of transgender individuals within the educational institution. This includes anti-discrimination policies, privacy protections, and guidelines for accommodating transgender students.

Transgender Pedagogy: The enormously different experiences of trans persons who refuse to be defined give rise to a critical transgender pedagogy... The persistent misery of trans people is due to the plain inadequacies of a prescriptive gender binary, not some erroneous knowledge of ourselves. We require pedagogies that investigate how our existing gender system restricts us all and interacts with other methods such as race, class, and ability. We need pedagogies that focus on the urgent need to avoid transgender murders and suicides, as well as prevent our delayed deaths at the hands of insufficient medical and legal institutions. We require pedagogies sensitive to transgender experience in all its manifestations (Keenan, 2017, pp. 552–553). Engage with the broader community to promote understanding and acceptance of transgender individuals. This may involve partnerships with parents, local organisations, and advocacy groups. Implementing transgender pedagogy in education is a continuous process that requires ongoing reflection, collaboration, and a commitment to creating an inclusive and equitable learning environment for all students.

References

Balabantaray, S. R., & Singh, A. (2020). Review of (revisiting) the transgender education in India: An analysis of the National Educational Policy 2020. *Journal of Public Affairs*. https://doi.org/10.1002/pa.2504

Chappell, S. V., Ketchum, K. E., & Richardson, L. (2018). *Gender Diversity and LGBTQ Inclusion in K-12 Schools: A Guide to Supporting Students, Changing Lives*. Routledge.

Gender: A Four-Lesson Unit Plan for High School Psychology Teachers. (n.d.).

Jecke, L., & Zepf, F. D. (2023). Delivering transgender-specific knowledge and skills into health and allied health studies and training: A systematic review. *European Child & Adolescent Psychiatry*. https://doi.org/10.1007/s00787-023-02195-8

Jerry-Peter-WW.pdf. (n.d.). Retrieved December 31, 2023, from https://supremoamicus.org/wp-content/uploads/2021/08/Jerry-Peter-WW.pdf

Kaplin, W. A., Lee, B. A., Hutchens, N. H., & Rooksby, J. H. (2019). *The Law of Higher Education, A Comprehensive Guide to Legal Implications of Administrative Decision Making.* John Wiley & Sons.

Keenan, H. B. (2017). Unscripting Curriculum: Toward a Critical Trans Pedagogy. *Harvard Educational Review*, *87*(4), 538–556. https://doi.org/10.17763/1943-5045-87.4.538

Khan, F. (2016). Khwaja Sira Activism: The Politics of Gender Ambiguity in Pakistan. *TSQ: Transgender Studies Quarterly*, *3*, 158–164. https://doi.org/10.1215/23289252-3334331

Khan, F. A. (n.d.). *Khwaja Sira: Culture, Identity Politics, and "Transgender" Activism in Pakistan.*

Khan, F. A. (2019). Institutionalizing an Ambiguous Category: <em>"Khwaja Sira"</em> Activism, the State, and Sex/Gender Regulation in Pakistan. *Anthropological Quarterly*, *92*(4), 1135–1172.

Lombardi, D., Shipley, T. F., Bailey, J. M., Bretones, P. S., Prather, E. E., Ballen, C. J., Knight, J. K., Smith, M. K., Stowe, R. L., Cooper, M. M., Prince, M., Atit, K., Uttal, D. H., LaDue, N. D., McNeal, P. M., Ryker, K., St. John, K., van der Hoeven Kraft, K. J., & Docktor, J. L. (2021). The Curious Construct of Active Learning. *Psychological Science in the Public Interest*, *22*(1), 8–43. https://doi.org/10.1177/1529100620973974

McGuire, J. K., Anderson, C. R., Toomey, R. B., & Russell, S. T. (2010). School Climate for Transgender Youth: A Mixed Method Investigation of Student Experiences and School Responses. *Journal of Youth and Adolescence*, *39*(10), 1175–1188. https://doi.org/10.1007/s10964-010-9540-7

Reddy, G. (2005). *With Respect to Sex: Negotiating Hijra Identity in South India.* University of Chicago Press. https://press.uchicago.edu/ucp/books/book/chicago/W/bo3534006.html

Reimagining our futures together: A new social contract for education—UNESCO Digital Library. (n.d.). Retrieved December 31, 2023, from https://unesdoc.unesco.org/ark:/48223/pf0000379707.locale=en

Right to Education | Ministry of Education, GoI. (n.d.). Retrieved December 31, 2023, from https://dsel.education.gov.in/rte

Shaikh, S., Mburu, G., Arumugam, V., Mattipalli, N., Aher, A., Mehta, S., & Robertson, J. (2016). Empowering communities and strengthening systems to improve transgender health: Outcomes from the Pehchan programme in India. *Journal of the International AIDS Society*, *19*(3S2), 20809. https://doi.org/10.7448/IAS.19.3.20809

Shrivastava, S. R., & Shrivastava, P. S. (2023). Transgender Health and Medical Education: The Existing Gaps and the Need for Curricular Reforms – A Systematic Review. *Journal of the Scientific Society*, *50*(2), 163. https://doi.org/10.4103/jss.jss_56_22

7

Psychosocial Well-being of Children with Learning Disabilities

Impact of Parental Support

Madhu Singh
Sana Fatima

Introduction

In our contemporary society, the perception of disability has evolved, recognising unique abilities in individuals traditionally labelled as disabled. This transformation extends to children with learning disabilities, who are increasingly integrated into mainstream education (Stahopoulou & Siskou, 2023). Despite advancements, youngsters diagnosed with specific learning disorders (SLDs) face academic challenges, often lacking motivation compared to their peers (Stahopoulou & Siskou, 2023). Common learning disabilities, such as dyslexia, highlight the need for tailored teaching methods (Stahopoulou & Siskou, 2023).

The research emphasises the link between learning disabilities and emotional/behavioural issues, with heightened susceptibility to anxiety disorders (Cavioni, Grazzani & Ornaghi, 2017). Cognitive studies reveal deficits in working memory and phonological processing among these children (Sofologi et al., 2022). Academic struggles contribute to emotional distress, emphasising the importance of addressing psychosocial well-being in this population (Cavioni, Grazzani & Ornaghi, 2017).

This study explores the differential impact of parental support levels on the psychosocial well-being of children with learning disabilities. By examining key psychosocial variables, including self-concept, social interaction, behaviour patterns, and home environment, we aim to uncover nuanced patterns that inform interventions for a more supportive educational environment.

Parental Support and Children with Learning Disabilities

Children diagnosed with learning problems often elicit distress in parents who struggle to accept this reality (Dyson, 2010). Instances of parental refusal or negligence contribute to high parental stress (Dyson, 2010). Mothers face elevated stress levels, expected to guide their children perfectly (Rogers, 2007).

Parental support emerges as a critical factor impacting the lives of children with learning disabilities. Those with secure support mechanisms demonstrate better-coping abilities, while those lacking support tend to experience greater challenges (Rogers, 2007). Insufficient support not only affects the child but can disable the entire family (Rogers, 2007). Research by Martínez (2006) suggests that children with learning disabilities receive less support from parents, friends, and teachers alike.

Interconnectedness of Psycho-Social Variables

The present study has explored five psycho-social variables namely self-concept, parental support, home environment, behaviour pattern and social interaction. Parents play a very crucial role in building up a home environment that is conducive and supportive as well as positively inclined for the growth of the children. Families where parents are not supportive and are ignorant about the inability of the child often seem to suffer harsh conditions. Parents are often held responsible for the building of the self-concept of children who suffer from learning problems. The children who lack parental support mostly are seen to have low self-concepts and in turn, are socially secluded. They fail to interact freely with their surroundings and they feel insecure in expressing themselves. This hampers their social interaction and the behaviours they exhibit. Dyson (2003) explored and concluded that children with learning disabilities had less social competence and many behavioural problems due to the stress their parents had regarding them. Such children also have a very low self-concept. (Brabcova et al. 2015), (Teimouri, Rezaei & Mohammadzadeh, 2020).

Hence, keeping in mind every aspect that gets severely affected by the support the parents of children with a learning disability get, it would not be unwise to state that one of the most important factors to boost the morale of such children is positive, motivating, and a high degree of parental support.

The Study

Rationale

Learning disabilities pose significant challenges, impacting both academic performance and psychosocial development in children. While academic aspects have been extensively studied, a gap exists in understanding the nuanced psychosocial dynamics influenced by parental support. This research addresses this gap by focusing on specific variables—Self-Concept, Social Interaction, Behaviour Patterns, and Home Environment—in the context of learning disabilities.

Understanding the role of parental support is crucial due to the unique social and emotional challenges faced by these children. Parents play a central role in providing necessary support, yet limited empirical evidence explores the differential impact on specific psychosocial domains. The study aims to uncover detailed patterns within the psychosocial landscape, contributing to both academic literature and practical knowledge for educators, parents, and professionals.

The interconnectedness of psychosocial variables underscores the complexity of challenges. By unravelling these relationships, the research informs targeted interventions for children with learning disabilities. The study's rationale lies in generating empirical evidence that guides academic research and practical efforts, filling critical gaps and positively impacting the lives of this vulnerable population (Dyson, 2010; Rogers, 2007; Martínez, 2006).

Objectives

1. To determine whether there are statistically significant differences in self-concept among children with learning disabilities characterised by high and low levels of parental support.
2. To investigate the extent to which the level of parental support influences Social Interaction among children with learning disabilities.
3. Explore and analyse if there are significant differences in behaviour patterns between groups of children with learning disabilities with high and low levels of parental support.
4. Assess and compare the home environment for children with learning disabilities based on differing levels of parental support.

Hypotheses

1. There is no significant difference in self-concept among children with learning disabilities with high and low levels of parental support.
2. The level of parental support does not significantly influence Social Interaction among children with learning disabilities.
3. There is no significant difference in behaviour patterns between children with learning disabilities with high and low levels of parental support.
4. The home environment does not significantly differ for children with learning disabilities with varying levels of parental support.

Methodology

Research Design: This study employs a quantitative research design to investigate the differential impact of parental support levels on the psychosocial well-being of children with learning disabilities. The chosen design aligns with the research objectives and allows for a systematic examination of specific psychosocial variables.

Sample and Sampling Technique: The population chosen for the study was children with mild or moderate disabilities studying in schools in Patna. The age group of the children was decided to be in the range of 8 to 20 years comprising both male and female children. The samples were chosen by purposive and snowball sampling methods to reach places where such children could be found. The study was conducted on 52 children diagnosed with mild or moderate learning disabilities by school counsellors or medical professionals and those who could understand and reply to the researcher.

Research Instruments Used: The study employed a psycho-social scale, meticulously crafted by the researcher. Its validation involved consultations with experts and a preliminary pilot study conducted on a sample of 5 children with learning disabilities. The scale encompasses five dimensions: parental support, self-concept, social interaction, behaviour pattern, and home environment. The data were collected from such children keeping in mind the ethical considerations and a proper protocol was followed by the researcher to enhance the authenticity of the research.

Ethical Considerations

The following considerations have been taken into account to ensure the welfare, confidentiality, and voluntary participation of all involved parties:

i *Informed Consent:* Obtained from participants or legal guardians, outlining the purpose, risks, and benefits. Child assent secured for those under 20.

ii *Confidentiality:* Participant identities were anonymized. Data is securely stored, with limited access.

iii *Voluntary Participation and Withdrawal:* Participation is voluntary, withdrawal is possible at any stage.

iv *Minimisation of Harm:* Measures were taken to minimise emotional distress. Debriefing was provided after participation.

Presentation of Statistical Analyses

The primary analysis utilized independent samples t-tests to examine mean differences between two groups: children with learning disabilities characterized by high and low levels of parental support. For each psychosocial variable, t-tests were conducted. The analysis is as follows:

Objective 1: To determine whether there are statistically significant differences in Self-Concept among children with learning disabilities characterised by high and low levels of parental support

$H_0 1$: There is no significant difference in Self-Concept among children with learning disabilities with high and low levels of parental support.

The mean Self-Concept scores were compared between the high parental support group and the low parental support group to determine if there was a significant difference in self-concept among these two groups. The results are shown in Table 1:

Table 1: Comparing Self-Concept Across Low and High Parental Support Groups

Parental Support	*N*	*Mean*	*S.D.*	*t-ratio*	*Remarks*
Low	11	13.09	3.26	3.65	Significant at 0.05 level
High	12	13.5	3.11		

In the independent samples t-test comparing the self-concept of learning-disabled children between the Low and High parental support groups, the calculated t-ratio was found to be 3.65. The critical table value for a two-tailed test at df=21 at a significance level of 0.05 is 2.080.

The null hypothesis is rejected based on the calculated value of 't.' The results suggest that there is a significant difference in the self-concept levels of the children who have high and low parental support. This in turn suggests that children who have good and high support from their parents seem to have a good self-concept and vice-versa.

Objective 2: To investigate the extent to which the level of parental support influences Social Interaction among children with learning disabilities.

$H_0 2$: The level of parental support does not significantly influence Social Interaction among children with learning disabilities.

The mean social interaction scores were compared between the high parental support group and the low parental support group to determine if there was a significant difference in social interaction among these two groups. The results are shown in Table 2:

Table 2: Comparing Social Interaction Across Low and High Parental Support Groups

Parental Support	*N*	*Mean*	*S.D.*	*t-ratio*	*Remarks*
Low	11	9	4.5	8.31	Significant at 0.05 level
High	12	13.83	3.15		

In the independent samples t-test comparing the social interaction of children with learning disabilities between the Low and High parental support groups, the calculated t-ratio was found to be 8.31. The critical table value for a two-tailed test at df=21 and a significance level of 0.05 is 2.080.

The calculated value suggests that the results are significant and the null hypothesis is rejected. This means that there is a significant difference in the social interaction of the children who experience high and low levels of parental support. The children whose parents are supportive are usually seen to have good interaction with society giving them the confidence their parents give and vice-versa.

***Objective 3*:** Explore and analyse if there are significant differences in Behaviour Patterns between groups of children with learning disabilities with high and low levels of parental support.

H_0 3: There is no significant difference in Behaviour Patterns between children with learning disabilities with high and low levels of parental support.

The mean behaviour pattern scores were compared between the high parental support group and the low parental support group to determine if there was a significant difference in behaviour patterns among these two groups. The results are shown in Table 3:

Table 3: Comparing Behaviour Pattern Across Low and High Parental Support Groups

Parental Support	*N*	*Mean*	*S.D.*	*t-ratio*	*Remarks*
Low	11	14.5	2.2	2.08	Significant at 0.05 level
High	12	14.4	3.3		

In the independent samples t-test comparing the behaviour patterns of children with learning disabilities between the Low and High parental support groups, the calculated t-ratio was found to be 2.08. The critical table value at df =21 at a significance level of 0.05 is 2.080.

The calculated value rejects the null hypothesis and establishes that there is a significant difference in the behaviour patterns of the children who receive a good level of parental support and those who do not have supportive parents. This finding suggests that the children who enjoy parental support are often seen to have less anxiety and frustration, exhibiting normal or good behaviour. Children who do not have supportive parents are often seen to be frustrated and anxious, resulting in them showing not-so-good behaviour patterns.

Objective 4: Assess and compare the Home Environment for children with learning disabilities based on differing levels of parental support.

H_0 4: The Home Environment does not significantly differ for children with learning disabilities with varying levels of parental support.

The mean home environment scores were compared between the high parental support group and the low parental support group to determine if there was a significant difference in the home environment among these two groups. The results are shown in Table 4:

Table 4: Comparing Home Environment Across Low and High Parental Support Groups

Parental Support	*N*	*Mean*	*S.D.*	*t-ratio*	*Remarks*
Low	11	12.45	3.11	3.91	Significant at 0.05 level
High	12	15.75	1.65		

In the independent samples t-test comparing the home environment of children with learning disabilities between the Low and High parental support groups, the calculated t-ratio was found to be 3.91. The critical table value at df =21 at a significance level of 0.05 is 2.080.

The results of the t-test reject the null hypothesis. The finding suggests that there is a significant difference in the home environment of the children who receive parental support and those who do not have supportive parents. It is indicated that the home environment of the children with supportive parents is usually conducive and supportive but this is not the case for those children whose parents fail to support them. Their home environment seems to become depressive and they find it hard to remain calm in such a situation.

Conclusion

The presence of support from the parents as well as its absence does affect the psycho-social well-being of such children. The presence of sound parental support makes the home environment of these children conducive and builds a sound self-concept in them. They are found to interact more when they feel safe and secure with their parents standing at their back. It is also known that children who are not fortunate enough to receive a good amount of parental support often find themselves low in self-concept and they feel hesitant in interacting with others. Even the environment of the house is not friendly and this impacts the psychological well-being of such children.

Conclusively it can be stated that parents do play the most crucial part in the lives of children. The well-being of each child is determined by the support, care and love he/she receives from his/her parents. Children with learning disabilities are no exception. These children also are in dire need of support from their parents as they face the harsh reality of facing inability to excel in their academics.

It is therefore the responsibility of the parents, teachers, and society to provide immense encouragement and support to such children and to enhance the strength of such children whichever area that may be. This will boost the morale of such children and they will never feel burdened.

Recommendations

i. Parental Engagement: Parents should be encouraged to actively advocate for their child's education.
ii. Parental Influence: The pivotal role of parents in a child's educational journey should be recognized.
iii. Strengths-Focused: Foster confidence by focusing on a child's strengths.
iv. Proactive Parenting: Parents should be urged to actively participate in educational decisions.
v. Holistic Well-being: Overall well-being for academic success should be promoted.

vi. Teacher-Parent Collaboration: Open communication between teachers and parents should be advocated.

vii. Positive Reinforcement: Consistent positive feedback for a supportive learning environment should be provided.

References

Better, O. N. D. (2016). Children and Young People with Learning Disabilities. Understanding Their Mental Health. https://scholar.google.com/scholar?hl=en&as_sdt=0%2C5&q

Brabcova, D., Zarubova, J., Kohout, J., Jošt, J., & Kršek, P. (2015). Effect of learning disabilities on academic self-concept in children with epilepsy and on their quality of life. *Research in developmental disabilities*, 45, 120-128. http://dx.doi.org/10.1016/j.ridd.2015.07.018 0891-4222/ 2015

Cavioni, V., Grazzani, I., & Ornaghi, V. (2017). Social and emotional learning for children with Learning Disability: Implications for inclusion. International Journal of Emotional Education., 9(2), 100-109. https://scholar.google.com/scholar?hl=en&as_sdt=0%2C5&q=Social+and+emotional+learning+for++children+with+Learning+Disability%3A+Implications+for+inclusion+International+Journal+of++Emotional+Education.%2C+9%282%29%2C+100-109&btnG=

Dyson, L. (2010). Unanticipated effects of children with learning disabilities on their families. Learning Disability Quarterly, 33(1), 43-55. https://doi.org/10.1177/073194871003300104

Dyson, L. L. (2003). Children with learning disabilities within the family context: A comparison with siblings in global self–concept, academic self–perception, and social competence. Learning disabilities research & practice, 18(1), 1-9. https://doi.org/10.1111/1540-5826.00053

Kimberly Newton, MS, LPE-I & Chair of LDA Mental Health Committee https://ldaamerica.org/lda_today/mental-health-and-ld/

Martínez, R. S. (2006). Social support in inclusive middle schools: Perceptions of youth with learning disabilities. *Psychology in the Schools*, 43(2), 197-209. https://scholar.google.com/scholar?hl=en&as_sdt=0%2C5&q=Social+support+in+inclusive+middle+schools%3A+Perceptions+of+youth+with++learning+disabilities.+Psychology+in+the+Schools%2C+43%282%29%2C+197-209.&btnG=

Matlon.R. (2019), 6 Ways to Support the Emotional Well-Being of Children with Learning Disorders https://ccy.jfcs.org/6-ways-to-support-the-emotional-well-being-of-children-with-learning-disorders/

Rogers, C. (2007). Disabling a family? Emotional dilemmas experienced in becoming a parent of a child with learning disabilities. British Journal of Special Education, 34(3), 136-143. https://doi.org/10.1111/j.1467-8578.2007.00469

Sofologi, M., Kougioumtzis, G. A., Efstratopoulou, M., Skoura, E., Sagia, S., Karvela, S., ... & Bonti, E. (2022). Specific Learning Disabilities and Psychosocial Difficulties in Children. *In Advising Preservice Teachers Through Narratives from Students with Disabilities* (pp. 31-54). IGI Global. DOI: 10.4018/978-1-7998-7359-4.ch002

Stahopoulou, A., & Siskou, K. (2023). Enhancing mental health promotion of students with learning disabilities: The role of motivation and digital technologies. GSC Advanced Research and Reviews, 16(1), 116-128. DOI:10.30574/gscarr.2023.16.1.0307

Teimouri, L., Rezaei, A., & Mohammadzadeh, A. (2020). A Comparative Study of Hope, academic achievement motivation, and academic self-concept among students with and without learning disabilities. Journal of Learning Disabilities, 9(2), 7-35. Doi 10.22098/JLD.2020.854.

8

Denotified Communities: Educational Status, Aspirations and Access

A Study of Sansi and Sapera Communities of Delhi

Shiney Vasishta

Introduction

India is a nation known for its rich cultural tapestry, encompassing a multitude of ethnicities, religious faiths, socio-economic statuses, and castes, all contributing to a diverse and pluralistic society. The Indian Constitution is designed to safeguard and strengthen this societal framework, ensuring the flourishing of individuals from various backgrounds. It not only acknowledges but also harnesses differences in caste, class, religion, and gender to identify marginalized populations. Numerous affirmative actions are implemented to cater to the requirements of these marginalised communities, safeguarding their constitutional rights. Positive discrimination stands as a pivotal method employed to achieve this objective.

After India gained independence from British rule in 1947, categories such as Scheduled Castes (SC), Scheduled Tribes (ST), and Other Backward Classes (OBC) were established to empower groups historically and socially marginalised. These categories not only offer privileges for development but also secure special rights through protective constitutional provisions.

Criminal Tribes Act (1871)

Before independence, the British administration classified certain communities as "Criminals" under the Criminal Tribes Act (CTA) of 1871. This legislation was specifically designed to label certain communities as inherently criminal. Approximately 200 communities were listed as Criminal Tribes (Radhakrishna, 2009). The British authorities identified communities with 'deviant behaviour' based on their own criteria and included them in the Criminal Tribes through Gazette notifications. These groups mainly consisted of entertainer tribes, nomadic communities, or those with distinct social characteristics. However, in 1949, two years after India gained independence, these communities were officially denotified of their criminal status, and the CTA was entirely abolished between 1950 and 1952 (Heredia, 2002).

Despite the repeal of the CTA, the impact continued as the Habitual Offender's Act of 1952 was enacted to monitor 'habitual offenders,' which still disproportionately affects these communities. Presently recognised as Denotified Tribes, these communities have faced continued discrimination due to the historical stigmatization and unfair treatment stemming from earlier legislations.

Denotified Communities and their Concerns

The Denotified communities, integral to Indian society, encompass groups like*Sapera, Kabelia, Gadia Lohar, Waghri, Madari, Nat,* and others, holding significant cultural heritage. Despite some communities being grouped under SC, ST, or OBC categories, inconsistencies persist, challenging their inclusion. Lingering historical stigma linked to past criminalisation renders their existence nearly invisible today, further marginalising them in education and socio-economic opportunities.

The Indian Constitution provisions, including Article 15, 29, 46, and 21-A, protect the rights of minority communities, empowering them with crucial incentives for societal progress. Education, a vital avenue for personal and communal growth, faces hurdles among Denotified communities due to factors like migratory lifestyles, poverty, and the stigma of past criminal identities. High dropout rates stem from discrimination in schools and a lack of tailored support mechanisms, hindering their access to welfare provisions.

Government initiatives like RTE, SSA, RMSA (now Samagra Shiksha Abhiyan), JNV, and Ashram Schools were introduced to integrate disadvantaged groups into formal education systems. However, achieving literacy remains a challenge due to a lack of awareness about education and persistent poverty within these communities. This situation disproportionately affects girls, often married off early with their education side-lined, while financial constraints hinder higher education after secondary schooling.

Insights from Literature Review

The extensive review of existing literature highlights a notable gap in research specifically focusing on the Delhi region regarding Denotified communities. While numerous studies have explored facets such as education, socio-economic status, stigmatisation, and marginalisation, the specificity to Delhi remains deficient. Studies concerning education shed light on pertinent issues like low enrolment rates, heightened dropout rates, inadequate contextualization of education, language barriers, lack of academic support at home, excessive household responsibilities for children, and resorting to begging to supplement family income, among others. However, a significant concern emerges regarding the lack of awareness and documentation among community members concerning available welfare provisions. This deficiency extends to accessing healthcare and socio-economic benefits, either due to a lack of knowledge about these schemes or an inability to avail themselves due to documentation constraints.

Stigmatisation of these communities emerges as a major issue, exacerbating their marginalisation. Instances of violence from upper-caste Hindus and police atrocities stem from the misguided perception that all community members are criminals. This not only affects their social lives and economic productivity but also results in disinterest in pursuing education, leading to increased dropout rates. The ongoing COVID-19 pandemic has significantly amplified their concerns.

A critical gap exists in studies that fail to capture the current challenges faced by Denotified communities residing in urban areas, particularly how they cope with the enduring stigma of criminality in this context. Additionally, a deeper exploration of educational issues from the perspective of urban living among these communities is warranted.

The Study

The study, titled 'A Study of Educational Status, Government Provisions, and Aspirations of Denotified Communities,' was conducted as part of a PhD programme, under the guidance of Prof. Fauzia Khan, at the IASE, Faculty of Education, in the esteemed Jamia Millia Islamia; with the post- doctoral award of ICSSR. The study focuses on understanding the lived experiences of two Denotified communities - *Sansi* and *Sapera* - residing in Delhi and aims to inform educational policymaking by providing insights into the challenges faced by these communities and advocating for comprehensive solutions to promote education among present and future generations. Thus, the study's foundation lies in comprehensively understanding the actual socio-economic, educational status, and social struggles of these communities to facilitate informed policy decisions promoting education within these groups.

Objectives

1. To identify the status of government schemes and provisions for the Denotified communities.
2. To assess the socio-economic status of Denotified communities.
3. To explore the educational status of children of Denotified communities.
4. To identify the factors leading to educational marginalisation of Denotified communities.
5. To understand the factors responsible for the stigmatisation of Denotified communities due to their past criminal identity.
6. To understand the issues related to women of Denotified communities.
7. To explore the vocational aspirations of youth of Denotified communities.
8. To assess the impact of COVID-19 induced lockdowns and restrictions on the education of children from Denotified communities

Design

This study followed a qualitative research design. Qualitative research is a continually evolving investigative approach that involves gathering data in a natural setting. In this type of study, significant emphasis is placed on comprehending human problems within their social context. The analysis of data utilises both inductive and deductive techniques to establish thematic patterns. The outcomes are presented through an extensive report, detailing descriptions of human issues and offering a profound understanding. This is complemented by a thorough review of related literature and recommendations for future initiatives in the particular field of inquiry.

There are five primary approaches to qualitative research: Narrative, Phenomenology, Grounded Theory, Ethnography, and Case Study. In this study, a Case Study approach was adopted in conjunction with Ethnography. While the study primarily followed an Ethnography approach, it cannot be strictly categorised as a pure Ethnographic study due to the identification of variables beforehand. However, considering that the study aimed to capture the multifaceted socio-cultural composition of the sample communities, the influence of Ethnography in shaping the study's perspectives cannot be overlooked.

Population and Sample

The population consisted of all the Denotified communities residing in the NCT Delhi region. Sample consisted of 100 families; 50 each from *Sapera* and *Sansi* Communities, residing in NCT Delhi. Settlements selected for the communities were– Molarband, a census town in South East District of the NCT Delhi; and Majnu-ka-tilla, a colony in Delhi, established around 1950, located in North Delhi district.

Snowball Sampling technique was used in this study. A Snowball Sampling technique, also called Chain- referral sampling, is used when the subjects are difficult to trace. It involves selecting the sample based on referrals from the population. It is a type of non-probability sampling that is most effective when one needs to study a certain cultural domain, but the participants are difficult to locate. As these communities are closed in nature, not many people were willing to participate. So, Snowball sampling technique was most effective to follow.

Tools and Data Collection

Data were collected using a self-constructed and validated tool-

- Settlement Observation Inventory
- Community Leader Interview Schedule
- Family Survey Questionnaire
- Separate FGD guidelines for Women, and Youth
- Teachers Interview Schedule

Data were collected in a phased manner and COVID-19 induced lockdowns highly impacted the data collection. The collected data was thematically analysed.

Findings

The major findings extracted from this study extensively support the research's objectives. They include:

1. *Socio- Economic Status and Livelihood*
   - *The Sansi* community exhibits a better overall socio-economic status compared to the *Sapera* community.
   - *B*oth communities faced significant livelihood losses due to COVID-19, resulting in increased financial struggles. *Sapera* women entered the workforce to support their families, gaining community acceptance.
   - *The Sapera* community experienced increased debts due to COVID-19, exhausting savings and selling assets. The *Sansi* community coped better due to substantial savings.
2. *Welfare schemes and Policies*
   - Both communities strive to utilise major government schemes and policies, both welfare and educational.
3. *Healthcare*
   - Government healthcare facilities are accessed by both communities, but *Sapera* women are dissatisfied with government hospital treatments; *Sansi* prefer private treatments.
   - Women from both communities prefer hospital births for access to birth control, yet *Sapera* women face difficulties due to traditional preferences for home births.
   - Sanitary napkin usage has increased among young girls and most older women in both communities.
   - *Sapera* women suffer from various health issues attributed to a lack of a nutritious diet, delayed medical interventions, and limited access to quality healthcare.
4. *Stigma and discrimination-*
   - Children from both communities' face discrimination and stigma at school due to their community background, impacting their confidence and well-being.
5. *Education*
   - Enrolment ratios have improved across generations, especially for women, due to increased access to educational schemes and growing awareness of education's importance.
   - Education for girls is less prioritized in the *Sapera* community, while the *Sansi* community encourages higher education, professional courses, and employment opportunities for girls.

- Educational attainment for women is considerably lower in the *Sapera* community compared to the *Sansi* community, where girls excel in higher education and competitive exams.
- Parents' involvement in their wards' education is lower in the Sapera community compared to the Sansi community.
- Dropping out around high school is common among *Sapera* children due to various factors, while *Sansi* children often progress to higher education.
- Both communities access government provisions for education, mostly enrolling in government schools or occasionally in private schools through the EWS category.
- COVID-19 affected children's interest and retention in schools due to difficulties adapting to online learning, especially for the *Sapera* community facing digital divide issues.
- Children from the *Sapera* community face multiple obstacles with online learning, leading to potential dropout risks due to inadequate resources.

6. *Aspirations*
   - *Sansi* girls aspire for high-level professions like joining the police force or civil services, while *Sapera* girls' aspirations are less ambitious, often aiming for careers as beauticians or boutique owners.
   - Vocational aspirations for *Sapera* boys are generally blue-collar jobs or traditional roles, while *Sansi* youth aim for higher professions with strong community and family support.
   - *The Sansi* community's youth have diverse vocational aspirations, aiming for jobs in civil services, sports coaching, teaching, among others, with robust community and family support.
7. *Other Issues*
   - The prevalence of illegal drug-selling businesses in the *Sansi* settlement and drug issues in the *Sapera* community contribute to societal stigma.
   - Early marriage is prevalent in the *Sapera* community, while the Sansi community delays marriage due to an emphasis on girls' education and employment.
   - Domestic violence is widespread in the *Sapera* community, while *Sansi* women are considered strong and not oppressed.
   - Both communities face police atrocities based on their stigmatised identities, often with complaints being disregarded.

The Sapera community faces educational marginalization due to various factors, while the *Sansi* community fares significantly better educationally, attributed to socio-economic conditions, family attitudes toward education, parental literacy levels, drug dependence, early marriage, and settlement environment.

These findings collectively provide a comprehensive understanding of the socio-economic, educational, and societal challenges faced by the *Sansi* and *Sapera* communities, illuminating the nuanced complexities within each community.

Suggestions and Recommendations

The recommendations suggested may provide a founding ground for future researches and policy making in the areas concerning Denotified communities. These recommendations are as follows:

1. *A dedicated National Commission for Denotified Communities* similar to existing commissions for Scheduled Castes, Scheduled Tribes, and Other Backward Classes, is imperative to address the unique challenges faced by these communities. Unlike other marginalized groups, Denotified communities lack a specific institution to voice their concerns and oversee their welfare. This proposed commission, operating under Article 8A, would vigilantly monitor and safeguard the rights of Denotified communities, addressing grievances, and devising policies for their socio-economic, cultural, and educational development. With a focus on human rights protection and policy implementation, this commission would serve as a crucial entity in advocating for the rights and advancement of Denotified communities in India.
2. *Rectifying Listing Anomalies:* Some denotified communities have been included in SC, ST and OBC lists; while some haven't been included in any schedule. Also, the included communities have different statuses in different states, due to lack of uniformity. The TAG Report (Ministry of Social Justice and Empowerment, 2006) also gave impressive recommendations in this regard.
3. *Population estimate:* In order to get an accurate picture of socio- economic conditions of these communities, effective policy making initiatives can be initiated. An alternative would be to enable the Indian Institute of Statistics to develop scientific and reliable population projections of DNT population.
4. *Constitutional safeguards* include abolishing Habitual Offenders Acts, specific constitutional acts and provisions for prohibiting any discrimination on the grounds of denotification, Prevention of atrocities act established on the similar grounds as SC and ST (prevention of atrocities) act (1989), political representation etc.
5. *Identification and documentation assistance* is provided to ensure that all DNTs have access to welfare provisions.
6. *Resource allocation* with respect to land and housing for community members living on the outskirts of villages and cities; in make-shift, semi- permanent, and slum dwellings, which lacks basic necessities like- sanitation, electricity, water etc. These should be covered under housing schemes as per requirement.
7. *Awareness, integration, and sensitisation* at the level of education, polity, and Ppolice services are necessary in order to integrate these communities in to mainstream society and reduce any stigma associated with them. Atrocities faced by these communities can be curbed in this manner.

8. *Education* can be made more contextual for these communities by including their community context in teaching and learning, and by providing education through different modes on need basis (considering the nomadic status of many communities). Teachers from these communities must be appointed to teach in their native language and contextual setting. Acceptance and sensitivity are required at the school level and incidents of discrimination must be addressed through strict disciplinary action and anti- bullying rules. Awareness must be created for the available Dr. Ambedkar Pre- Matric and Post-Matric Scholarships for DNT students. Students who are culturally adept at sports (gymnastics etc) and performing and fine arts must be motivated to nurture their talent.
9. *Livelihood* opportunities must be increased for these communities. Some of these communities have vast knowledge about Ayurveda, medicinal plants and traditional healing methods which have been there in our society for centuries. Their knowledge could be utilised by Naturopathy and Ayurvedic institutions. Also, there are certain communities which perform entertaining acts on the streets such as acrobatics, dancing and fortune telling. They are often wrongly booked under Beggary Prevention Acts, without understanding the traditional occupations of these communities. Efforts should be done to protect them by revisiting these acts and sensitising the police. For the communities that are still practicing their traditional livelihoods which are not yielding much income, they should be provided with skills so that they can effectively practice other occupations as well.
10. *Healthcare* must be addressed though awareness programmes, as communities lack awareness of the schemes and welfare provisions. Anganwadis can play a crucial role in densely populated areas. Awareness must be created regarding- immunisation, family planning, menstrual hygiene, pregnancy, childbirth, nutrition, the importance of a clean environment, health hazards of substance abuse, and the importance of regular health check-ups. It should be ensured that these communities have access to Anganwadi, ASHA workers, Government hospitals, and dispensaries. At the remote places which do not have a government hospital nearby, *Mohalla* Clinic, Mobile Clinics and Mobile Dispensaries should be made accessible.
11. *Women empowerment* must be another focus in order to curb atrocities faced by DNT women such as sexual exploitation and domestic violence. A separate cell in the National Commission for Women must be established to exclusively address the issues related to DNT women. Civil society organisations can play a crucial role in this.

Conclusion

Denotified communities endure a persistent stigma from their 'ex-criminal' label, alongside socio-economic hardships, limited awareness about welfare schemes, early marriages, and domestic violence within the *Sapera* community.

In contrast, the *Sansi* community demonstrates more stability in socio-economic status, education, and awareness of government initiatives. While *Sansi* prioritises girls' education and career aspirations, *Sapera* faces challenges with educational disparities, particularly exacerbated by COVID-19's digital divide. *Sansi's* better access to government schemes contrasts *Sapera's* limited uptake, reflecting significant socio-economic and educational gaps. Urgent attention is needed to raise awareness among *Sapera* members, address issues of drug dependence, domestic violence, and illegal activities, while empowering *Sapera* women and preserving their cultural heritage for potential utilisation.

References

Bokil, M. (2002). De-Notified and Nomadic Tribes: A Perspective. *Economic and Political Weekly*, *37*(2), 148–154. https://www.jstor.org/stable/4411599

Creswell, J. W., & Miller, D. L. (2000). Determining Validity in Qualitative Inquiry. *Theory Into Practice*, *39*(3), 124–130. https://doi.org/10.1207/s15430421tip3903_2

Creswell, J. W. (2006). *Qualitative Inquiry and Research Design: Choosing Among Five Approaches* (2nd ed.). SAGE Publications, Inc.

Department of School Education and Literacy & Ministry of Education, Government of India. (n.d.). *Samagra Shiksha*. Samagra Shiksha. Retrieved January 2, 2022, from https://dsel.education.gov.in/samagra-shikshaMinistry of Social Justice and Empowerment. (2006a). *Recommendations of the Technical Advisory Group*. Government of India. https://www.scribd.com/doc/933435/TAG-Report

Government of India. (2020). *The Constitution of India [As on 9th September, 2020]*. Ministry of Law and Justice Legislative Department. https://legislative.gov.in/sites/default/files/COI.pdf

Heredia, R. C. (2002). Review: Dishonoured by History, Branded by Law. *Economic and Political Weekly*, *37*(5), 391–392. https://www.jstor.org/stable/4411683

National Human Rights Commission Annual Report. (2001–2002). National Human Rights Commission. https://nhrc.nic.in/sites/default/files/Annual%20Report%202001-2002.pdf

NCERT. (2008). A Snake Charmer's Story. In *Environmental Studies LOOKING AROUND: Textbook for Class V* (1st ed., Vol. 1, pp. 15–21). National Council of Educational Research and Training. https://ncert.nic.in/textbook.php?eeap1=2-22

Radhakrishna, M. (2009). *Invented Pasts and Fabricated Presents: Indian Nomadic and Denotified Communities, Kunda Datar Memorial Lecture*. Gokhale Institute of Politics and Economics. https://dspace.gipe.ac.in/xmlui/bitstream/handle/10973/38576/kdl-2009.pdf?sequence=1&isAllowed=y

The Gazette of India: Extraordinary. (2019, February). *Ministry of Social Justice and Empowerment (Department of Social Justice and Empowerment) notification* (REGD. NO. D. L.-33004/99 PART II—Section 3—Sub-section (ii)). Government of India Press. http://socialjustice.nic.in/writereaddata/UploadFile/Gazette%20%20notification%20dated%2021022019.pdf

United Nations. (2007). *Report of the Committee on the Elimination of Racial Discrimination*. United Nations, New York. https://www.refworld.org/pdfid/473424062.pdf

9

As it Unfolds: Schooling, Aspirations, and Muslim Children's Lived Experiences in the Walled City of Delhi

Fariha Siddiqui
Sajjad Ahmad

Introduction

The idea of 'multiple childhoods' is a well-accepted shift in Indian childhood studies. This idea refers to the conscious acceptance of diverse cultural experiences of children. Thus, the idea of multiple childhoods is contrary to the generalised discourse of singular childhood that remains divorced from multi-cultural contexts. Numerous studies have interpreted Indian childhood from this wider lens rather than the 'normative' single childhood. Balagopalan (2011) highlighted that there has been much research on multiple childhoods in various disciplines like psychology (Kakar, 1982), sociology (Thapan, et al. 2014), anthropology (Veena Das and Froerer's work with Adivasi children), to name a few. Despite significant work within Indian childhood studies, only a few names emerge when the schooling or education of Muslim children is discussed. This shortage of research on Muslim children's life, their aspirations, schooling, and multiple childhoods set the backdrop of the present article.

The largest minority in India lags behind on most of the socio-economic indicators compared to other communities in India (Sachar, 2006; Shah, 2007; Haneefa, 2019). Their low literacy rate is attributed to the community's low socio-economic status as well as reform from within. Haneefa, (2019) suggests that their rate of progress and improvement in the context of their educational level have been the slowest compared to other socio-religious categories since independence. The National Education Policy, 1986 stated that Muslims and Neo-Buddhists are educationally backward and same was reiterated by the Sachar Committee in 2006. According to the Sachar Committee Report, "the recognition of their educational backwardness is quite acute among a large section of Indian Muslims" (pp. 14). Furthermore, the report highlights that "one-fourth of Muslim children in the age group of 6-14 years have either never attended school or are drop-outs" (pp. 58). For children above the age of 17 years, the educational attainment of Muslims at the matriculation level is 17%, against the national average of 26%. The report also hints at children's lack of interest in education or school since they do not see the long-term outcome of this (educational) investment. The same sentiment is reiterated by the report of the Standing Committee of the National Monitoring Committee for Minorities' Education (NMCME) indicating that Muslims lag at all educational levels and specifically at the primary education level (2013).

There have been a number of government policies and initiatives to uplift the education of marginal social groups. The National Education Policy 2020 (NEP 2020) also mentions the target of achieving a 100% enrolment ratio at all levels of schooling i.e. from early childhood to secondary levels by the year 2025. The NEP 2020 focuses on increasing enrolment and improving the educational status of marginalised or disadvantaged groups. Despite such initiatives the enrolment rate of Muslim children in the last decade has not changed much as highlighted by the NSSO survey 2018 (the Gross Attendance Ratio (GAR) of Muslims was 100 which is lower than SCs (101), STs (102), OBCs, and minorities). This indicates that Muslims (the second largest group in the total population) require preferential treatment, as the educational needs and learning context of their children may be different. The key observations of committees and reports reveal that due to a shortage of resources, most Muslim children attend government schools, followed by religious schools, with the lowest participation in private schools. This heterogeneity of the schooling system provides varying exposure to Muslim children and shapes their childhood.

The present study is formulated under these backdrops to explore the lived experiences of young Muslim children and their aspirations within the walled city (the old Shahjahanabad or Purani Dilli) of Delhi. Two primary schools (one government and one aided-school) were selected from the historically-rich walled city to explore the schooling of young Muslim children. The schools were selected from different localities within the walled city so that a multitude of experiences could be captured through these sites. One school (Public School) is situated in a buzzing market area around the old mosque and the private aided Muslim school is situated in a residential-cum-commercial area. Both of these schools are attended by a majority of Muslim children but have their own texture and intricacies (owing to different ownership and type of management).

Understanding Lived Experience and Schooling

Children are exposed to cultural practices early and learn shared meanings and lifestyles from their families. Recent trends show that research on children's lived experiences has gained momentum in childhood studies and children's geographical research (Holloway & Valentine, 2000; Ellis, 2005; Collins & Coleman, 2008). Children's agency and perspective are the critical units of analysis in these researches. Furthermore, children's everyday life is a product of social, historical, and cultural influences (James et al., 1998; Mayall, 2002; Qvortup, 1994). Daily cultural practices, materials, and spaces impact the growing child and shape their personality (Rasmussen, 2004).

Lived Experience

According to Given (2008), lived experience represents and understands a research subject's human experiences, choices, and options and how those factors influence one's perception of knowledge. It has a temporal and self-awareness structure and generally concentrates on every day and ordinary events in one's life like routines, rituals, languages, and communication. Understanding the lived experience of any person or community can help understand the context and avoid over-generalisation. Amin (2003) and Razzack (1991, 1994 and 2006) highlighted how Indian Muslims are represented using a few markers within the media and even in textbooks. They are reduced to wearing Gharaara, Topi, Beard, and Kohl and speak with a heavy Urdu accent. However, within the community exists huge variation that exploring lived experiences can bring forth. As Rogoff, et al. (2018) highlighted:

> *'Children observe, contribute to, discuss, and are instructed about cultural practices through everyday interactions with siblings, peers, parents, and other community members. While participating in cultural practices, children grow and transform their ways of being. Children's interactions are part of their community's ways of life, constituting those ways of life and constrained in some ways.'*
>
> (Rogoff et al., 2018, pp. 6-7)

Furthermore, lived experiences associated with space impact children's lives. In the last few decades, this association has been explored by different researchers (Soja 1989; Gulson and Symes 2007). Space has physical as well as social characteristics attached to it. Robinson (2009) points out that space should be considered continuously influenced by different actors and vice-versa, and not limited to being a stage. The conceptualisation of space as a product of social relations and materials is associated with French philosopher and sociologist Henri Lefebvre (1991). In his seminal work 'The Production of Space (1991), he developed a spatial triad to explain the relationship between the use of space by actors (people) and the actual space. The three dimensions of this triad are described in Figure 1.

Lefebvre's triad has been used in different disciplines to make meaning of the experience and impact of spaces. In school or classroom settings, this triad

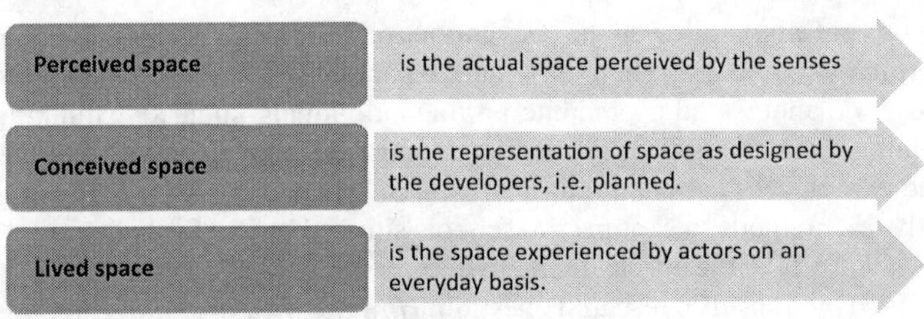

Figure 1: Lefebvre's space triad

has been used by a few researchers to make sense of the experiences of human beings and their relationship with the conceived spaces. For instance, Soja (1996) utilised Lefebvre's spatial triad and tried to explain the three types of spaces by introducing the concept of the third space. Furthermore, Kellock & Sexton (2017) used the triad to analyse children's everyday lived experiences in classrooms and spaces. The research revealed that children reimagine and renegotiate the conceived spaces every day.

Schooling

Schooling is when children learn skills and knowledge that they will later apply in the 'real world in addition to the *planned* or *intended* curriculum. It shapes a child's personality, attitudes, and values differently from home and prepares them to survive in the wider world. According to Thapan (2014: 2),

> *"Schooling in India is set in vastly different contexts that are dependent on a particular school's history and setting, institutional goals, location, available infrastructure, linguistic medium of instruction, the relevant school board to which the school is affiliated, the social class of students and the teachers, caste identities and a host of other influencing factors"*

The previous study conducted by Siddiqui (Unpublished M.Phil. thesis) in one of the minority schools in Delhi revealed that the students were provided with the 'official knowledge' (Apple, 1990) selected by the state. The 'official knowledge' presented their community to them through the lens of the 'majority' as people from the majority wrote the textbooks. The perspective about their community was shaped by the larger world's view, which could be confusing for children. Apple (1995) says that to understand the schooling process, one must explore children's perspectives and experiences along with the implicit and explicit curriculum, and teachers' perspective. Thus, the current study explored the voices of Muslim children related to schooling, lived experience at school and its impact on their lives.

The Study

Methodology

The present study followed the conventions of descriptive research utilising the interpretive paradigm. The interpretative paradigm is utilised when the study focuses on understanding and interpreting individuals' subjective thinking and meanings in contexts. Since understanding or inquiring about negotiations and lived experiences are central to the research. The study utilised ethnographic fieldwork methods to capture two schools situated in Old Delhi (referred to as the walled city in the article owing to the areas historical evolution). The study is guided by a specific research question: *How do Muslim children's schooling and engagement with space shapes their everyday life and choices*? To explore this research question, two objectives namely *'to explore children's everyday experiences about schooling in the walled city'* and *'to observe children's likes and dislikes within schools in the walled city'* were taken as the objectives of the study.

First setting (Muslim School)

The first site of the study is an aided-private minority school which has been serving the children of the Muslim ghetto in by lanes of Old Delhi area for almost a century. The school is located within Delhi's walled city, where inhabitants have been living since independence. The school serves children from nearby *mohallas.* The area around the school is a mixed locality of houses, factories, and shops. Around schools, there are many factories of iron, tools, etc.; above all, there are homes. The school runs in two shifts. First shift, all primary classes are taught for VI-XII class and in the afternoon. The school is a dilapidated old-style building. A small ground is there at the entrance though it is enormous compared to the walled city spaces. The building is built in Mughal style with arches and pillars.

Second setting (Public School)

The second school is situated near the famous Mosque in the walled city and is managed by the Department of Education (DoE), NCT Delhi. It is located in an urban area in the DoE block of the Central district of Delhi. The school consists of grades from 1 to 12. The school is for girls, and it has an attached pre-primary section. Urdu serves as the medium of instruction in this school. The school is a three-storied building and has no playground. The classrooms are spacious and well-lit and are decorated with charts. The pre-primary classrooms have desks (like older children) and the teaching-learning materials for children are also available which are stored in a big almirah. During recess, pre-primary children are allowed to play in the open veranda outside the classroom (since there is no playground).

Tools Used

The study draws from observations of school routines, rituals, events and drawing tasks. Several studies in early childhood education have used interviews or picture-association tasks to explore young children's experiences. On the contrary, this study used children's drawings to understand their life experiences. Alerby and Bergmark (2012) argue that visual art, including drawings, is a language, even though it does not consist of spoken words. Thus, pictures can be utilized as a tool to understand children's individual lived experiences. Along with this, informal interactions with children were held during the course of field work. I also conducted a few activities with children to establish rapport with them.

Children from grade 1 from both the schools constituted the sample for study. There was a total of forty students (eighteen students were in Class I at MS and 22 at PS). Informal interaction revolved around what do they like about school; their daily routines; play spaces and choices; home and neighbourhood. Since children were young (aged 6-7 years), the discussion only revolved around their lived experiences and not around abstract ideas like religion or gender.

Data Procedure and Analysis

Eighteen students were in Class I at MS and 22 at PS. They were asked to draw two pictures using a pencil. One of the pictures was about their favourite thing/place at school, and another was about what and where they play at home. The children were encouraged to draw whatever came to their minds. This free expression drawing task was difficult for most of them since it was a new task for children and they found the free-drawing task challenging. Children in early grades are used to drawing or copying simple objects like a flag, hut, apple, or typical scenery drawn by adults. However, I asked them to express their choice through drawing and it was difficult for them to think about it and visualise the same on paper. Thus, throughout the drawing task, I tried to interact with students to facilitate their drawing and help them visualise what they wanted to express. After each drawing, I asked the children to explain what they drew. In the following paragraphs, children's drawings and explanations are analysed under three themes: *Spaces of 'generous joy' at school, Aspirations and belonging in children's drawings and Children's lives outside the school.*

Spaces of 'Generous Joy' at School

Children's drawings about things or places they like in school indicate that school holds a special place in children's lives. Given the size of their homes in congested lanes and *mohallas* of Old Delhi, there was no open space for children at home. Eighty percent of children drew the school's physical infrastructure as their favourite thing. For instance, Figure 2a and 2b show drawings by two

Figure 2a: Play spaces in school

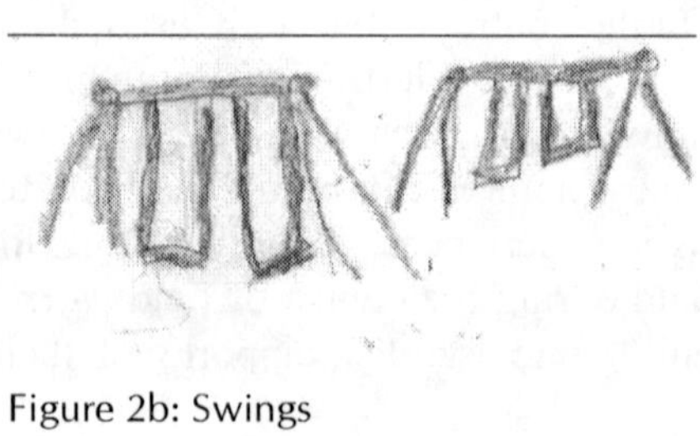

Figure 2b: Swings

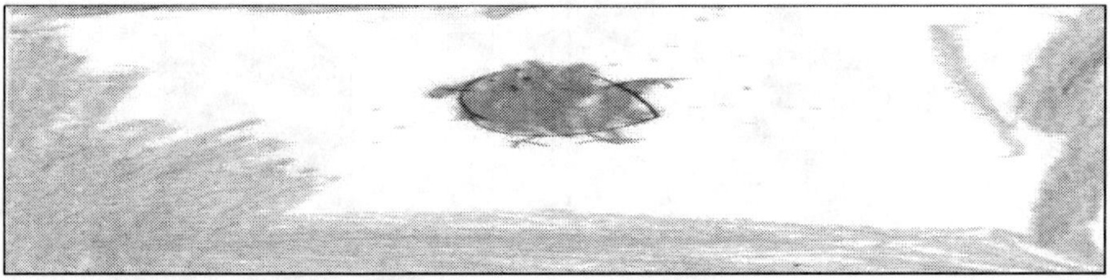

Figure 2c: Teddy bear and green space

girls from PS. Figure 2a shows the concrete play space (in black), two trees, two girls playing (one is the girl herself, and the other is her friend) and a toy. She also drew clouds above. In figure 2b, the girl drew swings. Through these drawings, the girls highlighted the missing elements from their home space and what they got to experience at school. While explaining her drawing (2a), she shared that the open hall space outside her classroom is her favourite place in school which she drew in black since she likes to play with her friends there. She further shared, *Ghar par to hum ghar mein hi khelte hain, ya kabhi kabhi gali ke bahar. Bahar ammi khelne ko mana karti hain kyuki khatra ho skta hai na!* (At home, I play inside the home mostly and sometimes outside the house since it may be dangerous). The drawings highlight the constrained spaces within homes and how school holds a special place in their lives. Their drawings show that children emotionally bonded with the school space since it gave them a sense of security and freedom.

Another common element in drawings of preschool was pictures of available toys within the classrooms. They had puzzles, puppets, and other educational toys in the classroom. Since these teaching-learning materials were visible to the children, they drew them as their favourite things at school. Figure 2c shows one such drawing of a *soft toy and a* lot of greenery by a girl. Many students drew similar pictures. The picture indicates that children love to play with teaching-learning materials which are not available at home. A girl shared, *Hume ye wale gudde se khelna acha lagta hai. Ghar par ye wala nahi hai. To jab ma'am deti hai tab hume acha lagta hai* (I like to play with this soft toy as I don't have it at home. When ma'am lets us play with this soft toy, I enjoy it!) Along with this, children also highlighted trees or greenery in their drawings of school. The greenery in the drawing depicts that for children having trees and plantation in the school is a variation from their home space since in their residential area, trees and plantation are a rare sight due to the scarcity of space.

On the contrary, the drawings of MS children were primarily abstractions like images of fans, tube lights, trees, or flowers (Figure 2d). Some of the students drew school elements like arches and flags. However, they could not share their reason for liking these elements.

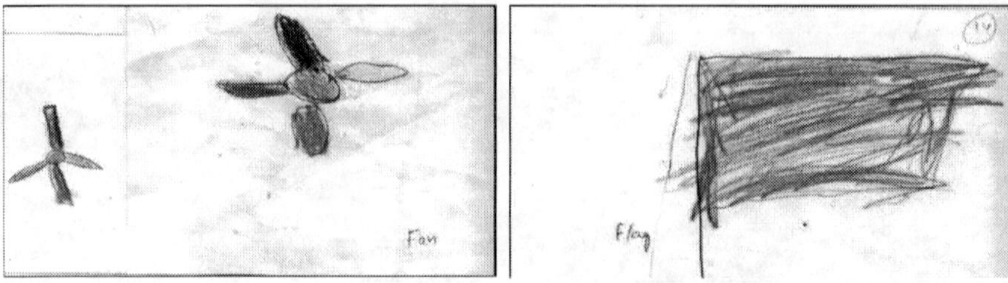

Figure 2d: Abstract images

Aspirations and belonging in children's drawings

The researcher asked children to draw their aspirations when they grow up. All children in both schools struggled with what to draw. Most of the children said, *Hume samajh nahi aa raha.* Gradually, they started drawing whatever they knew. Most of the children of both schools drew the Indian National flag on their sheets. To understand their experience with it, the researcher asked the children what they drew and why. The children responded that they only knew how to draw the picture of the flag, which was taught to them by their teacher.

Exploring it further, the researcher asked acha *aap bade hokar kya banna chahte ho.* Verbally they shared, and I asked them to draw that. Children's response revolved around the professions with which 'power' could be associated. There were drawings of soldiers, police man, doctors, advocate, scientist, and teachers. For instance, in figure 3a, a boy of MS drew *Fauji* (Army personnel). I tried to dig deeper into his reason, and he shared *Atankwadi ko maarne ke liye, jo humare jhande ko jhukhate hain. Hume uski raksha karni hai. Unme bahut takat hoti hai* (to kill terrorists who harms our National Flag and we want to protect our Flag. They have power.). He drew the army personnel along with the Indian National flag.

Similarly, in figure 3b, a girl from PS drew Doctor, and the national flag also accompanied her drawing. She explained that she wanted to be a doctor so that she could treat ill people.

Figure 3a: Child's aspiration to become soldier and protect the National Flag

Figure 3b: Child wants to be a doctor and protect the Flag

Furthermore, while explaining their drawings (drawings apart from soldiers or police as well) about aspirations, most of the children commonly used words like *desh* (country), *raksha* (safety), *madad* (help) and *takat* (power). The usage of these powerful words may be attributed either to children imitating each other to describe their aspiration or towards the influence of media on them. Since India is celebrating its 75 years of independence under the *Azadi ka Amrit Mahotsava*, Indian National Flag and other elements are visible in the physical environment, official curriculum and probably at home. One of the boys of MS shared that he saw videos of the National Flag and soldiers on his mother's phone while scrolling YouTube. The promotion of National Flag and Indian culture by media and government may be a reason that it has acquired significance in their mind, and it gets projected while explaining their aspirations.

Children's lives outside the school

In her article 'Silence and marginalisation,' Farooqi(2017) presented the lives of children studying in one of the Muslim minority schools in Delhi. The life of the child painted by Farooqi shows that Muslim children in the walled city of Delhi are closely intertwined with the community life and economic activities of their families. Due to economic burdens, they shoulder responsibilities with their parents/siblings from an early age and may not have leisure time to play and enjoy. Children's everyday routine is rigid as they have to balance work, education, and their desires. When I asked *Izza (*one of the girls in PS) about her routine at home, she shared, *"Hum school aate hain, phir ghar ja kar khana kha kar tuition jaate hain, sham mein thodi der khelte hain aur maal bhi lagate hain ammi ke saath aur phir so jaate hain"* (I attend school in the morning then have lunch at home, followed by tuition and some play time. I also work with my mother and then I sleep). I further inquired about "*maal konsa lagate ho ammi ke saath"*. (What do you work on with your mother?) She explained that they roll up local tobacco brands' wrappers and assemble the inside part of the switch. Many children from both schools shared similar stories. Muslim children studying at both the schools contributed to their families through their physical labour (helping in household chores or economic activities), time and other responsibilities. The life outside school shared by children from both the schools (MS and PS) indicates that their childhood is analogous to children belonging to poor households where contributing to the family through their labour is the norm.

Further, I prompted children to share their "favourite place in the neighbourhood and associated activities." Since PS is close to the *Old Mosque* (one of the oldest mosques with historical significance)and it holds a significant place in the social-cultural fabric of Old Delhi. Twenty out of twenty-three children of PS shared that almost every Friday or Sunday, they visit the mosque with their family in the evening. Children drew images of the mosque and activities they like to do there. In figures 4a and 4b, Sadiya and Fabiha drew arches of the *Old Mosque,* and they played with a ball and friends in the mosque's courtyard. Clouds and the sun are

Fig4a: Girl playing at the Old Mosque

Fig-4b: Girls playing in open verandah at the Old Mosque

Fig4c: Girl offering namaz at the Old Mosque

Fig4d: Child drew jalebis

also there in both the pictures symbolising the open space they experience in the open courtyards of the mosque. They further shared that *yahan hum bhaag bhaag bhi khelte hain* (We play racing as well here). I inquired if there was any space near their home where they could play outside. They said there is a park nearby *mohalla,* but there are drunkards, so they don't visit that place. Sadiya and Fabiha explained their pictures by saying they carry food from home and sometimes take money from their mother to buy ice cream. Another girl (Mantasha, Figure 4c) drew pictures of herself offering *namaz* (prayer) in the *Old Mosque* and there is a sun along a water body in her picture. She explained *hume namaz padhna acha lagta hai masjid mein* aur *Hauz mein muh dhona* (I like to offer namaz at the mosque and wash my face at the central tank of the mosque). While MS children shared that they like to visit their relatives in nearby areas on holidays. The common areas named by these students were Jafrabad, Seelampur, Nangloi and Okhla, to list a few. When asked about any other reason for liking these areas (apart of these being their relatives residence), they mentioned that people are rich in these areas and lives in big and clean houses. Their reasoning indicates that these localities are aspirational for MS children since these are comparatively newly developed areas; they have familial ties there and are Muslim pockets. None of the students named other nearby Cosmopolitan areas like *Karol Bagh* or *New Delhi. Khalid* of MS drew *Jalebis* in response to his favourite place/activity

(Figure 4d). He shared that once; he went to *nearby market area* with his brother and had tasty *Jalebis* there. So, for him, that was his favourite place and memory.

Discussion and Conclusion

Seeing these drawings of children of both schools highlights the diverse childhood experiences of Muslim children in the walled city of Delhi. The life of a Muslim child is deeply influenced by their expeiences outside school life. Children's lives and choices revolve around their immediate needs, open spaces, and missing elements in their lives such as toys, play time). School gave them escape from their congested, tangled and 'adult-like' life. Since there was shortage of open play spaces, for children open courtyard of Old Mosque or school hall served a luxurious and leisure purpose. Moreover, the old mosque holds a special place for children of PS. In the larger society, the majority narrative about mosques is perceived from religious Lense however, for PS children's lived experiences contradicted with this perceived notion. This concept is explained by Lefebvre as 'Lived space' in his space triad which depends on actors lived experience instead of the perceived notion. For Muslim children, mosque had religious significance as well as space for leisure and luxury which is reflected in their drawings and during informal interactions.

Children of both the schools highlighted the play opportunities they get at school and thus appreciated the school. On the contrary, none of the children from either school mentioned 'study,' 'books' or 'teachers' as their favourite things at school. This also highlights that they may not have developed a close connection or interest in education per se since it is divorced from their lived context. This gap between lived context and learning-context was also evident when I asked children about their aspirations. At first go, none of them understood the question/ task (to draw aspiration) since nobody asked them before and drawing such an open-ended thing is also a new thing for them. My cues and questioning supported their drawing task and one of the students even said '*ji humne khud se pehli baar aesi drawing bnayi hai school mein*' (This is my first such drawing at school). Considering children's age and context, teachers need to build upon their interest and life to retain their interest in school (or education).

Between the two schools, the PS children were much more oriented towards school life and tasks at hand. They understood the drawing task instructions and processed them accordingly. However, the MS children were clueless about processing open-ended drawing tasks (like the one I gave them). This could be a result of the differences between the teaching-learning processes followed at both the schools. PS follows directorate curriculum guidelines and provides age-appropriate tasks to children through a trained and qualified mother teacher. On the other hand, the MS school had no regular teacher for Class 1 (where the research was carried out). The coordinator at MS told me that every day they try to arrange a guest teacher or some other teacher assign those tasks (like writing counting, dictation, or textbook-based question answers). Thus, the MS children had problem in processing and articulating tasks other than the traditional paper-pencil tasks. (As discussed in preceding sections, MS children drew abstract elements like a fan, or a tube light in response to their favourite thing at school). The quality of the learning experience also varies between the two schools and may have a significant impact on retention rates in the future. The Sachar Committee (2006) highlighted that the learning context of Muslim children should be taken care of at school as it will help increase the retention rate.

Another emerging pattern from children's drawing and sharing was the necessity to portray Indian-ness or patriotism (flag or tricolour, national heroes) in front of a stranger (the researcher). During interaction with children, awareness about their position within the larger society and daily resistance was also evident. One of the MS students shared that he wants to be a police officer when he grows up. I further inquired about the reason for becoming a police officer to which he responded, "*Desh ki raksha karenge aur atankwadi ko pakdenge kyunki Muslim atankwadi nahi hote hain na* (I will protect my country and catch terrorists because Muslims are not terrorists). This same line was picked up by the remaining children of the MS school and they also highlighted the Muslim part of their identity and their integral role in the country. These sharings indicate that children imbibed the need for portraying themselves as loyal and patriotic without being asked to. The parents of these Muslim children must have shaped their minds for the same or it may have been picked up from the media. This could also be attributed to the national narrative infused in school education through various government programmes and policies. These everyday negotiations of minority and majority perspectives may have a significant impact on young Muslim children's identity development. And these children's portrayal of being patriotic can also be understood as an answer to the globally prevalent Islamophobia phenomenon.

Conclusion

Muslim children's childhood and everyday experiences are minimally discussed in recent years. Through the present study an attempt is made to explore Muslim children's lives and childhoods at a juncture where the socio-political scenario is becoming volatile for minorities. While exploring Muslim children's negotiations and life, the paper attempts to highlight the missing link between school and home life formally. Children have their personal reasons for liking school and spaces however school as a pedagogical site is ignorant to the lived experiences of children. Another important and unexplored theme is violation of Right to Play and leisure from Muslim children's life. Due to paucity of resources, space and leisure time, young children have minimal time to indulge in play at home and school. This has not been explored much within Indian context.

Lastly as Amatullah (2022) points out that at institutional spaces children deal with the issue of conformity and resistance for being Muslim. Children at both the schools projected their Indian identity above Muslim and they kept on negating the common narrative of Muslims being 'others' and 'outsiders.' These sensitive issues call for greater attention and (re)interpretation from educational researchers to dig deeper.

References

Alerby, E., & Bergmark, U. (2012). What can an image tell? Challenges and benefits of using visual art as a research method to voice lived experiences of students and teachers. *Journal of Arts and Humanities, 1*(1), 95-104.

Amatullah, S. (2022). Contesting the secular school: everyday nationalism and negotiations of Muslim childhoods. Children's Geographies, 20(6), 788-802.

Amin.S. Representing the Musalman : Then and now, Now and Then, in subaltern studies XII

Apple, M. W. (1990). Is there a curriculum voice to reclaim? *The Phi Delta Kappan, 71*(7), 526-530.

Apple, M. W., & Beane, J. A. (1995). *Democratic schools.* Association for Supervision and Curriculum Development, 1250 North Pitt Street, Alexandria, VA 22314 (Stock No. 1-95052; $14.95).

Balagopalan, S. (2011). Introduction: Children's lives and the Indian context. Childhood, 18(3), 291-297.

Berggren, L., Olsson, C., Talvia, S., Hörnell, A., Rönnlund, M., & Waling, M. (2020). The lived experiences of school lunch: an empathy-based study with children in Sweden. Children's geographies, 18(3), 339-350.

Borker,H.(2011) : Contesting Dilemma's: Muslim Identity and Education : A Case study of Jamia Nagar, New Delhi

Brenner, N., & Elden, S. (2001). Henri Lefebvre in contexts: An introduction. Antipode, 33(5), 763-768.

Collins, D., & Coleman, T. (2008). Social geographies of education: Looking within, and beyond, school boundaries. *Geography Compass, 2*(1), 281-299.

Das, V. (1989). Voices of children. Daedalus, 118(4), 262.

Ellis, J. (2005). Place and identity for children in classrooms and schools. *Journal of the Canadian Association for Curriculum Studies, 3*(2).

Froerer, P. (2012). Learning, Livelihoods, and Social Mobility: Valuing Girls' Education in Central India. Anthropology & Education Quarterly, 43(4), 344-357.

Farooqi, F. (2017). Silenced and marginalised: voices from a Sarkari-aided school of Delhi. Economic and Political Weekly, 52(38), 76-81.

Government of India Report of the Standing Committee of National Monitoring Committee for Minorities' Education (2013)

Govt. of India (2020). National Education Policy 2020. https://www.mhrd.gov.in/sites/upload_files/mhrd/files/NEP_Final_English_0.pdf

Gulson, K. N., & Symes, C. (2007). Knowing one's place: Space, theory, education. *Critical studies in education, 48*(1), 97-110.

Haneefa, M. (2019). Analysing the Outwardly Developed-Inwardly Backward Paradox Surrounding the Educational Status of Muslims in Kerala, India. Journal of Muslim Minority Affairs, 39(4), 478-492.

Holloway, S. L., & Valentine, G. (2000). Spatiality and the new social studies of childhood. *Sociology*, *34*(4), 763-783.

James, A., Jenks, C., & Prout, A. (1998). Theorizing childhood. *New York*, 81-104.

Kakar, S. (1978). The Inner World: A Psycho-Analytic Study of Childhood and Society in India.

Kaur, R. (2021). Constructions of Childhood in India: Exploring the Personal and Sociocultural Contours. Taylor & Francis.

Kellock, A., & Sexton, J. (2018). Whose space is it anyway? Learning about space to make space to learn. Children's Geographies, 16(2), 115-127.

Kipfer, S., Saberi, P., & Wieditz, T. (2013). Henri lefebvre: Debates and controversies1. Progress in Human Geography, 37(1), 115-134.

Lefebvre, H. (2012). From the production of space. In Theatre and performance design (pp. 81-84). Routledge.

Mayall, B. (2002). Understanding childhoods: A London study. In *Conceptualising child-adult relations* (pp. 128-142). Routledge.

Middleton, S. (2017). Henri Lefebvre on education: Critique and pedagogy. Policy Futures in Education, 15(4), 410-426.

Mohammad, P. H. (2022). Minorities and culture of learning: an anthropological study of the Muslim community in Telangana state in India. Asian Ethnicity, 23(2), 298-315.

Qvortrup, J., Bardy, M., Sgritta, G., & Wintersberger, H. (1994). Childhood matters: Social theory, practice, and politics.

Rasmussen, K. (2004). Places for children–children's places. *childhood*, *11*(2), 155-173.

Razzack, A. (1991, November). Growing up Muslim. In Seminar (387) (pp. 30-31).

Razzack.A. Confusion and Ambiguity within the secular. Rethinking Indian Secularism and the caste of Indian Muslim. In Kultur, The Indonesian Journal of Muslim culture, vol. 2.no. 1

Razzack.A. Musalman hone ki pehchaan, Hans, 1994

Razzack.A. Social Inclusion : The need to make schools 'Muslim friendly' , A review of books, October 2006

Robinson, C. (2009). 'Nightscapes and leisure spaces': an ethnographic study of young people's use of free space. *Journal of youth studies*, *12*(5), 501-514.

Rogoff, B., Dahl, A., & Callanan, M. (2018). The importance of understanding children's lived experience. Developmental Review, 50, 5-15.

Sachar, R., Hamid, S., Oommen, T. K., Basith, M. A., Basant, R., Majeed, A., & Shariff, A. (2006). Social, economic, and educational status of the Muslim community of India (No. 22136). East Asian Bureau of Economic Research.

Saraswathi, T. S., Menon, S., & Madan, A. (Eds.). (2017). Childhoods in India: Traditions, trends, and transformations. Taylor & Francis.

Shah, G. (2007). The condition of Muslims. Economic and Political Weekly, 42(10), 836-839. Retrieved from http://www.jstor.org/stable/4419332

Soja, E. W. (1989). *Postmodern geographies: The reassertion of space in critical social theory*. Verso.

Sudhir Kakkar (1982), Inner World: A psycho-analytic study of childhood and society in India, India: OUP

Thapan, M. (Ed.). (2014). Ethnographies of schooling in contemporary India. SAGE Publications India.

Veena Das (2006) Life and Words: Violence and the Descent into the Ordinary, California University Press

10

Inclusion and Minorities

A Special View on Madrasa Education System

Mahvish Bano
Vidyapati
J.P. Sahae

Introduction

India is best known for its unique characteristic which is cultural diversity. NEP 2020 emphasises valuable changes and focuses on the inculcation of human values such as respect for all persons, empathy, tolerance, human rights, gender equality, non-violence, global citizenship, inclusion, and equity. It calls upon stakeholders to overcome barriers and remove biases and stereotypes through sensitisation programmes. The policy aims to promote inclusion, bring out equity and develop respect for diversity through developing understanding about various cultures, religions, languages, gender identities, etc. among children, teachers, and other functionaries. Implementation of the policy will result in the empowerment of stakeholders through efficient manner of resourcing and a more robust and improved governance and monitoring mechanism with cooperation and support for education.

The study focuses on the present scenario of the Madrasa education system. We cannot neglect the fact that Madrasas, as places of education, have played a vital role in spreading literacy among the downtrodden segments of Muslim society.

The Study

Rationale

We live in a world today where education is in great demand. People are aware of the advantages of modern education and for an enlightened and inclusive democracy, it is necessary that all sections and classes of people are well-educated and intellectually equipped to shoulder the responsibility of developing the nation. Education occupies a unique role in the process of empowering minorities especially Muslims in the contemporary Indian context. As the Muslim community has lagged behind educationally over the decades, it is necessary to advance, foster and promote the education of this community at a quicker pace and as a matter of priority.

Madrasa Education seems to be working on old traditional patterns with less emphasis on research work. Therefore, research projects should be undertaken on various aspects of Madrasa education. Scholars associated with Madrasas Jamias and modern universities should be encouraged to work meaningfully in the area of Madrasa education.

In today's world the condition of the madrasas is not very appreciable. The present paper highlights the problems related to the Madrasa Education system with the help of the viewpoints of related stakeholders.

Objectives

1. To study the current status of Madrasas.
2. To know the curriculum and pedagogy of Madrasas.
3. To study the need for modernisation in Madrasas.
4. To study the government initiative for the development of Madrasas.
5. To know the access and attitude towards inclusion in Madrasas.

Sample

The sample for the current study includes teachers, administrators, and students of the Madrasas. The samples were collected randomly and the sample size is 60 which includes all the stakeholders.

Tool

For the purpose of collecting data a self-made tool with both open and closed ended questionnaire was used by the researcher. The questionnaire consists of the following dimensions –

1. The current state of Madrasas.
2. Curriculum and pedagogy of the Madrasas.
3. Need for modernisation of Madrasas.
4. The government initiatives for the development of Madrasas.
5. Access and attitude towards inclusion

Data Presentation

In this study the tool for data collection consists of 20 items with five dimensions related to the Madrasa Education system. The responses are given below in the form of percentages:

1-Current Status of Madrasa	*Unsatisfied %*	*Satisfied %*
1. Development initiatives	96%	4%
2. Quality perspective	98%	2%
3. Attitude of members and institutions	93%	7%
4. Support system	95%	5%

2-Curriculum and Pedagogy of Madarsa	*Disagree*	*Agree*
1. Well-designed curriculum	93%	7%
2. Curriculum need to be updated	11%	89%
3. Nature of the curriculum is traditional	2%	98%
4. Maths, Science, English are the integral part of the curriculum.	85%	15%
3-Modernisation of the Madrasa	*Disagree*	*Agree*
1. Positive scientific attitude	87%	13%
2. Science ,Maths and English are taught preferentially	83%	17%
3. Computer Based Education	4%	96%
4. Smart classroom	3%	97%
4- Government initiatives	*Unsatisfied %*	*Satisfied %*
1. SPQEM	75%	25%
2. Programmes for modernisation of Madrasa	85%	15%
3. NEP (1986) provision and implementation	50%	50%
4. NEP 2020 provision and implementation	47%	53%
Attitude towards Inclusion	*Positive*	*Negative*
1. Social Inclusion	21%	79%
2. Academic Inclusion	25%	65%
3. High Enrolment	30%	60%
4. Retention	31%	69%

Data Analysis

The present paper highlights the quality concerns and issues of the Madrasas. Data has been taken from the related stakeholders including teachers, administrators and students and the responses and interpretations are given below-

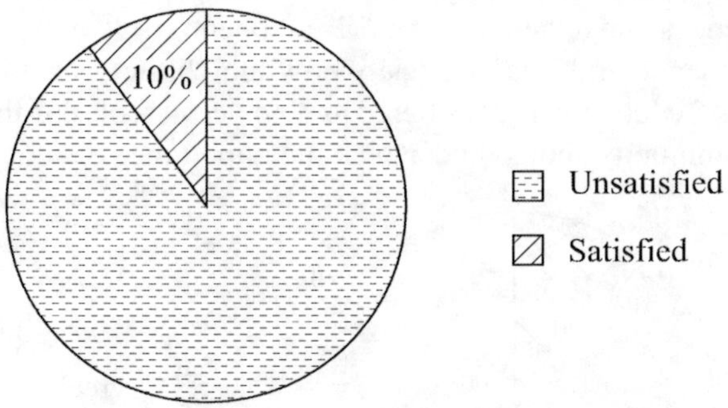

Figure 1: Current Status of Madrasa in Quality Perspective

The current state of the Madrasa education system is not quite good. Most people are unsatisfied with the current state of Madrasas due to a lack of development initiatives and proper support systems. Quality education is not seen in the Madrasas and the attitudes of other members also do not seem to be positive. These are the major issues faced by these types of institutions.

The government should take remedial action regarding this issue. On the other hand, people should also try for the Upgradation and upliftment of these types of institutions at their own pace.

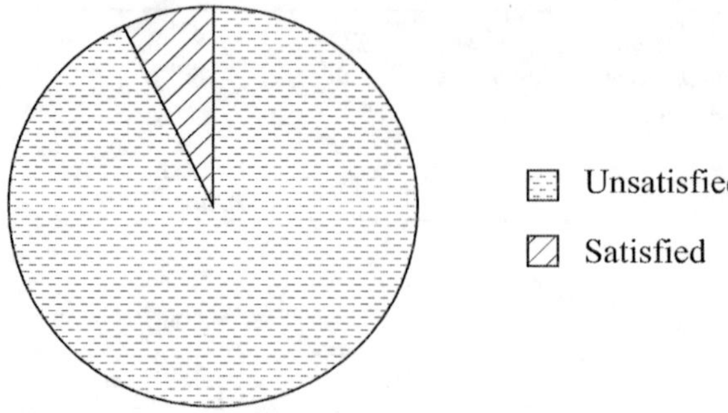

Figure 2: Curriculum and Pedagogy of the Madrasas

From the data, we can see that most people are unsatisfied with the present curriculum and pedagogy of the Madrasa education systems. There is a lack of a well-designed curriculum. The nature of the curriculum is traditional and rigid with Maths, Science and English not being integral parts of the mainstream curriculum.

The curriculum should change timely according to the needs of society. There should be timely and regular updates to ensure the curriculum is keeping abreast of the latest trends and changes. Students must be equipped with the skills necessary to develop their potential. It is important for Muslim minorities to cope with the new challenges and understand the present phenomena of the globalisation, industrialisation, and an IT-based society providing basic skills to adjust. with, For this purpose, education is considered as a powerful tool. So, all members of the Muslim community should understand the importance of education.

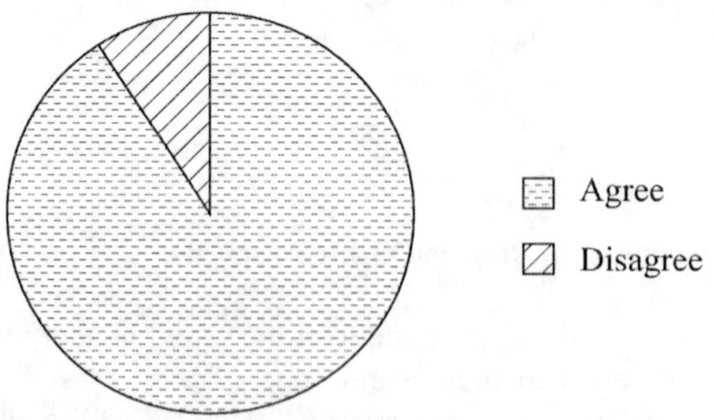

Figure 3: Modernisation of the Madrasas

Around 90% of the people have positive attitude towards the modernisation of Madrasas as they agree with concepts such as smart classrooms and computer-assisted education. As mentioned above Madrasa is the place where education is given from the very beginning of the Islamic Education. Perhaps in the present era, Modernisation is an important need in every institution. So, it is felt that Madrasa should also modernised.

It is also suggested that trained teachers for this new modernised programme should be in Madrasa education system.

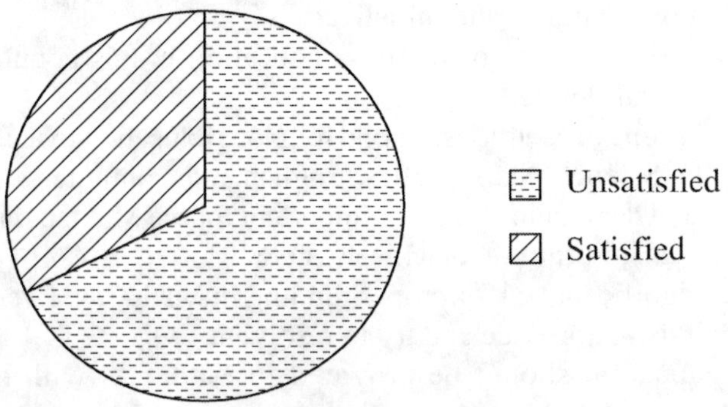

Figure 4: The Government initiatives

Most people are unsatisfied with the government's policies and initiatives. There are many more policies to make Madrasa education more acceptable. Various efforts have been made by the government to modernise the system.

The High-Power Panel on Minorities (1980) and the Group on Minorities Education (1990) set up by the Department of Education advocate relevant changes in the curriculum. The National Policy on Education (1986) and Programme of Action (1992) and the Prime Minister's 15 Point Programme for Welfare of Minorities suggested the modernisation of traditional Madrasas, and the "Scheme of Modernisation of Madrasa" was launched as a Centrally sponsored scheme in 1994 suggesting the introduction of English, Science, Mathematics and Hindi subjects on a voluntary basis. In 2004, the Standing Committee of the "National Monitoring Committee for Minorities" was constituted for the development of the Madrasa education system but in reality, it is not implemented truly and also did not fulfil the desired objectives.

We cannot neglect the fact that Madrasas play an important role in the enhancement of the literacy rate of Muslim minorities, so the government should also take remedial decisions for these institutions.

Most people have positive attitude towards inclusion. Inclusion should be in terms of pedagogy curriculum, institution, students, teachers, subject matter etc. However, the problem is related to the enrolment and retention ratio of students There are very few people who are not aware of the importance of education so that everyone should look upon these issues. So that we can also contribute to overcome the problems of wastage and stagnation.

Suggestions

Few suggestions for the improvement and upliftment of Madrasa education are given below:

- The government should encourage these institutions through different monitoring programmes and initiatives.
- The aims and objectives of Madrasa education in this country should be specifically well-defined.
- Expand the scope of Madrasas beyond religious education to include teaching subjects like Science, Mathematics, English and Computer.
- Infrastructural development is very important for the Maktabs and Madrasas, like classrooms, Furniture, blackboards etc
- There is a significant lack of proper funding in Madrasas. Everyone should look upon this major issue and try to resolve it.
- Quality education should be provided in Madrasas with emphasis on Information and Communication Technology.
- There should be a provision for teachers training programme for the teachers and teachers should uplift the morale of the students of the Madrasas.
- Madrasas need to encourage community outreach programmes, such as sports competitions, essay writing competitions, quizzes etc, in which students from both Madrasas and modern educational institutions can jointly participate. (*Ali.M)*

Conclusion

This study highlights Madrasa education and its contribution to the empowerment of Muslims. It discusses the current status of Madrasa education system, curriculum and pedagogy of the Madrasas as well as the inclusion of these institutions. It also explores important initiatives being taken by the Indian government and the problems faced by Madrasas. The study offers suggestions for improving the educational status of Indian Madrasas. The Madrasas will need to be revitalised to meet the challenges of the modern world. Strong emphasis will need to be laid on the quality of education and expanding the base of science, information and technology, because this is the need of our present era of competition. The contribution of these Madrasas has been so important that one cannot strategise any policies or programmes for the educational development of Muslim community by neglecting or overlooking the important existence of these Madrasas.

References

Beg, M.A. & Kidwai, A.R.(2012). *Empowerment of Indian Muslims: Perspective Planning and Road Ahead.* Concept Publishing Company Pvt. Ltd.[2].

Shazli T. and Asma S. Role of Madrasa Education in Empowerment of Muslims in India, IOSR *Journal Of Humanities And Social Science* (IOSR-JHSS)Volume 20, Issue 2, Ver. V (Feb. 2015), PP 10-15e-ISSN: 2279-0837, p-ISSN: 2279

Ali, M. (2015) An overview on Madrasa Education in India, *IJDR* Vol5, Issue3, pp 3714-3716

Durrani, K. (1986). *Muslim Educational Reform*, Islamic Book Service, Lahore.[3].

Erfan, N. & Valie, Z.A. (1995). Education and the Muslim World: Challenge and Response. Institute of Policy Studies The Islamic Foundation, U.K.[4].

Jain, S. (1986). *Muslims and Modernisation.* Jaipur: Rawat Publications. [5].

11

Madrasas and Other Minority Educational Institutions

Issues and Concerns

Mohammad Haider Raza

Introduction

Officially, India is a secular democratic nation. Its constitution empowers the country's people with many rights, providing various types of freedom to the citizens. No doubt, the right to freedom of religion is one of the biggest aspects of this, guaranteed through Article 25, which gives the freedom to not only profess and practice any religion but also the right to propagate itThis freedom includes the right to religious education. Articles 29 and 30 are very much related to this cause.

Article 29 of the Indian Constitution empowers people by giving them the right to conserve and promote their distinct language, script and culture, while Article 30 gives citizens the right to establish and maintain educational institutions of their choice. Not just this, these articles along with their clauses and sub-clauses, prohibit the denial of admission to government-aided educational institutions on any basis, be it religion, language, race or caste. Further, they strengthen the educational institutions run by minority communities by prohibiting the government from any kind of discrimination (Constitution of India, 1950).

Despite all these provisions existing in the Constitution of India, *Madrasas* and other minority educational institutions (OMEIs) of the country are facing a lot of difficulties. While some of the issues are of internal nature; others come from external forces. This is how this author perceives them. This paper aims at dealing with both of these concerns.

Although the title includes both Madrasas and other minority educational institutions; the paper focusses on the former. And, for this, there are three major reasons:

(a) The writer comes from a Madrasa background. So, he has more knowledge and understanding of Madrasas than that of any other minority educational institution.

(b) The role Madrasas play in Muslim community is bigger than that of other minority educational institutions in their respective communities. Perhaps, this is why Madrasas have their distinct identity: a complete and religious one.
(c) As far as the author's understanding is concerned, majority of issues and concerns that Madrasas face, are the same other minority educational institutions might suffer from. Hence, description of one should suffice for the others, to a large extent.

The Study

Significance

Religion plays much important role in people's daily lives. However, as a secular country, the Indian education system does not allow religious education in schools funded by the government. Yes, a negligible number of private schools run by some Muslims offer religious education in their school curricula. But, in a country holding the second largest Muslim population in the world, that is obviously not enough. Hence, in order to make students equipped with the knowledge of religion and religious affairs, madrasas (in the case of Muslims) or other minority educational institutions are of utmost significance.

Despite this much importance, Madrasas and other minority educational institutions (OMEIs) are facing a lot of difficulties. So many challenges and issues are there, in front of them. This paper will try to describe them one by one in some details along with some suggestions for the stakeholders so that the problems could be resolved or minimised at least.

Objectives

Objectives are as follows:
- To describe what Madrasas are
- To shed some light on the role of madrasas and OMEIs
- To highlight the problems and issues that Madrasas and OMEIs are facing
- To recommend solutions to the issues and concerns
- To give a few suggestions for future researchers in the field

What are Madrasas?

Etymologically, *Madrasa* is an Arabic word, derived from a triconsonantal Semitic root, *dars,* which means: to learn, or to study. It is on the morphological form/template of *maf'ala,* meaning 'a place where something is done or something takes place.' Therefore, the literal meaning of Madrasa is: a place where learning takes place (irrespective of the type of learning being imparted). So, literally, it includes every educational institute (Wikipedia, 2023).

However, in today's world, madrasa is being used in slightly different contexts. In the Arab world, it refers to what the word 'school' stands for in

English (a system of education from nursery/kindergarten/pre-primary to senior secondary). And, for university, the language has another word: *Jamia.* Thus, contemporary usage of the word doesn't cover (in totality) what the literal meaning encompasses. Still, it is very close. But, outside the Arab world and especially in the Indian subcontinent, madrasa has been specifically used for a system of education where religious learning takes place only. This difference can be understood more easily by this example:

Jamia Millia Islamia's senior secondary school, is a Madrasa in the context of Arab world, not in the context of Indian subcontinent. So, Arabs will call it Madrasa. However, non-Arabs do not apply the term Madrasa on it. By this, they only mean the likes of Al Jamiatul Ashrafia Mubarakpur, Darul Uloom Deoband, Nadwatul Ulama Lucknow, Jamia Salafia Banaras, etc.

In Arabic grammar, madrasa is pluralised as *Madaris,* on the morphological form of *mafa'il.* However, in English, the plural is made by just adding 's' to the word, like it is done in most of the cases.

Role of Madrasas and OMEIs

Madrasas and OMEIs have much important role to play in their respective communities. From the very beginning, they have been a source of guidance for their people. And, no matter, how much technological advancement takes place in the history of human civilisation, these institutions, more or less, will keep lighting the lamp and enlightening human minds.

The biggest role Madrasas and OMEIs play is that they guide followers of respective religions, in their day-to-day life activities. Each and every aspect of their life is governed by the teachings taught there. Whether it is marriage ceremony or funeral, they have their contribution in one way or the other. These institutions not only equip students with moral values; but also propagate them among the masses.

Not just the above, Madrasas and OMEIs provide job opportunities to their graduates in different walks of life. In fact, their contribution is much more than what has been mentioned. However, this paper is not meant to deal with all that. Still, it was appropriate to shed some light on their role. It will make their issues and concerns more appealing and subsequently, may urge the stakeholders to be more sensitised to solve the problems.

Issues and Concerns of Madrasas and OMEIs (Alongside their Solutions)

Internal Issues

By internal issues, the author means issues and concerns that originate within Madrasas and OMEIs. Thus, they do not come from somewhere else; rather, they arise from the institutions themselves. They are as follows:

a. *Outdated Curricula:* One of the major internal problems of Madrasas and OMEIs is that the current curricula are not getting updated according to the needs of time. There are some subjects/topics which have no relevance any longer. For example, ancient Greek philosophy has no usage in today's world. Therefore, this writer feels that keeping the original spirit of these institutions alive and maintaining their actual purposes, a change in their curricula is inevitable. So, in place of irrelevant subjects/topics, those should be included in the syllabi which have applicability in the contemporary world.

There needs to be more emphasis on English and Hindi. Beyond the boundaries of addition, subtraction, multiplication and division, mathematics should be taught. Science subjects can also be appropriately accommodated.

It is true that some Madrasas have modified their curricula in recent times. So, now, English enjoys a more respectable place there. Still, much work needs to be done in this regard. It will not only benefit the students in their day-to-day life and future careers; but also help these institutions grow in relevance.

b. *Rigid and Old-Fashioned Pedagogies:* A lot of changes are occurring in the way the teaching-learning process is taking place in today's classrooms. However, Madrasas and OMEIs, in this respect as well, are not keeping up with the pace of the times. The pedagogical approaches being applied there are still old-fashioned. And, they are even more rigid, in this regard.

Textbooks used in lower classes of Madrasas and OMEIs are not according to the nature of early-stage learners. Similarly, either there are no exercises in the books (where the application of knowledge is important) or they are not sufficient. The usage of teaching-aids in classrooms is almost nil.

So, along with the curricula, changes are also required in pedagogies and the overall Madrasa education system. The books of the lower grades should be beautified. There should be maximum opportunities for the practical application of knowledge. The Braille system should also be used to some extent for blind students. So far, at least, this author has not heard about Braille books in any Indian seminary. May be that's why visually-impaired children don't even think of getting education there (however, with the help from their friend(s), some blind children memorise the Holy Qur'an).

c. *Lack of Regular Income Sources:* Students studying in Madrasas and OMEIs, get education completely free. There are no charges at all for their lodging and accommodation, as well. Even, many Madrasas don't charge students for their food. In case some institutions charge money for the food, the amount happens to be very low. Thus, learners get complete free education, free accommodation, and even almost free food.

So, another big concern for Madrasas and OMEIs is the lack of permanent funding resources. These institutions totally depend on donations and charities from the public. In the case of Madrasas, these funds come mostly during Eid al Fitr (Ramadan) and Eid al Adha. A major part of the revenues for Madrasas of Bihar, U. P., and other poor states, gets generated, from big cities like Mumbai, Ahmedabad, Surat, Hyderabad, Delhi, etc. And, since travel was banned during the covid19 lockdown; a number of small Madrasas were forced to be closed permanently.

Time has arrived when Madrasas and OMEIs should think of generating revenues on their own. For this, various techniques can be adopted. An affordable amount of money can be fixed for every student. Further, those who can pay, should be charged fully. This is a path every huge or small madrasa can walk on. And, there is a way which can be adopted only by big institutions and that too in town areas: creation of income sources by shop/flat construction for rent. Nadwatul Ulama of Lucknow is a live example in this respect. This madrasa manages a major portion of its expenses through this.

This writer finds both of the above-mentioned techniques very helpful. And, he believes that if Madrasas and OMEIs adopt them, it will certainly minimise their dependence on donations and charity funds.

d. *Un-Organised System of Teachers' Hiring:* In Madrasas and OMEIs, there is no proper mechanism for the appointment of teachers. The contemporary method of hiring professionals is rarely followed there. Thus, neither eligible candidates are invited to apply for teaching posts, nor interviews are held for this purpose. In exceptional cases, application forms are filled and interviews are conducted.

Yes, Madrasas aided by the government are an exception in this regard. Vacancies are advertised and interviews are held. However, all this is done just for the sake of formality. Otherwise, all the things are already settled outside.

In such a scenario, it is a welcome move from the side of a few state governments to announce the holding of Teacher Eligibility Test (TET) for the recruitment of teachers in aided Madrasas as is done for government schools' teachers. *The Indian Express* reported "TET to be Made Mandatory for Recruitment of Teachers in UP Madrasas," (2022).

The author is of the opinion that in order to hire more competitive and experienced teachers, private madrassas and OMEIs should also follow the contemporary method. They are advised to invite applications from eligible candidates and then hire those who are really talented and interested by conducting interviews.

e. *Absence of Teacher Training:* There is a popular saying that goes like this: "Practice makes a man perfect." This is the reason professionals get training. And, school teachers are not an exception in this regard. However, when it comes to madrasa teachers, there is no concept of pre-service or in-service teacher training. Thus, teachers teaching in these institutions and OMEIs are not trained.

The writer understands well that it is not easy to run a programme like B. Ed. for the training of Madrasa teachers. Still, he is of the belief that there must be some kind of teaching practice, before the graduates of Madrasas and OMEIs enter the field of real teaching. For example, students of final year can be sent to nearby Madrasas for practice under the supervision of expert teachers.

f. *Private Possession of Public-Like Institutions:* Madrasas and OMEIs are constructed and run by charity funds collected from the respective communities. So, in a way, these institutions are like the public ones. There is a similarity: if state-run institutions are funded by the government; Madrasas and OMEIs function with the help of donations from respective communities.

   However, there is a difference: state-run institutions are owned by the government, but Madrasas are not owned by the public. Rather, the founders/directors happen to possess the institutions built and run by public money. Though it is not as big an issue as the above-mentioned issues, it is still a concern.

   Yes, directors should take care of the Madrasas and OMEIs they have built. But they should not act like their owners. Responsible and well-informed committees consisting of honest, genuine and serious members should be there. And, founders must be accountable to them.

External Issues

By external issues, the writer means issues and concerns that do not originate from Madrasas and OMEIs. Rather, there are some outside forces which time and again try to demoralise these institutions. They are as follows:

i. *Interference in the Name of "Modernisation":* One of the major external concerns Madrasas are suffering from is unnecessary interference of the government in their internal affairs. Since long, this has been doing the rounds. And, all this is being done in the name of "modernisation".

   The most recent example of this interference is what the Assam government did by converting all the state-run Madrasas into modern schools. They not only converted them, but also renamed the Madrasas as 'Middle English Schools' and even withdrew subjects like Islamic Studies and the Quran, as reported by *The Hindu* ("1281 Madrasas Renamed in Assam as 'Middle English' Schools" 2023).

   It is true that Madrasas are not keeping up with the pace of the times. As said earlier, it is high time these institutions should make necessary changes in their curricula and pedagogical approaches. And, this must be done keeping in mind the actual purposes of their establishment. Hence, any changes that interfere with the very basic nature of Madrasas, can't bc allowed.

ii. *Denigration Under the Guise of Terrorism:* Another big concern for especially Madrasas is the hate and humiliation they have to go through, due to the allegation of spreading terrorism. These institutions are a very easy target. Anyone can hurl abuses towards them and say whatever they wish.

U. P. government's 2022 decision of conducting a survey of "unrecognised" Madrasas across the state was a testimony to this humiliation. Therefore, it was heavily criticised by concerned public and the opposition political parties alike, as reported by *Hindustan Times* ("UP Govt's Madrasa Survey Sparks Political Row," 2022).

If an individual says something ill about madrasas and OMEIs, it is not a big deal. But, when an elected government discriminates with minority educational institutions on the basis of religion, it is very much unfortunate. Neither Indian constitution allows this nor any civilised society can even think of it.

Table 1: Issues and Concerns of Madrasas and OMEIs

Sr. No.	*Internal Issues*	*External Issues*
1	Outdated Curricula	Interference in the Name of Modernisation
2	Rigid and Old-Fashioned Pedagogies	Denigration Under the Guise of Terrorism
3	Lack of Regular Income Sources	
4	Un-Organised System of Hiring	
5	Absence of Teacher Training	
6	Private Possession	

Recommendations

In the previous pages, the writer has dealt with the issues and concerns that Madrasas and OMEIs are going through. And, towards the end, alongside each problem, its solution was discussed. Now, the stakeholders are recommended and requested to apply those remedies as much as possible so that the issues can be resolved at least to a certain extent and these institutions can achieve their aims and objectives in a better way.

Suggestions

Research is a never-ending process. Moreover, the nature of social science is so divergent that no paper/study can be considered complete. According to his understanding and experience, this author has tried to deal briefly with the issues and concerns Madrasas and OMEIs are going through.

Further researches on this topic can be conducted where the problems are discussed in details. There is a huge possibility that some other issues are existing in Madrasas and OMEIs which this writer could not see through.

The above-described concerns are so big that separate studies can be carried out on each of them. And, for this, data can be collected through questionnaire. This will increase the value of those works.

Conclusion

It can be concluded that this paper highlights the complicated challenges confronting Madrasas and other minority educational institutions (OMEIs). From navigating pedagogical approaches and curriculum discrepancies to grappling with financial obstacles and teacher recruitment drawbacks, these institutions face an intricate landscape. Not just that! From these internal concerns to external issues like intervention in the name of modernisation and intimidation under the guise of terrorism, Madrasas have to deal with all, that too very patiently.

Identifying and then addressing these problems is very much important not just for the sake of safeguarding the constitutional rights of minority communities, but also for fostering inclusivity and ensuring the overall development of students studying in Madrasas and OMEIs. This paper urges all the stakeholders to heed the solutions given above and take them into consideration.

References

Constitution of India. (1950). Articles 25, 29 and 30.

Madrasa. (2023, December 20). In Wikipedia. Retrieved January 5, 2024. https://en.wikipedia.org/wiki/Madrasa

TET to be made mandatory for recruitment of teachers in UP Madrassas. (2022, July 31). *The Indian Express.* https://indianexpress.com/article/jobs/tet-to-be-made-mandatory-for-recruitment-of-teachers-in-up-madrassas-8062280/

1,281 Madrasas renamed in Assam as 'Middle English' schools. (2023, December 24). *The Hindu.* https://www.thehindu.com/news/national/other-states/1281-madrasas-renamed-in-assam-as-middle-english-schools/article67637509.ece

UP govt's Madrasa survey sparks political row. (2022, September 02). *Hindustan Times.* https://www.hindustantimes.com/india-news/up-govt-s-madrasa-survey-sparks-political-row-101662056256019.html

12

Educational Status of Muslims of India

The AISHE Report 2020–21

Mohd Farhan
Aerum Khan

Introduction

For the development of any country, every person, class, race, and gender should participate equally in every field including the education sector. India is the most populous nation in the world .One of the major challenges for the Indian government is to ensure that everyone has access to quality education so that we can be a developed country. The educational status of Muslims in India is a matter of grave concern for the nation.

During the British colonial period, Muslim education faced many obstacles, including resource scarcity, limited access to formal education, and discrimination. Nonetheless, inspiring leaders like Sir Syed Ahmed Khan played a pivotal role in promoting education among Muslims. He founded the Muhammadan Anglo-Oriental College in 1875, which later evolved into Aligarh Muslim University. The university's mission was to provide modern education to Muslims, fostering their social and economic progress. Today, Aligarh Muslim University is one of India's prestigious educational institutions, offering diverse courses across various disciplines.

To examine the educational and socio-economic status of Muslims in India, the government set up a committee called the "Sachar Committee" in 2006. The report suggested various measures such as increasing public spending on education for Muslims, providing scholarships to more minority educational institutions , enhancing access to quality schools and colleges in Muslim concentration areas, ensuring adequate representation of Muslims in teaching and non-teaching staff, promoting vocational and technical education for Muslims etc.

The education ministry has been conducting AISHE (All India Survey on Higher Education) since 2011, covering all higher education institutions in the country. The survey collects detailed information on different parameters, such as student-teacher data, infrastructural information and financial information.

In the recent AISHE report 2020-2021, Muslims are identified as the most educationally backward community. in the country, lagging behind scheduled castes scheduled tribes and other backward classes in terms of enrolment, attainment and representation in higher education. The report shows that total student enrolments in higher education increased to nearly 4.13 crore in 2020-21 from 3.85 crore in 2019-20.India witnessed a 7.5% increase in student enrolment across the country compared to 2019-20. However, the survey also shows that the Muslim community's enrolment declined by 8% at a time when the enrolment of SCs STs and OBCs improved by 4.2%,11.94%and 4% respectively, compared to 2019-20. This indicates that the Muslim community is not only deprived of quality education but also losing its share in the educational opportunities available in the country.

The report also depicts that in the Muslim community the female students have outnumbered male students in terms of enrolment at higher education level. This is a positive sign that indicates that Muslim girls and women are breaking the barriers of patriarchy and conservatism that restrict their access to education.

While in some states, West Bengal, Telangana, and Kerala have bucked the national trend of the Muslim students enrolled for higher education.

Literature Review

Sacher committee report (2006) while examining the Socio-Economic and Educational status of the Muslim community of India found that the growth of the Muslim community has been higher than average. It also revealed that the literacy rate among Muslims in 2001 was 59.1% below the national average (64.8%). Despite a common belief that a large number of Muslim children attend s for primary , only 3.1% of Muslim children among the school-going age go to Madrasas. According to the committee 7% of the population aged 20 years and above are graduates or hold diplomas while only 4% among the Muslim population do and this gap increases as the level of education increases.

Worker population ratios for Muslims are significantly lower than for all other SRC (socio religious categories) in rural areas, but only marginally lower in urban areas. This is due to less participation in –economic activities by Muslim women. According to the report, Muslim workers were much engaged in self-employment activities like traditional manufacturing and trade (especially wearing apparel, auto-repair etc.). The committee also highlighted that in majority Muslim population areas there is no proper social and physical structure.

About one-third of small villages with high concentrations of Muslims do not have any educational institutions. About 40% of large villages with a substantial Muslim concentration do not have any medical facilities.

The report also says that Muslims face a fairly high level of poverty. According to NSSO data, overall, 22.7% of India's population was poor in 2004-5 with SC/STs together as the worst off (35%) followed by Muslims at 31%.

In a case study of Maharashtra and Gujarat, Muslim higher education data was collected from Pune and Ahmedabad.The major finding of this case study is that the main constraint to attaining Higher education are:

a) Financial constraints: This is the main constraint in entering higher education. Since school education acts as the base of an educational career, when asked whether their school was good enough to build a good career, most of them responded that due to financial problems they couldn't attend a good school. It was also observed that most students went to school at a greater distance. One thing was also pointed out that financial problems being the prime reason in way of attaining higher education, the number of males students was less than the number of female students because most of the boys enter small business or jobs to support the family after school. A male respondent answered that we learn basic calculation skills and how to read and write, that is enough to get a job and support the family. Almost 90% of the sample belonged to only 1 earning member, that's why it becomes difficult to avail quality education to all.
b) Lack of Information and motivation is another reason as 40% of the sample did not have any knowledge about their nearest university for higher education or any scholarships for higher education, except for the Maulana Azad fellowship and minority scholarship.
c) Feeling of Religious Discrimination - Most respondents say that religious discrimination is also a major factor in not attending higher education. Females highlighted the issue with more emphasis on wearing a burkha and they also add that in recent years they have started feeling it more. Most of them also raise issues about not being able to get a PG or rent a house due to their beliefs and dress code.
d) Lack of infrastructure - Muslims do not want to send their children far from schools and colleges, the reason is safety for girls, and boys to help in the family financially. And most of the schools and colleges are far away from residential areas. So, the government should take initiative to provide closer educational facilities, including hostels and coaching services, which would greatly benefit society.
e) Madrasa education, mentality of people and female education are other constraints. Most of them attend Madrasa for Quran/ Arabic studies and some of them also attend for primary education which is totally in Urdu. If we add modern education in Madrasa infrastructure, it would be a good initiative. Additionally, most of the sample respondents said that females did not have much variety in their ambitions. The mentality of people is

that Muslims don't get jobs after studying, and they also believe in early marriage for girls in certain regions. All these are the major case studies.

- (G0I.2012) Majority of Muslims have a negative attitude towards girls' education, and due to hurdles from their parents, brothers or elders, girls lose interest in academics. If they are allowed to go school then they are often discouraged to go for higher education.
- As identified by the Sachar Committee that normally Muslim settlements are systematically deprived of access to infrastructure and public services like power, piped water supplies and sewerage. Muslim community is living in low income, filthy and poor living conditions (GOI, 2006).
- The anti–Muslim attitude taken by the British before independence to curtail the educational and employment opportunities of the community has laid a drastic impact on their socio-economic condition (Khan and Butool, 2013). The Muslims are facing the same problem even today. This attitude towards Muslims has pushed them into more backwardness.
- In the report titled 'Six Years After Sachar,' by Abusaleh Shariff (January, 2013), the participation of Muslims in higher education has been analysed. It is found that Muslim OBCs are much behind Hindu OBCs, SCs and STs. Even the general category of Muslims is far behind SCs and STs. Worryingly, it has been noted that the general category of Muslims has seen a 1.5% decline between 2004-05 and 2009-10 (p. 22). The study has also noted that there has been a massive increase in the participation of students in higher education in the age group of 17-29, in general. In 2004-05, the percentage of participation in this age group in higher education was 6 % and it has risen to 11% in 2009-10. However, the Muslim community has not been able to get the benefit of higher education despite the Sachar Committee Report and some steps taken by the government to address the situation. We strongly feel that there is a need to take concrete steps to improve the participation of Muslims in higher education by making it mandatory for universities, institutions and colleges to try to achieve diversity in their student population. Scholarships, fee waivers and other facilities like hostels etc. given to SC students also need to be made available to Muslim students so that poverty does not come in the way of their participation in higher education.

Review of AISHE Report 2020-21 with Reference to the Status of Muslims in Higher Education

The AISHE report 2020-21 was reviewed with reference to the status of Muslims in higher education. The researcher had a thorough analysis and the following points were found:

- On page no.32 in point 2.2.3 Representation of Minority students, the report states that 4.6% students belong to Muslim minority and 2% from the other minority and the notable feature is that female students are more than male students in another minority and Muslim minority.

- On page no. 45 in point 2.5 Teaching position ,the report states that the total no. of Teachers for the year 2020-2021 are 15,51,070. Out of this 56 .2% teachers belong to the General category, 32.2% OBC, 9.1% SC and 2.5% are ST .While 5.6% teachers come from muslim community , and the other minority groups are 8.8%.
- On page no. 46 under the same point report states the no. of female teachers per 100 male teachers , for Muslim it is 59 female teachers per 100 male whiles at the all-India level its 75 female teachers per 100 male teachers. In SC there are 60 female teachers per 100 males, in ST it is 75 and in OBC it is 71 female teachers per 100 male teachers. Whereas for other minorities, there are 156 females per 100 male teachers.
- On page no. 48 under the point 2.6 non-teaching staff, the report states that the non-teaching posts are 13,95,868 which is divided into four groups- A,B,C and D and it shows that the male non- teaching staff is 65.9% while female non- teaching staff 34.1% which is less than male. The average no. of females per 100 male non-teaching staff is approximately 52. In case of minorities, Muslim female non- teaching staff per 100 male is 34,which is the lowest per 100 male non- teaching staff, as other minority communities have 85 females non- teaching staff per 100 males. And SC, ST, OBC and PWD has 60,58,64 and 37 females per 100 males.
- On page no. 114 in Table 11: Programme-wise Enrolment, the report shows the enrolment of Muslim in various programmes.
  Continued.... Refer to AISHE Report for the detailed tables through this link: aishe 2020-21 https://aishe.gov.in/aishe/BlankDCF/AISHE%20Final%20 Report%202020-21.pdf
- On page no.126 in Table 11(a), the report shows the programme wise enrolment of muslim and other minority communities in distance mode.
- On page no.136 in table 15, the report shows the State wise enrolment of Muslim, PWD and other minority communities
- On page no.156 in table 21(b) , the report shows state wise number of teachers in Muslim, PWD and in other minority communities
- On page no.167 in table 24(b), the report shows state wise non-teaching staff in muslim, PWD and other minority communities. The table 28 of the report shows PWD and Minority enrolment in various types of universities. The table 30 of the document shows social group-wise number of teachers in various types of universities.
- On page no. 198 in table 34(a), the report shows the programme-wise passed out students in Muslims and in other minority communities.

- On page 255 in table 46 , the report shows the enrolment in muslim , PWD and other minority communities from 2016-17 to 2020-21 which clearly shows that the enrolment of muslim decrease in the year of 2020-2021. Refer to AISHE Report for the detailed tables through this link: aishe 2020-21 https://aishe.gov.in/aishe/BlankDCF/AISHE%20Final%20Report%20 2020-21.pdf for the detailed tables.

Conclusion

The All-India Survey on Higher Education (AISHE) provides a complete picture of Higher Education in India. The comprehensive data on several parameters such as teachers, student enrolment, programmes, examination results, educational finance, infrastructure etc. are being collected and indicators of educational development are calculated from the data collected through AISHE, annually. These are useful in making informed policy decisions. The AISHE, 2020-21 report's review in the context of the status of Muslims in higher education done through this research work is an eye opener. The review points display the minute details of the status of Muslim education in our country. The policies and schemes specialized for addressing the issues can use the points as ready reckoner. The most important point in this direction will be once the government takes the issues into consideration and starts working on those to address the issues of Muslim's education in India.

References

GOI (2006), —Social, Economic and Educational Status of the Muslim Community of India – A Report‖, Prime Minister's High-Level Committee, Cabinet Secretariat, Government of India (Chairperson- Justice Rajindar Sacher). New Delhi. Retrieved from:
http://www.minorityaffairs.gov.in/newsite/sachar/sachar.asp

GOI, (2012). Committee on Girls Education, National Commission for Minority Educational Institutions Ministry of Human Resource Development, New Delhi. Retrieved from: http://www.mospi.gov.in

Khan, J. H., Butool, F. (2013). Education and development of Muslims in India: A comparative study. Journal of Humanities and Social Science, 13(2), 80-86.

All India Survey On Higher Education 2020-21, (2018) Government of India, Ministry of Human Resource Development Department of Higher Education New Delhi.

Census of India, (2011). Religion wise population details. Directorate of Census Operation, New Delhi. Retrieved from: http://www.censusindia.gov.in

13

Exploring Teachers' Perspective for Dysgraphia Learners in Inclusive Classrooms

Mohd Zuber
Eram Nasir

"When we care for the children, we care for the future"

-Joyce Kristen

Introduction

Every child has creativity. When a child first steps into the world, he has no idea how complicated it is. His mind is empty, and as he engages more with the world around him, he gradually starts to absorb and make room for ideas, enabling him to progressively adjust to his circumstances. During the involvement and adjustment phase, he succeeds with certain things but finds it difficult to learn others. Consequently, it seems that the child is struggling to acquire a number of abilities that are essential to his development.

In a definition given by Kirk in 1962**,** "A learning disability (LD) is defined as a disorder, retardation, or delayed development in one or more language, reading, spelling, writing, or math processes that can be caused by emotional or behavioural disturbances, mental retardation, sensory deprivation, or cultural or instructional factors.".

Learners who face problems in writing exhibit poor handwriting that is difficult to read, pressure on the hand during writing, a mismatch between capital and tiny letters, incorrect word and letter spacing,. reflect writing, reversals, letters that are not on the line, and a lack of writing fluency. Dysgraphia is the term used to describe these writing impairments.

Dysgraphia is the medical word for a brain disorder that results in issues with spelling, putting thoughts on paper, or performing the physical parts of writing (e.g., awkward pencil grip or poor handwriting). A person with an illness writes erroneously or in twisted ways.

Dysgraphia is a unique type of learning disability that impairs writing skills. Spelling, penmanship, and difficulty putting ideas on paper are some of the ways it can show up. "It's a particular type of learning disability that impacts children's ability to learn written language and communicate ideas through written language."

The word dysgraphia is Greek in origin. The hand's role in writing and the letters it forms are both mentioned in the basic word graph. The prefix "dys" denotes disability. Graph describes the process of creating shapes of letters by hand. The word "condition" is indicated by the suffix 'ia.' Consequently, dysgraphia is the term used to describe the impairment of handwriting or, occasionally, spelling in letters.

Dysgraphia sufferers typically have some degree of writing ability but frequently struggle with other fine motor abilities, making simple things like tying shoelaces challenging. Additionally, they may struggle with basic spelling (such as the words "b," "d," "p," and "q") and frequently spell words incorrectly while attempting to put their ideas on paper. While additional learning challenges may be present in children with this illness, societal or other academic difficulties are typically absent.

It is crucial to try to make sure that pupils' handwriting is as legible and smooth as possible. Identifying the types and variations of dysgraphia that our teachers see most often in pupils is crucial to creating a curriculum that is diagnosis, prescriptive in nature remedial, or preventive for kids who have the disorder.

Additional factors contributing to dysgraphia include underlying issues with orthographic coding, the orthographic loop (word storage based on hand-eye coordination), and graphomotor skills (writing movements made by the hands, fingers, and executive functions involved in writing letters). The orthographic loop occurs when written words are sequentially processed by the fingers in the mind's eye, resulting in motor output from the hand and visual feedback.

Instructors must recognise the indications of dysgraphia and not write off a child's handwriting as merely sloppy. A teacher should investigate whether a student has dysgraphia if they notice a pattern of unintelligible writing. Instructors ought to record the steps in the writing process that a youngster finds most challenging. Despite the fact that dysgraphia frequently coexists with another impairment, many dysgraphia children also achieve scholastic success in other disciplines.

Review of Literature

Indian Paediatrics (2013) the KEM Hospital in Mumbai's Learning Disability Clinic examined the characteristics of kids who perform poorly in school and reported on the causes of poor scholastic performance (PSP). The study examined children's impairments in western India during a 12-month period. The most frequent cause of subpar academic performance (73.76%) was specific learning difficulties, such as dyslexia, dysgraphia, and dyscalculia.

Akhil, J. (2013), conducted an experimental investigation on the incidence and nature of learning difficulties in school children. Boys and girls in rural Jaipur schools using Hindi and English as their medium of instruction were the samples chosen at random for the study. School instructors and pupils were the ones that provided the data. The age range of the 1116 total population was 6–13 years old, with 668 boys and 448 girls. 33 students (22.0%) out of them had dysgraphia. The majority of pupils also face a language barrier. As per the study's conclusion, It is more common for boys to have writing problems.

In India, according to reports from 2014, the prevalence of learning disorders ranges from 9 to 39%, while the incidence of dyslexia, dysgraphia, and dyscalculia among elementary school pupils is 2-18%, 14%, and 5.5%, respectively. The prevalence of dysgraphia in children aged 8 to 11 is measured by the department of paediatrics at JN Medical College in India, based on data from primary school students in a city in south India. Of them, dysgraphia affected 12.5% and dyscalculia affected 11.2%. Writing difficulties impact 42% of school-age children in Tamil Nadu. Compared to girls, boys are more impacted.

According to the World Health Report, a significant 15% of kids suffer from learning impairments. According to an ICMR epidemiological study on child and adolescent psychiatric disorders, 12.5% of Indian children and adolescents overall have mental and learning abnormalities.

(Karande and Kulkarni, 2005; Karande, 2008), In Indian classrooms, 15% to 20% of students have specific learning problems. A quarter of the students in schools have both specific academic challenges and physical limitations. These kids really have the potential to be school dropouts. Unfortunately, a widespread lack of understanding in India causes many learners with learning issues to go untreated, which can result in persistently low academic performance, class detention, or even dropping out of school.

The Study

Objectives

(1) To study teachers' perspective about student with Dysgraphia in inclusive classroom.
(2) To explore difficulties and challenges faced by teachers to deal with student with dysgraphia.
(3) To explore the pedagogical practices to deal with students with dysgraphia.

Significance

The importance of this research resides in sharing information on the challenges and experiences teachers have when instructing students with Dysgraphia in Delhi government schools. It attempts to identify the gaps in education and support for these pupils by examining the views and difficulties faced by teachers in inclusive classrooms. It is critical to comprehend the constraints that school educators have while attempting to assist Students with Dysgraphia with their writing assignments. In order to improve inclusive teaching methods, support networks, and teacher preparation, this study aims to provide workable solutions. It tackles the lack of awareness, preparation, and teamwork among educators, highlighting the necessity of better resources and expertise to assist dysgraphia learners who struggle with writing. In the end, this study is a vital first step in identifying and addressing structural problems in education, and will also fixing systemic flaws in education, opening the door for improved assistance for pupils with dysgraphia in Delhi government schools.

Methodology

Qualitative Research Design: The main aim is to find the challenges faced by special educators while dealing Dysgraphia learners and how they try to overcome them. We have to explore teachers' perspective about dysgraphia and their experiences in dealing students with dysgraphia. We have to find out which kind of pedagogical practices they are using in schools in teaching dysgraphia learners. The study's qualitative technique is appropriate given the necessity to comprehend societal issues from a variety of angles; qualitative research has the benefit of providing rich data on real-life situations.

Research Method: This paper is an Exploratory Research based and the population of the research is Delhi Govt Schools & Delhi Govt special education teachers where teachers are working in inclusive setup and addressing the needs of pupils with disabilities including Dysgraphia learners. 30 Special Educators have been selected purposefully. These educators were purposefully selected based on their minimum two-year experience teaching students with Dysgraphia in mainstream classes.

Instruments and Gathering Data

Information was gathered using unstructured questionnaires and interviews. The questionnaires and semi-structured interview procedures were employed to collect data from participants. Questionnaires were used because the subjects were always free to answer. Furthermore, questionnaires provided respondents with enough time to answer questions. Questionnaires were easy to administer as they were distributed to a small sample that was easy to manage. The questionnaire, structured across six domains, gathered comprehensive insights.

1: Teaching Methodologies and Pedagogical Strategies
2: Personalised Planning and Assistance
3: challenges Encountered and Techniques Employed
4. Collaboration & Awareness
5: Ongoing Development and Professional Advancement
6. Educating Students with Dysgraphia: The Experiences of Special Educators

Discussion

When working with students with dysgraphia, it is important to talk about the relationship between parents and educators for students who have unique requirements, the educational benefits of teaching dysgraphia students in inclusive settings, and collaborating with specialists involved in the daily activities of dysgraphia students. The kind of difficulties educators have while working with students with Dysgraphia. How teaching children with dysgraphia has benefited from their experiences. The other queries dealt with the teachers' ongoing professional development and progress. distinct instructional techniques and pedagogical approaches that are unique to each student. The study's author circulated the questionnaire to the teachers and then had it collected. The confidentiality of the answers was maintained with care.

This study examines how educators deal with students with Dysgraphia in inclusive classrooms and evaluates the pedagogical effects of various instructional strategies. It looks at the relationship that exists between teachers and parents of special needs students as well as how they work together with other professionals involved in the lives of pupils.

When providing dysgraphia help to students, teachers may face a variety of difficulties. This interview explores these issues and looks at how instructors' experiences have influenced the way they teach dysgraphia-affected kids. It also explores the specialised teaching for students with dysgraphia, especially in the government-run inclusive schools in Delhi.

The questionnaire primarily aims to gather information about teachers' experiences working with Dysgraphia learners in the Delhi government's inclusive school system. It seeks to reveal the methods, techniques, and individualised approaches that educators employ to address the unique requirements of students with dysgraphia in these contexts.

The questionnaire also emphasises instructors' professional development and ongoing progress. Its inquiries into different pedagogical approaches and instructional methodologies cater to the particular requirements of every student. The author carefully circulated the questionnaire and ensured that it was collected under tight confidentiality guidelines.

Data Analysis

The response of the participants from the questionnaire was first recorded and then analysed qualitatively. The qualitative analysis was conducted under six domains produced important themes and sub-themes based on the teachers' reaction. The interviews were conducted in the bilingual language.

Examining the results of the interviews and questionnaires reveals the complex environment for educating students with dysgraphia in Delhi government schools. Despite the difficulties mentioned—such as a shortage of training, excessive workloads, and inadequate resources—teachers' commitment is evident. Resource rooms and individualised methods are crucial for supporting dysgraphia learners, as demonstrated by these effective techniques. Despite these victories, there is a resounding cry for improved teacher preparation, more consciousness, and teamwork. Gaining an understanding of these complex viewpoints prepares the ground for systemic changes, such as updating training curricula, reducing non-teaching duties, and promoting collaborative workplaces. These findings provide a road map for establishing more understanding, accommodating, and supportive environments for dysgraphia learner in Delhi's educational system.

Delimitation

- A sample of schools wills we taken from East of Delhi only.
- Only Govt Schools Teachers has been taken for the study.

Results

Goal 1

(1) *To study teachers' perspective about learner with Dysgraphia in inclusive classroom.*

Ninety percent of teachers (n = 27) expressed enthusiasm for teaching students with dysgraphia in inclusive environments, while realizing the need for individualised approaches based on their experiences. But because there was no specialized training available regarding subject adaptation specific curriculum content to address the unique requirements of students with disabilities, 100% (n=30) of the teachers faced several difficulties. As such, they mainly depended on instinct and imagination that came from their experiences as teachers. Large class sizes, insufficient customized instructional resources, and a lack of time all contributed to this.

Surprisingly, every participant (100%) mentioned that the Inclusive Education Branch (IEB) of the Delhi Government works with several organizations to offer in-service training for teachers on cross-disability. The goal of this program is to improve teachers' abilities to accommodate students with dysgraphia and other difficulties.

Remarkably, every single respondent (n = 30) acknowledged the existence of resource rooms or corners in Delhi government schools. Teachers can work one-on-one with pupils who have dysgraphia and other difficulties in these settings through activities and sessions. Especially noteworthy are the resource rooms' ample supplies of tools, equipment, and materials created especially to help dysgraphia pupils' hand-eye coordination and grasping skills.

The importance of tailored engagement with kids who have dysgraphia in improving their academic performance was acknowledged by all participants. It is noteworthy to mention that a staggering 97% of participants (n=29) said that their special needs children had Individualised Education Programs (IEPs).

Furthermore, sixty percent of the participants (n = 18) mentioned that teachers' capacity to assist students with dysgraphia was hampered by the absence of specific training in the field. While 80% (n=24) reported stigma and low knowledge of dysgraphia among children, parents, and educators, 70% (n=21) indicated difficulties with verbal expression.

90% of educators (n=27) said they are committed to inclusive education, emphasising the value of fostering a welcoming and understanding environment. They frequently talk about how difficult it can be to help children who face challenges with writing and can use creative teaching techniques to make these pupils succeed.

Of the participants, around 77% (n = 23) had attended training workshops related to dysgraphia or learning disabilities, and 75% of them thought these sessions were helpful. The training sessions are regarded by teachers as "a very good chance to exchange experiences" in addition to offering information on interesting subjects.

Furthermore, every single participant (100%, n = 30) reported that the Delhi government schools had adopted the resource room approach to enhance inclusive education. For special students, including those with dysgraphia, this designated area is run by a resource room teacher and functions as a specialized classroom. Here, all teachers work with dysgraphia students, providing them with specialized attention and support. This room serves as a multipurpose center that gives parents and other experts involved in the students' education in collaborative manner, They also stores a library-like collection of special education books, and provides individualised assistance by the support teacher.

Goal 2

(2) *To explore difficulties and challenges faced by teachers to deal with dysgraphia learners.*

Despite having specialised degrees in a single disability area, 70% (n=21) of teachers experienced uneasiness when dealing with pupils who had several kinds of disabilities. Based on each person's specific requirements, none of the participating teachers thought that they were sufficiently equipped to work with special needs students. For example, there was no material on the various types of disabilities and associated specific academic needs in their pre-service teacher education program. They lacked the necessary training to handle various disabilities.

All participants (100%) noted that learning Hindi and English presents major problems for dysgraphia learners. Individuals with this disability encounter difficulties with letter construction and thought expressing when writing. Remarkably, 80% of participants (n=24) reported having inadequate access to tools designed especially to alleviate dysgraphia in Hindi instruction.

Furthermore, all thirty (100%) agreed that spelling and grammar mistakes have an impact on written English. 90% of participants (n = 27) said they struggled with fine motor control, which affected their ability to write in both languages for assignments. Large class sizes and time constraints exacerbate this issue.

Surprisingly, 100% of respondents (n=30) agreed unequivocally that the amount of paperwork assigned by higher authorities and non-teaching responsibilities has increased dramatically. Teachers' attention has been continually distracted from teaching by this rise. Teachers are frequently diverted to other tasks by the sudden deluge of orders and notices, which makes it difficult for them to offer full-time support to children with special needs, including those who have dysgraphia.

About 70% (n=21) of teachers at Delhi government schools voice worries about time constraints, big class numbers, and resource limits when it comes to meeting the requirements of pupils with dysgraphia. Peer-assisted learning, routines, and making use of available technology to improve learning experiences are some of the strategies used to lessen these difficulties.

90% of participants (n=27) emphasized how difficult it is to give individualized support to pupils with dysgraphia because of the difficulties brought about by big class sizes and added responsibilities.

Additionally, eighty percent (n=24) of the teachers stressed how urgently it is important to educate coworkers, principals, and higher authorities about disabilities like dysgraphia. It's thought that this deeper comprehension is essential to creating a welcoming atmosphere that accommodates kids with a range of learning requirements.

Goal 3

(3) To explore the pedagogical practices to deal with dysgraphia students. 90% (n=27) of the participants, drawing from their vast experiences, strongly suggested that special educators be relieved of their non-teaching duties; they suggested that these duties be allocated exclusively in cases of urgency. With this change, teachers would be able to give pupils with a variety of requirements, such dysgraphia, the time and attention they need, and prioritize those needs.

Educators in Delhi government schools discuss students with dysgraphia are in inclusive classes from a variety of angles. 90% of the participants, or 27 students, highlight the importance of providing individualized attention. They recognize that each dysgraphia learner has unique demands., and they adjust their teaching strategies accordingly.

Ninety percent of educators (n=27) plan fun, engaging activities, such as role-playing games, to help Dysgraphia pupils improve their comprehension and communication abilities. Resource rooms are used by them to hold these sessions.

Every respondent (100 percent, n = 30) acknowledged that Delhi government schools offer therapeutic interventions. These interventions, such as physical therapy, occupational therapy, and speech therapy, aim to improve writing ability and fine motor coordination in all pupils, including those diagnosed with dysgraphia.

Furthermore, all (30 participants, 100%) agreed that it is a good idea to hold customized sessions to give Dysgraphia students the specialised attention and support they need to improve their writing abilities."

The use of fine motor activities, such as utilising tiny tools or manipulatives to develop hand muscles, to increase fine motor skills was confirmed by 100% of participants (n = 30). They include pupils in puzzle-solving, sketching, and tracing exercises that enhance hand-eye coordination.

Ninety percent of the participants, (n = 27) in all, attested to the use of assistive technologies, such as word prediction or speech-to-text software, in helping dysgraphia pupils with their writing assignments. Authorities supported chances for learning and training in response to the pandemic.

Furthermore, eighty percent of participants (n = 24) agreed that the availability of Special Writing Tools—such as customised grips or adaptable utensils—improved writing control.

Additionally, every participant (100 percent, n = 30) supported the application of tailored techniques, particularly involve making strategies that are especially customised to everyone's needs (dysgraphia-related difficulties). Each student receives customised case studies, functional tests, and Individualised Education Plans (IEPs) in addition to one-on-one meetings in resource rooms along with full classroom instruction.

Furthermore, every single participant (100 percent, n = 30) attested to the application of adjustments and accommodations based on the severity and demands of the students, providing Adaptive Instruction. The delivery of information and teaching strategies are modified to meet the unique learning requirements of dysgraphia students."

Additionally, every participant (100 percent, n = 30) agreed that resource rooms ought to be utilised for particular tasks that improve motor skills, coordination, and writing ability. Depending on the needs and skill level of the students, these resource rooms are adapted to provide customised exercises and assignments created especially to address the areas of difficulty faced by student with dysgraphia.

87% of teachers (n = 26) think that collaboration between parents, specialists, and school staff is crucial to providing complete support. They promote ongoing development of their careers to increase their ability to fulfil the needs of dysgraphia learners.

Every teacher agrees that it's critical to maintain positive relationships with the parents of their pupils. But after some consideration, they claim that the method isn't always straightforward. The notion that their children require special education and an IEP is frequently rejected by the guardians of children who had been originally identified as having special needs. Nonetheless, the relationship eventually improves when parents are recognized as partners in the process of learning and are requested for help.

In terms of Collaboration and Awareness, around 80% (n = 24) of teachers in government schools in Delhi highlight how crucial it is for educators to work together as a team with parents, specialists, and school administration. They emphasise the necessity of raising awareness and knowledge of dysgraphia among the school community in order to create an inclusive setting that can successfully accommodate students with a range of learning needs.

Moreover, these educators work to promote awareness and acceptance in the classroom, creating an environment where each kid feels capable and respected despite their difficulties. Using each student's unique talents and abilities, they aim to give dysgraphia students a sense of empowerment and community.

Furthermore, every participant (i.e., 100%, n = 30) emphasised the significance of working with a range of experts, including general teachers, principals, counsellors, music and sports teachers, therapists, and various other experts. This cooperation is thought to be essential to enhancing the overall process of teaching and learning.

In addition, these educators work to provide a setting in the learning environment where each student feels respected and capable, regardless of their difficulties, by promoting acceptance and awareness. To help dysgraphia kids feel empowered and like they belong, they place a strong emphasis on making use of each learner's individual strengths and abilities.

The results have been organised based on the primary areas of the study. The preparation of teachers, the pedagogical implications of teaching inclusive classes, the interaction with parents of special students, working with other professionals, providing administrative, material, and human support, and the perceived efficacy of the current incentives for including special needs students in mainstream classes are the main ones.

Teachers' perspective about positive aspects for students with dysgraphia in Inclusive Classrooms

1. *Recognition of the Significance of Individualised Work*: Everyone agrees that individualized work plays a critical role in helping students with dysgraphia achieve academic success. The importance of providing individualised attention for dysgraphic learners is acknowledged.
2. *Tailored Support and Resource Rooms*: The availability of well-equipped resource rooms for kids with particular needs, such as dysgraphia, enables focused activities and one-on-one sessions. A proactive approach to meeting the requirements of kids with dysgraphia is demonstrated by the availability of resource rooms equipped with specialised aids and support materials.
3. *Diverse Pedagogical Strategies*: These techniques include the use of therapeutic treatments, fine motor exercises, assistive technology, and personalised plans, all of which highlight attempts to address particular difficulties presented by students with dysgraphia. Diverse tactics being used show that difficulties associated with dysgraphia are being addressed.
4. *Collaborative engagement:* It is a concept that emphasises the value of inclusive environments by acknowledging the combined efforts of educators,

experts, parents, and school administration. Stakeholder collaboration is highlighted, demonstrating a dedication to inclusive education.

5. *In-Service Training:* The partnership with different organisations offering in-service training that *crosses* disabilities suggests a proactive strategy to improve instructors' abilities. Collaborating for in-service training on cross-disability represents a step toward improving instructors' capacities.
6. *Resource Room Implementation*: Making use of resource rooms with specialised assistance shows that students' needs are being met proactively. Use of resource rooms effectively for targeted activities, specialised sessions, and exercises designed for learners with dysgraphia.
7. *Educators are passionate* about teaching in inclusive environments and recognise the importance of tailored education. Interactive and enjoyable activities are given priority while trying to help dysgraphia students learn better.
8. *Innovative Techniques*: To improve learning opportunities, teachers use a range of strategies, including role-playing, therapeutic interventions, and fine motor exercises.
9. *Adaptive Instruction:* Utilising instructional techniques and the delivery of materials that are adapted to the particular learning needs of kids with dysgraphia. Teachers employ adjustments and adaptations extensively to meet the demands and capabilities of their dysgraphia students.

Teachers' perspective about negative aspects for students with dysgraphia in Inclusive Classrooms

1. *Resource constraints*: The stigma associated with dysgraphia is not well-known to parents, teachers, or students, and there are little resources available in Hindi for teaching about the disorder.
2. *Administrative pressures and workload*: Overwhelming paperwork and non-teaching duties take instructors' attention away from instructing students and offering full-time help to those with special needs. Support for kids with dysgraphia is impacted when teaching is neglected due to an excessive administrative workload.
3. *Difficulties with Managing Diverse Disabilities:* Despite specialised degrees in a single disability field, there is uneasiness and insufficiency while managing pupils with diverse disabilities. Teachers, especially those with degrees specialised in a specific area of disability, report feeling uncomfortable working with students who have a variety of difficulties.
4. *Instructors lack specialised training* in adapting curriculum to meet the requirements of students with disabilities. Curriculums for pre-service education do not adequately prepare students to deal with a range of difficulties.

5. *Limited resources for* teaching Hindi and English to dysgraphia learner.
6. *Stigma and Awareness*: Difficulties in receiving support and understanding stem from a lack of knowledge and misconceptions regarding dysgraphia.

Conclusion

Delhi Government schools are doing a great job of providing inclusive education to students with dysgraphia. Special education teachers do this by providing specialised attention, creative surroundings, and cutting-edge teaching methods. These initiatives demonstrate a dedication to individualised assistance and cooperative participation. Lots of in-service trainings organised by Inclusive Education Branch for the professional development and provided good infrastructure in schools including resource room to special education teacher to conduct one on one session with disabled students. Optimal support is hampered by enduring issues such as a shortage of dysgraphia awareness, administrative hassles, and resource constraints. Instructors that are passionate about inclusive education encounter challenges when it comes to accommodating an extensive variety of disabilities because they haven't gotten enough specialist training or curriculum adjustments. These difficulties are exacerbated by the lack of resources available to instruct Hindi and English, and the stigma associated with dysgraphia makes it more difficult to get understanding and support. But educators face a variety of difficult situations. Teachers faced challenges such as time restrictions, non-teaching work, stigma and awareness gaps, and managing a variety of disabilities with specialised degrees only in one disability.

The gap between the recognition of the need for customised care and the availability of resources highlights the pressing need for improved training, more effective use of resources, and focused awareness efforts. Support for students is impacted when specialised teaching is neglected due to an abundance of administrative responsibilities. An all-encompassing strategy, including thorough teacher preparation, more funding, and active awareness campaigns, is needed to close these disparities. For students with dysgraphia enrolled in Delhi Government schools, inclusive education would be strengthened by providing teachers with substantial training, an abundance of resources, and increased stakeholder awareness. In order to guarantee that these children receive the specialised assistance they require to succeed in inclusive settings, such initiatives are essential.

Recommendations and Suggestions

With the help of these suggestions, students with dysgraphia should be able to receive better assistance and instruction in Delhi government schools, creating an atmosphere that will help them succeed both academically and socially.

1. *Programmess for Specialised Training*: Provide extensive, mandated training curricula designed to address certain learning difficulties such

as dysgraphia. Identification, comprehension, and effective teaching strategies—including curriculum material modification—should be covered in these programs. Work together with professionals to create and carry out these initiatives.

2. *Enhancement of the Curriculum:* Modify modules on different disabilities, such as dysgraphia, and their academic needs in pre-service teacher education. In order to effectively serve diverse learners, introduce specialised courses covering instructional techniques, interventions, and tactics.
3. *Resource Allocation:* Provide additional resources, particularly in the area of Hindi education, that are expressly designed to combat dysgraphia. Make sure resource Rooms are equipped with everything they need in both English and any other language that is widely spoken in the area.
4. *Raising Awareness and Eradicating Stigma:* To combat misunderstandings and lessen stigma associated with dysgraphia, start awareness initiatives aimed at educators, parents, and students. Create a welcoming atmosphere that promotes empathy and assistance for students with a range of learning needs.
5. *Reducing Non-Teaching Duties:* Promote a streamlined administrative procedure to help educators specially educators who work with these children who have special needs handle less paperwork and non-teaching duties. Stress that these assignments should only be given in an emergency so that teachers can concentrate on properly instructing and assisting students.
6. *Increased Collaborative Efforts:* Promote and assist increased cooperation between educators, experts, guardians, and school administration. In order to fully address the diverse requirements of dysgraphia learners, this teamwork is essential.
7. *Personalised and Adaptive Instruction:* Stress the value of using tailored and flexible teaching methods for dysgraphia learners. Keep creating and implementing specialised plans, interventions, and instructional strategies based on the unique needs and abilities of every student.
8. *Technological integration:* To support Dysgraphia kids, promote the continued incorporation and use of assistive technologies in schools. Make that educators are knowledgeable the use of tools to improve learning experiences and have received the necessary training.
9. *Parent-Teacher Collaboration*: Keep encouraging parents and teachers to get along. Employ techniques that highlight the significance of parents' involvement in assisting their child's education and include them as participants in the educational journey of kids with dysgraphia.
10. *Longitudinal Research and Ongoing Professional Development:* Promote the use of longitudinal research to monitor the development of learners with dysgraphia. Promote ongoing professional development initiatives as well in order to keep teachers informed about the newest techniques and approaches in the area of special education.

11. *Holistic Approaches to Inclusive Education:* Promote an inclusive education strategy that emphasises social and emotional components besides academic support. Create programmes that assist students with dysgraphia in enhancing their social skills, self-worth, and confidence.
12. *Peer-Assisted Learning activities:* Create and carry out organised activities for students that aid one another in learning in the classroom. This strategy can aid in developing a helpful atmosphere where students help one another, encouraging empathy and peer cooperation.
13. *Advocacy & Policy initiatives:* Promote policy modifications or efforts that require and endorse inclusive teaching methods. Encourage the allocation of more funds, resources, and policies to guarantee that learners with dysgraphia receive specialised help.
14. *Continuous Assessment & Monitoring:* Use tools for continuous assessment to track the development of learners with dysgraphia. On the basis of each student's development, regular evaluations might assist in customising interventions and instructional methods.
15. *Community Involvement*: Promote collaborations with advocacy groups that focus on dysgraphia or special education, as well as community organisations and non-governmental organisations. Work together to bring in outside knowledge, materials, and student and teacher support networks.
16. *Professional Support Networking:* Create forums or professional networks for educators who deal with dysgraphia learners. By providing a forum for the exchange of best practices, materials, and life lessons, these networks can help teachers build a strong sense of community.
17. *Cultural sensitivities and Linguistic variety:* When treating dysgraphia, take into account and acknowledge linguistic and cultural variety. Promote the creation of resources and interventions that are adapted to the diverse language and cultural backgrounds that are common in the area.
18. *Research-Based Intervention and support :* Fund studies aimed at comprehending the particular difficulties encountered by dysgraphia learners in their particular setting. Create evidence-based strategies and interventions based on these findings.
19. *Parental Training Programs:* Provide seminars or other events with the goal of teaching families about dysgraphia, its symptoms, and practical strategies for helping their kids at home. This will guarantee that the requirements of students with dysgraphia are met both in the home and in the classroom.
20. *Extended-Duration Service Frameworks:* Provide Dysgraphia students with long-term assistance, even when they leave the resource rooms or advance to higher grades. Make sure the support doesn't stop in order to help them succeed and advance farther.

These suggestions are meant to establish a more all-encompassing and encouraging environment in Delhi government schools, with an emphasis on enhancing the learning environment and results for pupils who have dysgraphia.

References

Javed, M., Juan, W. X., & Nazli, S. (2013). A study of students' assessment in writing skills of the English language. *Online Submission*, 6 (2), 129-144.

Gill,M.D.K (December7,2018) . Dysgraphia: Symptom, Causes, treatment, Mannagement on line article.

Gunning, T. G. (1998). *Assessing and Correcting Reading and Writing Difficulties*, Allyn and Bacon, Boston, 1998, pp. 3

Venkatesan, S.(2017c). Development and validation of a graded reading test for children with learning disabilities. *Journal of Psychology*,8(1), 11-20.

Graham, S., & Perin, D. (2007). Writing next-effective strategies to improve writing of adolescents in middle and high schools. *The Elementary School Journal*, 94 (2),169-181.

Venkatesan, S. (2016). A Concept Analysis of Learning Disability Based on Research Articles Published in India, 43 (2), 97-107.

Silver C H, Ruff R M, Iverson G L, Barth J T, Broshek D K, Bush S S, Koffler S P, Reynolds, C. R. (2008). Learning disabilities: The need for neuropsychological evaluation. *Archives of Clinical Neuropsychology,* 23, 217–219.

Singh, S., Sawani, V., Deokate, M., Panchal, S., Subramanyam, A., Shah, H. & Kamath, R. 2017. Specific Learning Disability: a 5-year Study from India. *International Journal of Contemporary Paediatrics*, 4 (3), 863-868

Gupta, S.K. & Venkatesan, S. 2014. Efficacy of Training Program on Executive Functions in Children with Learning Disabilities. *Guru Journal of Behavioural and Social Sciences*, 2 (2), 283-291.

Geremew, L. (2016). A Study of the Requirements in Writing for an Academic Purpose at Addis Ababa University. Unpublished PhD Dissertation. Addis Ababa: Addis Ababa University.

Gill,M.D.K (December7,2018) . Dysgraphia: Symptom, Causes, treatment, Mannagement on line article.

Gunning, T. G. (2008). *Assessing and Correcting Reading and Writing Difficulties*, Allyn and Bacon, Boston, 1998, pp. 3.

Parker, S. (2003). The craft of writing. Paul Chapman Publishing: London.

Rostami, A., Allahverdi, F., Mousavi, F. (February, 2014) Dysgraphia: The Causes and Solutions. *International Journal of Academic Research in Business and Social Sciences* Vol. 4, No. 2 ISSN: 2222-6990 .http://dx.doi.org/10.6007/IJARBSS/v4- i2/582

Zeleke Arficho (2018). Students' Perceptions and Teachers' Practices of Teaching and Learning Writing Skills: The Case of Four Selected Secondary Schools in Hawassa City Administration, South Nations, Nationalities and Peoples' Regional State of Ethiopia.

14

Sustainable Development through Inclusive Education

A Focus on Twice-Exceptional Learners in Inclusive Schools

Tanvi Pahwa
Mohd Faijullah Khan

Introduction

Twice-exceptional (2E/2e) learners are those who are identified as gifted or talented while also having a disability. The term "twice-exceptionalism" refers to the dual exceptionalities of these individuals. The identification and support of learners who are both intellectually gifted and have learning disabilities discuss the ambiguity surrounding the definitions of intellectual giftedness and learning disabilities, and present an argument against using profile analysis to identify gifted learners with learning disabilities. Intellectually gifted learners are those who demonstrate exceptional ability and it is argued that school districts choose to define giftedness based on general intellectual ability, often using IQ tests. Similarly, learning disabilities are defined as a significant discrepancy between a student's performance in a particular academic area and their general intellectual ability, which cannot be explained by a lack of educational opportunity.

The concept of "masking" is introduced, suggesting that gifted learners with learning disabilities may exhibit patterns of strengths and weaknesses that make it challenging to identify them as both gifted and learning disabled. It is recommended by longitudinal data collection to identify declining achievement, proposing that larger than expected declines in academic achievement could be a cause for concern and lead to further assessment. (Baum et al., 2001)

The study focused on identifying and comparing prospective twice-exceptional students with non-twice-exceptional peers based on their strengths in math or reading. The results showed that students potentially gifted in reading did not differ significantly in end-of-year reading outcomes, while twice-exceptional students potentially gifted in math performed significantly lower in both math and reading outcomes. The study highlighted the challenges in identifying twice-exceptional students due to the masking effect, where giftedness may obscure the need for a learning disability diagnosis and vice versa. The findings also suggested that reading deficits may negatively impact math performance on standardized tests. (Bell et al., 2015)

Need and Importance of Inclusive Education for Twice-exceptional Learners

The need for this research to create differential identification procedures for gifted learners with learning disabilities. Inclusive education is paramount for twice-exceptional learners, who possess both exceptional intellectual abilities and disabilities. Embracing inclusivity ensures that these learners receive tailored support, addressing their unique strengths and challenges within mainstream classrooms. It fosters a diverse and accepting learning environment, encouraging social interactions and understanding among peers. Inclusive education also nurtures the talents of twice-exceptional learners, allowing them to contribute meaningfully to the academic community while fostering a sense of belonging. By recognizing and accommodating their dual exceptionalities, inclusive education empowers twice-exceptional learners to reach their full potential, promoting equity and fostering a positive educational experience. Education is key to achieving gender equality and empowering women. When girls and women have access to education, they are more likely to participate in decision-making, have control over their lives, and contribute to the development of their communities. It can also play a role in promoting peace and security. When people are educated, they are more likely to understand different cultures and perspectives, and to resolve conflicts peacefully. Sustainable development helps ensure that education is essential for achieving all of the Sustainable Development Goals. It is the foundation for a sustainable future, and it can help us to address the challenges of climate change, poverty, inequality, and hunger.

Sustainable Development Goal 4 (SDG 4), also known as Quality Education, aims to ensure inclusive and equitable quality education and promote lifelong learning opportunities for all. Addressing the educational needs of twice-exceptional learners aligns with SDG 4 by promoting inclusive education, ensuring equal access to quality education, and supporting teacher training and development to create learning environments that cater to the diverse needs of all learners. Sustainable Development Goal 4 (SDG 4) focuses on ensuring inclusive and equitable quality education for all. Twice-exceptional learners often face challenges in traditional educational settings due to the simultaneous presence of their giftedness and disability. Inclusive education practices aim to cater to the diverse learning needs of all learners, including those who are twice-exceptional. The need for all learners to acquire knowledge and skills that promote sustainable development. (Sharma & Vinaya, 2023)

Twice-exceptional learners may have unique talents and abilities that need to be recognised and nurtured, contributing to the overall quality of education. Addressing their specific needs ensures that the education provided is comprehensive and effective. Twice-exceptional learners, like all learners, should have equal access to education. Ensuring that educational programmes are designed to accommodate the diverse needs of learners, including those with dual exceptionalities, supports the goal of providing equal opportunities for learning. Teachers, special educators and parents play a crucial role in supporting the education of twice-exceptional learners. It emphasises the importance of building and upgrading educational facilities that are child, disability, and gender-sensitive and providing safe, nonviolent, inclusive, and effective learning environments for all.

Findings

This dual exceptionalism can manifest in various combinations, such as giftedness coupled with attention deficit hyperactivity disorder (ADHD), dyslexia, or autism spectrum disorder and various comorbid conditions. Identification of twice-exceptional learners is challenging due to the paradoxical nature of their abilities and disabilities. As noted by Baum, Schader, and Owen (1995), traditional assessment methods may overlook these learners, as their strengths may mask underlying struggles, and vice versa. For instance, a gifted 2E student with dyslexia may exhibit advanced verbal skills but struggle with reading comprehension, making identification complex for educators and specialists. The impact of twice-exceptionality on learning and development is multifaceted. Researchers like Mullet and Callahan (2008) emphasise that 2E individuals often face asynchronous development, where their intellectual, emotional, and social growth occurs at uneven rates. This can result in a mismatch between their cognitive abilities and emotional maturity, affecting their social interactions and self-esteem. Moreover, the learning experiences of twice-exceptional learners may be influenced by the extent to which their educational environment recognizes and accommodates their unique needs. (Ruban, 2005; Reis, 2022)

The intricate nature of twice-exceptionality requires a nuanced understanding of both the gifted and disabled aspects. Recognition of the challenges in identification and comprehension of the impact on learning and development is essential for educators, parents, and policymakers to design inclusive and supportive environments that empower 2E learners to thrive academically and socially. (Mohammad, 2018)

Best Practices and Innovative Strategies: By integrating the principles of differentiated instruction, strengths-based approaches, UDL, personalised learning, social-emotional learning, IEPs, peer support, and ongoing professional development, educators can better address the unique needs of twice-exceptional learners and contribute to the achievement of SDG 4 goals.

Differentiated Instruction: Recognising and addressing the diverse learning needs of learners. Implement differentiated instruction by providing various learning pathways, materials, and assessment methods. Tailor the curriculum to accommodate both the gifted and disabled aspects of 2E learners.

Strengths-Based Approach: Building on individual strengths to promote learning. Identify and leverage the strengths of 2E learners. Provide opportunities for them to explore and develop their talents, fostering a positive self-concept while addressing challenges through appropriate support.

Universal Design for Learning (UDL): Creating flexible and accessible learning environments. Implement UDL principles to make curriculum materials and assessments more flexible and accommodating. Provide multiple means of representation, engagement, and expression to meet the diverse needs of 2E learners.

Personalized Learning Plans: Tailoring education to individual needs and preferences. Develop personalised learning plans for 2E learners that take into account their strengths, challenges, and learning styles. Collaborate with learners, parents, and specialists to create a plan that supports their unique profile.

Social-Emotional Learning (SEL): Recognising the importance of emotional well-being in learning. Integrate social-emotional learning into the curriculum to help 2E learners develop self-awareness, self-regulation, and interpersonal skills. Foster a supportive and inclusive classroom environment to address their social and emotional needs.

Individualized Education Programs (IEPs): Providing customised educational plans for learners with disabilities. Develop comprehensive IEPs that address the specific needs of 2E learners. Include goals, accommodations, and modifications that support both their gifted and disabled aspects. Regularly review and update the IEP in collaboration with parents, teachers, and specialists.

Peer Support and Collaboration: Promoting collaborative and inclusive learning environments. Encourage peer support and collaboration among learners. Foster a sense of community in the classroom where 2E learners can work with their peers, sharing strengths and learning from each other.

Professional Development for Educators: Supporting teachers in understanding and addressing diverse learning needs. Provide ongoing professional development for educators to enhance their understanding of twice-exceptional learners. Equip teachers with effective strategies, tools, and resources to create inclusive and supportive learning environments.

Practical Approaches for Classroom Implementation: Implementing effective strategies for twice-exceptional (2E) learners in the classroom involves a combination of differentiation, individualised education plans (IEPs), and creating supportive learning environments.

1. Differentiation Strategies

Tiered Assignments: Provide tiered assignments that allow learners to engage with content at varying levels of complexity based on their abilities.

Flexible Grouping: Implement flexible grouping to allow 2E learners to work with peers who complement their strengths and support their challenges.

Varied Assessments: Offer a range of assessment methods, including project-based assessments, verbal presentations, and written assignments, allowing learners to showcase their talents in different ways.

2. Individualized Education Plans (IEPs)

Collaborative Goal Setting: Collaborate with parents, special education professionals, and the student to set personalised academic and social-emotional goals based on their strengths and areas of growth.

Accommodations and Modifications: Clearly outline accommodations and modifications within the IEP, ensuring that classroom materials and assessments are tailored to the student's needs.

Regular Progress Monitoring: Conduct regular assessments and progress monitoring to track the effectiveness of interventions and adjust the IEP as needed.

3. Creating Supportive Learning Environments

Fostering a supportive atmosphere is crucial for the well-being of 2E learners.

Social-Emotional Learning (SEL): Integrate SEL activities into the curriculum to help 2E learners develop emotional regulation and interpersonal skills. This can include mindfulness exercises, peer mentoring, and explicit instruction on social skills. (King, 2005)

Teacher Training: Provide professional development for educators on identifying and supporting 2E learners. Equip teachers with the knowledge and skills to create inclusive and positive classroom cultures.

Peer Support Systems: Establish peer support systems where learners work together on projects, fostering a sense of community and understanding. Peer support can enhance the social experiences of 2E learners.

Conclusion

Combining differentiation, individual educational plans, and a supportive learning environment creates a comprehensive framework for meeting the unique needs of twice-exceptional learners. These practical approaches enhance academic achievement, social-emotional development, and overall well-being, aligning with the principles of inclusive education fostering universal design of learning and contributing to the realization of SDG 4 goals. Research indicates that these approaches contribute to improved outcomes for 2E learners. According to a study by Reis and McCoach (2000), differentiated instruction positively impacts the academic performance of gifted learners. According to McCoach (2001), the best practices for identifying and serving gifted learners with learning disabilities, emphasise the need for comprehensive assessment, including behavioural observations, individual intelligence tests, cognitive processing measures, and a full achievement battery. It suggests that educators should allow these learners to work at an appropriate level in each subject area, even if this results in grade level asynchronies within the student's educational programme. Additionally, it highlights the importance of interventions for these learners, stating that they should have opportunities for enrichment as well as remediation.

References

Baldwin, L., Baum, S. E., Pereles, D. A., & Hughes, C. (2015). Twice-exceptional learners. *Gifted Child Today*, *38*, 206–214. https://doi.org/10.1177/1076217515597277

Baum, S., Cooper, C. R., & Neu, T. W. (2001). Dual differentiation: An approach for meeting the curricular needs of gifted students with learning disabilities. *Psychology in the Schools*, *38*, 477–490. https://doi.org/10.1002/PITS.1036

Baum, S., Schader, R. M., & Hébert, T. P. (2014b). *Twice-exceptional learners through a different lens : Reflecting on a strengths-based , talent-focused approach for.*

Beckmann, E., & Minnaert, A. (2017). Non-cognitive characteristics of gifted students with learning disabilities: An in-depth systematic review. *Frontiers in Psychology*, *9*, null. https://doi.org/10.3389/fpsyg.2018.00504

Bell, S. M., Taylor, E. P., McCallum, R. S., Coles, J., & Hays, E. (2015). Comparing prospective twice-exceptional students with high-performing peers on high-stakes tests of achievement. *Journal for the Education of the Gifted*, *38*, 294–317. https://doi.org/10.1177/0162353215592500

Brody, L. E., & Mills, C. J. (1997). Gifted children with learning disabilities: A review of the issues. *Journal of Learning Disabilities*, *30*, 282–296. https://doi.org/10.1177/002221949703000304

Danika. (2018). The identification of students who are gifted and have a learning disability: A comparison of different diagnostic criteria. *Gifted Child Quarterly*, *62*, 175–192. https://doi.org/10.1177/0016986217752096

Dare, L., & Nowicki, E. (2015). Twice-exceptionality: Parents' perspectives on 2e identification. *Roeper Review*, *37*, 208–218. https://doi.org/10.1080/02783193.2015.1077911

King, E. (2005). Addressing the social and emotional needs of twice-exceptional students. *TEACHING Exceptional Children*, *38*, 16–21. https://doi.org/10.1177/004005990503800103

L. Barnard-Brak, Johnsen, S., Alyssa Pond Hannig, & Wei, T. (2015). The incidence of potentially gifted students within a special education population. *Roeper Review*, *37*, 74–83. https://doi.org/10.1080/02783193.2015.1008661

Lee, K. M., & Olenchak, R. (2015). Individuals with a gifted/attention deficit/hyperactivity disorder diagnosis. *Gifted Education International*, *31*, 185–199. https://doi.org/10.1177/0261429414530712

Lovett, B. J., & Sparks, R. (2013). The identification and performance of gifted students with learning disability diagnoses. *Journal of Learning Disabilities*, *46*, 304–316. https://doi.org/10.1177/0022219411421810

M. Foley-Nicpon, S. Assouline, & Colangelo, N. (2013a). Twice-exceptional learners. *Gifted Child Quarterly*, *57*, 169–180. https://doi.org/10.1177/0016986213490021

McCallum, R. S., Bell, S. M., Coles, J., Miller, K. C., Hopkins, M. B., & Hilton-Prillhart, A. (2013). A model for screening twice-exceptional students (gifted with learning disabilities) within a response to intervention paradigm. *Gifted Child Quarterly*, *57*, 209–222. https://doi.org/10.1177/0016986213500070

McCoach, D., Kehle, T. J., Bray, M., & Siegle, D. (2001). Best practices in the identification of gifted students with learning disabilities. *Psychology in the Schools*, *38*, 403–411. https://doi.org/10.1002/PITS.1029

Mohammed, A. (2018). Twice-Exceptionality in the Kingdom of Saudi Arabia: Policy Recommendations for Advances in Special Education. *International Journal of Special Education*, *33*(2), 397–415. https://eric.ed.gov/?id=EJ1185585

Morrison, W. F., & Rizza, M. G. (2007). Creating a toolkit for identifying twice-exceptional students. *Journal for the Education of the Gifted*, *31*, 57–76. https://doi.org/10.4219/jeg-2007-513

Mullet, D. R., Kettler, T., & Sabatini, A. (2018). Gifted Students' Conceptions of Their High School STEM Education. *Journal for the Education of the Gifted*, 41(1), 60-92. https://doi.org/10.1177/0162353217745156

Neihart, M. (2008). *Identifying and providing services to twice exceptional children*. https://doi.org/10.1007/978-0-387-74401-8_7

Nielsen, M. (2002). Gifted students with learning disabilities: Recommendations for identification and programming. *Exceptionality*, *10*, 111–193. https://doi.org/10.1207/S15327035EX1002_4

Reis, S. M., Madaus, J. W., Gelbar, N. W., & Miller, L. J. (2022). Strength-Based Strategies for Twice-Exceptional High School Students With Autism Spectrum Disorder. *TEACHING Exceptional Children*, 004005992211088.https://doi.org/10.1177/00400599221108899

Reis, S., Baum, S., & Burke, E. M. (2014). An operational definition of twice-exceptional learners. *Gifted Child Quarterly*, *58*, 217–230. https://doi.org/10.1177/0016986214534976

Ruban, L. (2005). Identification and assessment of gifted students with learning disabilities. *Theory into Practice*, *44*, 115–124. https://doi.org/10.1207/s15430421tip4402_6

Ruban, L. M. (2005). Identification and Assessment of Gifted Students With Learning Disabilities. *Theory into Practice*, *44*(2), 115–124. https://doi.org/10.1207/s15430421tip4402_6

Sharma, K., & Vinayan, S. (2023). Education and Leaving No One Behind: A Critical Analysis of Law and Policy for Children with Disabilities in India. *NUJS Law Review*, *16* (3).

Wormald, C. (2017). *An enigma: Barriers to the identification of students who are gifted with a learning disability*. https://doi.org/10.1007/978-981-10-6701-3_15

Wormald, C., Rogers, K. B., & Vialle, W. (2015a). A Case Study of Giftedness and Specific Learning Disabilities: Bridging the Two Exceptionalities. *Roeper Review*, *37*(3), 124–138. https://doi.org/10.1080/02783193.2015.1047547

Wormald, C., Vialle, W., & Rogers, K. (2014). Young and misunderstood in the education system: A case study of giftedness and specific learning disabilities. *Australasian Journal of Gifted Education*, 23, 16.

15

Issues and Challenges for Students with Disabilities while Accessing Higher Education in India

Nayab Parveen

Introduction

Disability is acknowledged as "an evolving concept" in the Preamble to the Convention on the Rights of Persons with Disabilities (CRPD), but it also emphasises that disability comes from the interaction between individuals with impairments and environmental and attitudinal barriers that prevent them from fully and equally participating in society. If disability is defined as an interaction, then "disability" is not a personal characteristic. It is possible to improve social participation by removing the barriers that people with impairments experience. Internationally, at the beginning of the 1990s, there was an effort to create a more inclusive educational system and promote the process of getting education for individuals with disabilities. The adoption of equity and the universalisation of education for all children was first acknowledged at the World Conference on Education for All in 1990, which took place in Jomtien, Thailand. Education for all became even more important globally after the 1994 Salamanca Conference on Special Needs Education in Spain, where the Salamanca Statement was published, stressing the construction of inclusive education for all children, including children with disabilities. According to Vislie (2003), the Salamanca Statement's introduction has made inclusive education a global standard. Signatories to the declaration have pledged to prioritise the adoption of inclusive policies and programmes (Ainscow & Sebba, 1996; Singal, 2005). However, promoters of inclusion acknowledge that there are differences in the paths taken by industrialised and developing nations towards inclusive education and inclusive schooling due to the concept's varied application (Armstrong et al., 2011). For example, inclusive education aims to include students with disabilities in conventional classrooms in most Western nations (Miles & Singal, 2010); Ainscow & Sebba (1996) suggested restructuring curriculum organization and provision; Florian & Linklater (2010) suggested increasing inclusive pedagogies; Avramidis et al. (2000) suggested improving teaching attitudes toward learning. However, addressing disability and inclusion is not a major concern for developing nations like India (Singal, 2010). As a result, implementing inclusive education in such countries has many challenges (Srivastava et al., 2015).

The higher education system introduces diversity into the context of disability. It is not a given that the inclusion of students with disabilities in elementary, upper elementary, and secondary school will translate to higher education. To proceed to the post-secondary education level, a self-sufficient personal and social identity must be formed. Different kinds of students with disabilities face many obstacles and difficulties in meeting their basic needs in daily life. Most of the same challenges are observed in their academic pursuits in higher education. Although these students face a variety of challenges in higher education, despite their willingness to enroll, continue, and complete their education, this may be something that needs to be looked at and provided a higher priority. Several issues that affect higher education for students with disabilities often result in extended studies or students failing to complete their studies (Zuber & Ramakrishna, 2021). Higher education not only ensures employment but also develops analytical and critical thinking skills. It makes someone a thoughtful, educated citizen who can support the development and success of their country. The population of each country determines its level of development. All citizens are important in advancing their country, and people with disabilities are not excluded. Their contributions are invaluable (Pandey, 2021).

The Study

Objectives

This research investigated the challenges faced by students with disabilities at Indian Higher Education Institutions.

Methodology

This paper is mainly based on secondary sources, data collected from various books, journal articles, census data, and AISHE reports, etc.

Status of Students with Disabilities in Higher Education

About 2.68 million persons in India have been identified as "disabled" making up 2.21% of the country's total population (Census, 2011). 22% population with disabilities between the ages of 20 to 39 years have locomotor disabilities, while 18% have hearing disabilities. 15% have difficulty seeing, 8% have difficulties with speech, and 6% have multiple disabilities. Over 55% (1.46 million) of the total persons with disabilities are literate. 45% of all persons with disabilities are illiterate, 13% have matric/secondary education but are not graduates, and

5% have a bachelor's degree or above. Given the ratio of illiterates, it is safe to say that such a large population cannot even be taken advantage of. It is a significant loss of human capital and a major source of concern. There were 1,113 Universities, 43,796 Colleges, and 11,296 Stand Alone Institutions registered (AISHE, 2020-21). The total number of students enrolled in higher education increased by 28.80 lakh from 3.85 crore in 2019–20 to approximately 4.13 crore in 2020–21. Over time, there has been an improvement in the annual rate of enrolment growth. The enrolment increases in 2020–21 over 2019–20 is 7.4%; in 2019–20, it was 3%, and in 2018–19, it was 2.7%. Moreover, enrolment has increased by 20.9% overall between 2014 and 2015. 2.12 crore (51.3%) male students and 2.01 crore (48.7%) female students were enrolled in higher education. There were 1.89 crore female students enrolled in 2019–20, compared to 1.96 crore male students.

Only 0.56% of students with disabilities enroll in higher education institutions, even though 5% of Indian students should be in higher education (RPWD ACT, 2016), according to the National Centre for Promotion of Employment of Disabled People from 150 top colleges/universities, and institutes. There are only 8,449 students with disabilities among the 15,21,438 students enrolled in these educational institutions. which is hardly 0.56%, whereas 5% is the expected number that should be in higher education (RPWD Act, 2016).

The AISHE report estimates that 38.5 million students were enrolled in higher education state-wide in 2020, with 92,831 students with disabilities enrolling compared to 85,877 in 2019. Let us contrast this figure with those of the other marginalised groups. It is the lowest of all, clearly showing that their population is growing over time and that only a small percentage of these people pursue higher education. The state of Uttar Pradesh had the highest enrolment (18,050), primarily due to the establishment of two universities: Jagadguru Rambhadracharya Handicapped University and Dr. Shakuntala Mishra National Rehabilitation University (50% of seats reserved for students with disabilities). After Uttar Pradesh, the highest percentages are found in Tamil Nadu and Delhi; in contrast, there are only three students registered in higher education institutions in Daman and Diu. Lakshadweep and Ladakh have no students with disabilities enrolled in higher education. These low enrolment figures are concerning.

Empirical research on the first-hand experiences of disabled students at higher education institutions is lacking. The work that already exists that shows the connection between social discrimination, education, and disability focuses mostly on the school level of education (Das & Kattumuri, 2011; Sawhney, 2015; Singal, 2005; Singal et al., 2009; Vik & Lassen, 2010). These studies typically found barriers that can be seen as effective barriers to high-quality instruction. Unfair leadership and ideology toward education (Kavoori,

2002), social attitudes against students with disabilities (Tulli, 2002), rigid curriculum design (Anita, 2000; Jha, 2008), inadequate role of instructors (Dev & Belfiore, 1996), and infrastructural hurdles (Sawhney, 2015) are examples of these obstacles.

Theoretical Framework of the Study

Interactionist Model of Disability

According to Evans and Broido (2011), interactions between the environment, the person, and their disability determine their ability to learn in a specific setting. Each aspect is dynamic: the environment can be enabling or disabling, people can make effective decisions, and impairments can range from minor to severe. The three factors also affect one another. The environment may help to improve an individual's ability to make effective choices, and individuals may affect the circumstances they face, people's ability to make effective choices can be influenced by their level of disability, and the choices they make can change the impact of the environment (depending on the type of disability). In the context of Indian Universities, this model emphasises how the interaction between a student's disability and the university environment affects their experience.

Students with disabilities face several challenges in Indian higher education institutions, including issues with accessibility, support services, attitudes, and inclusivity. Despite the efforts to implement inclusive policies and provide adjustments, there are frequently gaps between legislation and reality. Efforts to address these concerns include campaigning for better policies, increasing disability awareness, improving accessibility, providing required accommodations, and cultivating a more inclusive campus culture. Collaboration is essential for building an environment in which students with disabilities can succeed academically and socially. Collaboration between disability service offices, faculty, administration, and students themselves is essential.

Challenges Faced by Students with Disabilities in Accessing Higher Education

Although the Government of India has attempted to create policies and legislative acts for students with disabilities, their implementation efforts have not resulted in an inclusive environment for the universities, nor have reached their goal of "education for all" across the country (Kohma, 2012). It is because of various challenges which are both external and internal as well (Johan, 2002 & Jha, 2007). The status of students with disabilities in Indian higher education has seen improvements in recent years but continues to face significant challenges. Efforts have been made to promote inclusivity, such as the Rights of Persons with Disabilities Act in 2016, mandating a 5% reservation for students with disabilities in educational institutions. Despite this, several challenges were faced by them.

Students with disabilities have equal rights, these include the freedom to be citizens of the nation, the right to self-determination, the right against discrimination, and the right to self-respect and dignity. Every individual may become more competent through education, which contributes to their overall development in several areas. To meet the needs of students with disabilities in higher education to compete in areas of life that are usually created in society and lead to a better and more effective life, the rights behind all programs, policies, benefits, and provisions for these students should be given top priority. Their issues and challenges in pursuing higher education include issues like the educational institution's physical infrastructure, transportation facilities, the availability of assistive technology, and support services, and the need to increase financial aid for their benefits (Zuber & Ramakrishna, 2021).

Challenges to Higher Education

- *Physical Accessibility:* Physical access to the institution in which they are educated is seen as one of the most significant impediments for students with disabilities. Access concerns are being noted increasingly frequently on institutional campuses (Zuber & Ramakrishna, 2021). This is one of the biggest challenges for students with disabilities. Most school and college facilities lack the infrastructure required to make the institution physically accessible to students with disabilities. These schools lack wheelchair ramps and sufficient tactile paths for students with visual impairments. There is a lack of elevators and lifts in multi-story buildings. Toilets are frequently inaccessible. Institutions are inaccessible to students with disabilities due to heavy doors and narrow, dimly lighted entrances. Many universities lack the necessary infrastructure and facilities to accommodate students with disabilities. Wheelchair ramps, accessible restrooms, Braille, signage, and assistive technology are all examples of physical challenges they faced on the campuses. A lack of these resources restricts their mobility and access to educational opportunities.
- *Attitudinal Barrier:* Students with disabilities are socially isolated by students without disabilities in less developed communities due to fear, ignorance, and a lack of knowledge. Poverty, gender, and caste all marginalize many people (Dr. Vandana Dua & Dr. Ankur Dua, 2017). Acceptance by peers is a considerably harder difficulty for college/university students with disabilities. Negative peer attitudes are a major impediment to full social inclusion for students with disabilities at school (Dutta & Banerjee). The attitude of regular teachers is another significant barrier that students perceive. Attitudinal barriers complicate the inclusion process in educational

institutions/universities for students with disabilities in higher education (Rao & Gartin, 2003).

- *Institutional Barrier:* Faculty, staff, and students are frequently unaware of the needs and challenges that students with disabilities experience. As a result, insensitivity, discrimination, and inadequate support systems might arise. Specialised support services such as sign language interpreters, note-takers, exam scribes, and accessible learning materials may be lacking at universities. This absence can have a substantial influence on students with disabilities and their learning experiences. Many students with disabilities may find it difficult to afford assistive devices, specialist software, or personal assistance. The lack of financial assistance or scholarships available expressly for these students increases the problem.

Milestone in Disability-Inclusive Education

- **1999:** Adopted the National Trust for Welfare of Persons with Autism, Cerebral Palsy, Mental Retardation, and Multiple Disabilities Act.
- **2005:** The National Curriculum Framework, which promotes respect for learner diversity was adopted.
- **2006:** The National Policy for Persons with Disabilities.
- **2008:** The Convention on the Rights of Persons with Disabilities was ratified.
- **2009:** The Right of Children to Free and Compulsory Education Act.
- **2015:** Accessible India Campaign (Sugamya Bharat Abhiyan).
- **2016:** The Rights of Persons with Disabilities Act was passed.
- **2018:** Samagra Shiksha, the national flagship education program was launched.
- **2020**: The National Education Policy.

Conclusion

In terms of accessibility and support systems, nearly all the participants listed several challenges they experienced with technology, academic knowledge, and physical access. Most students stated that the main obstacle faced by study participants was inappropriate architectural access. In response to questions about accessibility, participants brought out the institutional disregard for infrastructure and even for distinction when it comes to various forms of assistance like technical devices, scholarships, training, and placement. Even though India has implemented several policies and programmes aimed at attaining the goal of universal education, the objective would remain unattainable unless students with disabilities are included.

To solve these issues, efforts must be made to develop inclusive policies, provide the required infrastructure and resources, educate the university community, provide financial assistance, and establish an inclusive and supportive environment for students with disabilities. Legal frameworks such as India's Rights of Persons with Disabilities Act, 2016, try to address these concerns, but implementation and awareness are essential for lasting change. One of the major challenges for students with disabilities pursuing higher education in India is a lack of accessible facilities, including classrooms, laboratories, libraries, dining halls, restrooms, and dining halls. Another significant hurdle for young people with disabilities in higher education is a lack of physical and social access.

References

Ahmad, W. (2012). *Higher Education for Persons with Disabilities in India Challenges and Concerns*. [online] Available at: https://www.researchgate.net/publication/325619759_Higher_Education_for_Persons_with_Disabilities_in_India_Challenges_and_Concerns

Bera, M., & Parmanik, Dr. K. C. (2023, August 8). *Access Challenges For Students With Disabilities In Higher Education*. https://ijcrt.org/papers/IJCRT2308503.pdf

AISHE. (2010-20). *All India Survey on Higher Education*. Ministry of Human Resource Development, Department of Higher Education, Government of India

Armstrong, D. (2003). *Experiences of Special Education*. https://doi.org/10.4324/9780203380550

Avramidis, E., Bayliss, P., & Burden, R. (2000). A survey into mainstream teachers' attitudes towards the inclusion of children with special educational needs in the ordinary school in one local education authority. *Educational Psychology*, *20*(2), 191–211. https://doi.org/10.1080/713663717

Census of India. (2011). *The First Report on Disability*. Registrar General and Census Commissioner, New Delhi, India

Das A., & Kattumuri R. (2011). Children with disabilities in private inclusive schools in Mumbai: Experiences and challenges. *Electronic Journal of Inclusive Education*, 2(8). https://corescholar.libraries.wright.edu/ejie/vol2/iss8/7/

Dua, Dr. V., & Dua, Dr. A. (2017, January). Inclusive Education: Challenges and Barriers. *World Wide Journal – PIJR* https://www.worldwidejournals.com/paripex/page/p/author-guidelines

Florian, L., & Linklater, H. (2010). Preparing teachers for Inclusive Education: Using inclusive pedagogy to enhance teaching and learning for all. *Cambridge Journal of Education*, *40*(4), 369–386. https://doi.org/10.1080/0305764x.2010.526588

Government of India. (2017). *Notification. Ministry of Social Justice & Empowerment, Department of Empowerment of Persons with Disabilities*. Retrieved from https://enabled.in/wp/wp-content/uploads/2017/03/Draft-RPwD-Rules2017.pdf

Mohan, M. (2012). *School Without Walls: Inclusive Education for All*. Oxford: Heinemann

Khan, A. (2019). Disability and Education: Assessment of Enrollment of Disabled People and Their Empowerment in Higher Education. *International Journal of Science and Research*. https://doi:10.21275/SR20922210332

Madan, J. (2007). Barriers to Access and Success: Is Inclusive Education an Answer? Retrieved on August 16. 2023 from www.col.org/pcf2/ papers%5Cjha.pdf https://www.unicef.org/education/inclusive-education

Miles, S., & Singal, N. (2009). The education for all and Inclusive Education Debate: Conflict, contradiction or opportunity? *International Journal of Inclusive Education*, *14*(1), 1–15. https://doi.org/10.1080/13603110802265125

MHRD (2019). *All India Survey on Higher Education.* Ministry of Human Resource Development, Department of Higher Education, New Delhi.

MHRD (2020). *All India Survey on Higher Education.* Ministry of Human Resource Development, Department of Higher Education, New Delhi.

NCPEDP. (2001). *National Centre for Promotion of Employment of Disabled People.* Status of mainstream education of disabled students in India.

NCPEDP. (2015). *National Centre for Promotion of Employment of Disabled People.* Status of mainstream education of disabled students in India.

National Education Policy 2020 - Ministry of Education. (n.d.). https://www.education.gov.in/sites/upload_files/mhrd/files/NEP_Final_English.pdf

Pandey, A. (2021). Roadblock on the way of disabled students in the higher education. *Issues and Ideas in Education*, *9*(2), 97–102. https://doi.org/10.15415/iie.2021.92009

RPWD. (2016). The rights of persons with disabilities act, 2016 ... - *legislative*. (n.d.). from https://legislative.gov.in/sites/default/files/A2016-49_1.pdf

Sawhney S. (2015). Unpacking the nature and practices of inclusive education: The case of two schools in Hyderabad, India. *International Journal of Inclusive Education*, 19(9), 887–907. https://doi.org/10.1080/13603116.2015.1015178

Sebba, J., & Ainscow, M. (1996). International developments in inclusive schooling: Mapping the issues. *Cambridge Journal of Education*, *26*(1), 5–18. https://doi.org/10.1080/0305764960260101

Srivastava, M., et al., (2013). Inclusive Education in developing countries: A closer look at its implementation in the last 10 years. *Educational Review*, *67*(2), 179–195. https://doi.org/10.1080/00131911.2013.847061

Rao, S., & Gartin, B. (2003). Attitudes of University Faculty toward Accommodations to Students with Disabilities. *The Journal for Vocational Special Needs Education*, 25(2). Retrieved from http://www.specialpopulations.org/Vol%2025%20-%20Chapters/10Rao.pdf

UNESCO. (1994). *The Salmanaca Statement and Framework for Action on Special Needs Education.* Paris: UNES. [Google Scholar]

Zuber, M., & Ramakrishna, P., (2021). Challenges encountered by persons with disabilities in accessing higher education in India. *Journal for the Child Development, Exceptionality and Education*, 2(1), 11-17.

16

Employment Challenges and Support Strategies for Dyslexic Adults

A Literature Review

Sana Mukhtar Khan
Eram Nasir

Introduction

Adulthood is a phase of life that marks a significant transition from adolescence to maturity. It is a period characterised by increased independence, responsibility, and self-discovery. As adults, we assume various roles and responsibilities, such as pursuing higher education, establishing a career, managing finances, and building personal relationships. This stage often comes with its fair share of challenges, requiring us to make important decisions, face the consequences of our actions, and learn from our mistakes. Adulthood provides opportunities for personal growth and development as we navigate through the complexities of life, shaping our identities and aspirations. It is a time when we strive to find a balance between our personal goals and societal expectations, while also contributing to the well-being of our communities. Ultimately, adulthood offers us the chance to embrace our individuality, face challenges, and create a fulfilling and meaningful life.

In the realm of cognitive diversity, the experiences of people with learning difficulties shed light on a complicated and often misunderstood environment. Learning disabilities, which include a range of conditions like dyslexia, dysgraphia, and ADHD, are defined by constant problems with knowledge acquisition, processing, and application. Learning difficulties, in contrast to temporary setbacks or barriers in the classroom, are chronic disorders that continue into adulthood. Adults having difficulties in their learning face unique challenges in navigating the complexities of everyday life. Learning disabilities can manifest in various ways, affecting an individual's ability to acquire, process, or retain information. These challenges may impact their educational pursuits, career opportunities, and personal relationships. It is important to recognise learning disabilities as conditions that continue throughout life to be able to promote empathy, understanding, and the application of supporting strategies that enable people to successfully manage their own learning journeys throughout their lives.

Specific Learning disorders are neurological disorders that influence a person's ability to process, store and propagate information. These disorders are detected in early school aged children and sometimes not diagnosed until adulthood. Besides having low academic achievement, learning disorders can create problems like an increased risk of greater psychological distress, poor mental health, underemployment, unemployment and dropping out of school.

Dyslexia is a difficulty in the acquisition of literacy skills (ability to read, write, speak, and comprehend written and spoken language) that is neurological in origin. The World Health Organisation defines it as a distinct type of learning disability characterised by particular deficiencies in information processing that lead to challenges with speaking, listening, reasoning, writing, spelling, or performing mathematical computations. Therefore, dyslexic students tend to avoid activities that involve reading; they also show problems in remembering the sequence of things and most usually are not able to sound out the pronunciation of (more or less) unfamiliar words. Early identification and treatment are directly linked to better educational achievement and quality life.

Researchers and other experts have been perplexed by the actual cause of dyslexia for nearly a century and a half (Nicolson & Fawcett, 2010), but no clear definition or fundamental causes of dyslexia have been identified. The main signs of literacy deficit are not as readily apparent in adulthood compared to when they were in childhood because of corrective techniques that have evolved, making the diagnosis of dyslexia more difficult (Leather et al. 2011). For instance, a child, who had dyslexia as a child, overcame difficulties by getting early interventions. The effective utilization of assistive devices and audiobooks in adulthood can cover the long-lasting impact of dyslexia on literacy.

Spelling and reading issues have a variety of effects on people's educational and professional paths. Compared to their secondary school peers, young people with these issues typically select less rigorous academic programmes. (Savolainen, Ahonen, Aro, Tolvanen, & Holopainen, 2008). While attaining adulthood many people find it difficult to enter college, career school or a full-time job after completing high school. Either they explore short term jobs one after another or they stay at home in their 20s' which makes them more depressed and life gets meaningless for them with no full-time employment. In comparison to their classmates without learning disabilities (LDs), vocational trainees have lower graduation rates (Stein, Blum, & Barbaresi, 2011). Additionally, they frequently demonstrate underachievement, which can result in feelings of alienation and low self-worth (Leather, Hogh, Seiss, & Everatt, 2011). These young people experience great distress in expressing themselves and understanding verbal, nonverbal and written communication. Additional longitudinal research has shown that persons with LDs work fewer hours, earn less money (Vogel, Murray, Wren, & Adelman, 2007), and hold lower-skill jobs than adults without LD (Stein et al., 2011).

Young people need encouragement, experience, and exposure to new opportunities in addition to extensive support to make them mature enough to become self-sufficient. The adults addressed here need more than what a normal young person needs i.e. acknowledgement of their strengths. They require step-by-step directives on how to perform important life tasks and encouragement to plan their own activities. Parents play a pivotal role in reinforcing their action success by assigning responsibilities to the children in appropriateness to their abilities.

The Study

Rationale

When talking about learning disabilities we always focus upon students in school and the type of support services they need to learn better, but young adults with learning disabilities are still ignored or less addressed. Many researches have been conducted on students with learning disabilities and their challenges in school environment but there is still a dearth of researches when it comes to adults with LDs and their challenges. This paper focuses on exploring the challenges faced by dyslexic adults during their employment and provides appropriate support strategies.

Review

Rutledge, H. (2002) in her study "Dyslexia: Challenges and opportunities for public libraries" tried to investigate about the availability of materials in a public library for those who are dyslexic. Results from a questionnaire survey administered to 114 library authorities were compiled, along with an extensive review of the literature. The study found that resources that would help dyslexic people overcome their challenges are not being appropriately promoted by public libraries. When it comes to taking the initiative to provide resources for individuals with dyslexia, library professionals and influential dyslexic organisations are helpless.

Illingworth, K. (2005) in his study "The effects of dyslexia on the work of nurses and healthcare assistants" investigated, using a sample of seven participants, the impact that dyslexia had on the work lives of nurses and health care assistants and what could be done to enhance their working conditions. A qualitative approach was undertaken which consisted semi-structured interviews and interpretative data analysis. The findings suggest that dyslexia affect everyone differently and might affect career choice and career progression. The participants identified dyslexia friendly strategies and made suggestions for improvements.

Morris, D. & Turnbull, P. (2007) in their study "A survey-based exploration of the impact of dyslexia on career progression of UK registered nurses" investigated the impact of dyslexia on the practice and advancement of registered nurses employed in the United Kingdom. A total of 116 dyslexic nurses were included in the sample, and information was gathered using a 12-item questionnaire that asked for both qualitative and quantitative answers. Data analysis of quantitative data was done through descriptive analysis and content analysis was used in case of qualitative data. The findings suggest that dyslexia have a major impact on work life of nurses, written and verbal communication were central but literacy, numeracy, memory, and verbal communication were identified as problematic in varying degrees.

Tanner, K., (2009) in the study "Adult dyslexia and the Conundrum of failure" focuses on the deficit perspective of failure. The study was conducted over a period of three years during TAFE (Technical and Further Education) course specifically designed for adults with dyslexia. The sample consisted 70 students with a mixed gender balance with the majority in the 22-45 age group. Varied tools were used for data collection like focus group discussions, illustrated personal profiles and one-on-one interviews. The findings show that all the students had experienced a sense of adversity in terms of their educational experience. The majority used passing techniques to enable them to operate within a literacy focussed society.

Major, R., & Tetley, J. (2010) in their study "Effects of dyslexia on registered nurses in practice" tried to investigate how dyslexia might affect registered nurses with prime focus on practice. A sample of 14 nurses (3 male & 11 female) who have dyslexia was taken across Great Britain and semi structured in-depth interviews were conducted. Template analysis of the interviews developed five main themes: career choices, decision to disclose, effect on practice, compensatory strategies, and support from others . The study showed that there is still a perception of stigma associated with having dyslexia and that colleagues still don't understand it, which has an impact on disclosure and getting help. Nonetheless, to practice efficiently, registered nurses developed a range of compensating measures, and they placed a high priority on patient safety.

Eila, B., & Bell, S. (2010) in the study "Voices of teachers with dyslexia in Finnish and English further and higher educational settings" tried to discover the challenges faced by them in teaching process what they feel about being dyslexic teachers. A qualitative approach was opted in which data was collected through narrative interviews and further thematic analysis was done of the same. The sample consisted of six teachers (two females & four males). The narratives disclosed that the teachers had accepted their difficulties and come across their own robustness to overcome it. The data also revealed that the teachers appreciate their teaching role and acknowledge the importance of empathy and understanding towards the students.

Burns, E. et al.,(2010) in their study "Resilience strategies employed by teachers with dyslexia working at tertiary level" aimed to deepen our understanding of how educators—in this case, dyslexic educators—developed and applied resilience techniques to address the challenges they encounter in the workplace. Empirical data was collected from six participants through narrative interviews. The results showed that a variety of resilience tactics were used, including task-related strategies, customizing work environments, leveraging social support networks, and fostering self-efficacy and self-esteem. Creating customized plans is essential to achieving a prosperous career in higher education. To develop the tactics that help educators meet professional requirements and give them a sense of autonomy and self-efficacy in their work, self-awareness is a prerequisite.

Glazzard, J. & Dale, K. (2012) in their study "Trainee teachers with dyslexia: personal narratives of resilience" examined the ways in which the individual experiences of two dyslexic trainee teachers during their academic careers influenced their perception of themselves and their professional selves. A sample of two trainee teachers were drawn through purposive sampling and life history approach was applied. Narratives of the participants illustrated that dyslexia had negative effects on self-concept and poor internal locus to control. Personal experience of dyslexia has helped to inculcate a sense of empathy in their teaching practices and has aided them to adopt a particular teacher identity which is built on caring and supportive values.

De Beers, J. et al., (2014) in their study "Factors influencing work participation of adults with developmental dyslexia: a systematic review" seeks to identify the obstacles and opportunities that affect the engagement of people with developmental dyslexia who are categorised based on the ICF dimensions in the workplace. 33 papers in all were qualified for a comprehensive review, four of which concentrated on the experience of dyslexia in everyday life, including the workplace. Eight studies focused on dyslexia in the workplace: two examined the condition generally, five examined professions like teaching or nursing, and one examined young women just starting their careers. Two studies investigated the status of employees with dyslexia after protective laws were introduced in the US and Canada. Two researchers examined the impact of the Anger Management Programme and the introduction of assistive technology on learning disabilities (LD). Only one study looked at the employer's perspective on LD. A distinction between qualitative and quantitative studies was drawn in this review.

Locke, R.et al., (2016) in their study "Doctors with dyslexia: study and support" tried to study the dyslexia's effects on clinical practice as well as coping mechanisms used by doctors to minimise the effect. Six doctors participated in semi structured interviews, six took part through online survey and two doctors were interviewed 'In situ' to allow for observations and coping mechanisms. In addition, employers and educators were also consulted. The participants revealed that they faced various difficulties but had drawn various strategies to cope up with the challenges and never let dyslexia hold them back.

Taylor, K. (2017) in the study "A social constructionist inquiry study on the lived experiences of educators with dyslexia overcoming workplace barriers and increasing their capacity for success" explored the lives of dyslexic educators and how they overcome obstacles at work. A qualitative study was designed to construct reality by interpreting the viewpoints of group of educators built on their experiences and social dynamics. One-on-one interviews, observations and artefacts were used as primary data. Findings suggest that educators experienced various workplace barriers like reading, writing, speaking and social-emotional challenges. Findings also disclosed that these educators use their strengths to stay motivated, endure and self-monitor despite their difficulty.

Wissel,S.,et al. (2022). The study "You don't look dyslexic: Using the Job Demands-Resource Model of Burnout to Explore Employment Experiences of Australian Adults with Dyslexia" tried to explore experiences held by adults with dyslexia in seeking and retaining employment. Fourteen dyslexic adults participated in this study. The JD-R Model was used together with in-depth interviews to investigate possible connections between workplace features and worker wellbeing. Participants from minority groups reported receiving helpful and positive assistance from their teammates. The bulk of participants faced a wide range of difficulties, such as the possibility of mental exhaustion, prejudice, a lack of resources, and fatigue which made them vulnerable to burnout at work.

Wissel,S.,et al., (2022). In their study "Leading Diverse Workforces: Perspectives from Managers and Employers about Dyslexic Employees in Australian Workplaces" attempted to look at the viewpoints and experiences of employers managing dyslexic workers within the company. Using a purposive sample approach, four managers—three female and one male—who have experience managing dyslexic personnel were interviewed in-depth as part of a qualitative research design. A deductive approach was used to analyse the data and categorise the responses. The responses indicated that dyslexia is not well understood in the workplace.

The studies reviewed above highlight various challenges that are faced by employees as well as employers within organisational setups which can be a cause of hindrance in their work efficacy and which need to be addressed with supporting strategies to cope up with them. These challenges are listed hereunder.

Dislexia Challenges in Workplaces

Self-disclosure

The term "dyslexia" still has stigmas that prevent people from admitting they have the condition or that it is a disability. One of the most significant challenges the respondents faced was comprehending and understanding their problems (Eila, B., & Bell, S. (2010). Employees who self-reported their difficulties in research reported a variety of obstacles, including feelings of embarrassment, anxiety, and shame, as well as a lack of confidence to speak up for themselves when disclosing their difficulties. Some workers anticipated potential repercussions after disclosing their dyslexia to a manager because they believed the employee may have had bad experiences in the past (Wissel, S., et al, 2022). Dyslexic employees find it harder to work after self-disclosure since company policies and procedures aren't altered to provide a more inclusive environment. According to research done on dyslexic workers, they struggled with whether or not to check the box indicating that they had a handicap or medical condition. Fears of mocking, losing one's job, being victimised, and thinking that people don't understand the nature of the work were among the reasons given for either selective or non-disclosure (Morris, D. & Turnbull, P. 2007).

Attitudinal Barrier

Attitudinal barriers refer to the negative attitudes, stereotypes, or prejudices that individuals or groups may hold toward others based on characteristics such as race, gender, age, disability, or other personal attributes. These are particularly relevant in the framework of diversity and inclusion.

Employer's perspective: In a report prepared by Alex Woodley and Nadine Metzger with assistance from Sacha Dylan for the Ministry of Social Development, New Zealand (2022) one employer felt that a dyslexic staff member required more supervision and this was more costly in terms of the additional time required to check written work.

Colleague's perspective: The communities of the dyslexic adults fail to provide them with appropriate support due to their prejudiced views and negative attitudes held by non-disabled people. Due to stereotypical attitudes of people around it becomes very difficult for people with dyslexia to disclose their disability to the supervisor due to which they are unable to demand *support required by them for efficiently working in the organisation.*

Organisation of work: The organisation of work in the workplace is a critical aspect of optimising productivity, efficiency, and overall well-being for employees. This involves structuring tasks, roles, and responsibilities in a way that aligns with the goals of the organisation and promotes a positive working environment but it could be challenging for dyslexic adults.

Language- related barriers: Dyslexic employees struggle with email construction, spelling and grammar issues, delayed processing of written material, and the requirement for extra time to perform jobs that require reading and writing (Wissel,S.,etal,2022). These difficulties include matching invoices to product numbers, writing down phone numbers and people's names, comprehending written material, and engaging with people who speak English as a second language (Wissel,S.,etal,2022). Writing briefs, preparing tenders, and developing government documentation are all issues in the non-profit industry. Dyslexic employees in management roles face performance challenges in the construction and manufacturing industries, particularly when required to provide instructions for team members in written format (such as step-by-step instruction manuals) or when required to work at a fast pace (Wissel,S.,etal,2022).

Contractual barriers: At the time of appointment, the newly appointed has to sign a lengthy contract of agreement for which they are given very little time making it difficult for dyslexic employees to comprehend it.

Documentation-related barriers: Documentation was most frequently described as an area of concern for respondents with reading affected by word blindness, handwriting and spelling being the most prominent descriptors (Morris, D. & Turnbull, P.2007). In a study by Locke, R. et. al, (2016), difficulties doctors have encountered in carrying out their clinical duties were reported to be remembering the names of patients, structuring and wording referral letters, and taking case histories. In the education sector, dyslexic teachers reported that it was challenging for them to attend meetings and note down minutes of the meeting.

Financial Management

Financial management involves the activities of planning a budget, setting aside savings, making investments, controlling expenditures, and generally supervising the use of financial resources by an individual or a group. Because of the way dyslexic adults' brains work, getting and handling a salary might be difficult. It can be difficult to figure out how much money you have, make a spending and saving plans, and prepare for the future.

Money management: According to a report submitted by DOSH Ltd. in 2014 physical access to branches; access to cash via ATMs and counters; use of telephone and internet banking; security requirements such as a PIN; accessible information; support from branch staff; and absence of cooperation with support staff and family members are an overwhelming number of difficulties faced by adults with learning disabilities.

Mathematical Challenges: Dyslexia is not limited to reading difficulties; it can also affect mathematical processing. Dyslexic adults may encounter challenges in performing calculations, which are crucial for tasks like budgeting, tax preparation, or investment planning.

Budgeting: Budgeting is a major challenge for employed adults with learning disabilities because when these individuals receive their salaries, it becomes very difficult for them to allocate this money proportionately, whether it be for savings, shopping, monthly groceries, excursions, etc.

Shopping: When it comes to going for shopping or even through online platform, people with learning disabilities find it difficult to calculate the discounted price of any item or even find it strenuous to fill out the available coupon codes to avail discount.

Investment: Investing money can be hard for dyslexic adults because reading and understanding complex financial stuff is tough. Figuring out where to put their money, what the risks are, and what's happening in the market can be confusing.

Using Debit/Credit card: Dyslexia can affect number recognition and sequencing. This may make it more difficult for people with dyslexia to enter their credit card or account information accurately while doing digital transactions. Remembering these numbers or codes may also be challenging. Digital currency interfaces, which often contain multiple elements and data, can be overwhelming for individuals who struggle with visual processing. Some individuals with dyslexia may have difficulties with visual processing, especially when presented with crowded or busy screens.

Job Burnout

In jobs that require a significant amount of reading or writing, dyslexic individuals may experience fatigue and frustration. Dyslexic adults may experience increased stress and pressure in the workplace, particularly when they perceive a need to compensate for their learning difference or fear being judged.

Mental fatigue has been indicated many times as dyslexic employees would require more time to do a task comparatively. They would come in early and stay up late or even skip lunch to do work.

Employees with dyslexia who believe they have unstable employment and unsupportive working conditions are more likely to suffer from poor mental health, happiness, and early burnout on the job.

Time Management

Time management is the synchronisation of tasks and activities to optimise an individual's efforts. It is also the practice of planning and organising how to split your time between various tasks.

In a study by Locke, R.et. al, (2016), doctors with dyslexia mentioned various challenges like prioritising work, sequencing the order of tasks, handover and multitasking difficulties, managing and completing tasks on time and managing administrative work.

Drug administration and calculation were commonly cited as aspects of practice affected by dyslexia. Concerns for patient safety prompted this group of respondents to take more time with these activities or check the accuracy of the drug and calculation with others Morris, D. & Turnbull, P. (2007).

Navigational Challenges

Dyslexia can affect spatial awareness and the ability to visualise and mentally manipulate objects in space. This may make it harder for some dyslexic individuals to understand and interpret maps accurately. Maps often utilise symbols and icons to represent various features such as landmarks, roads, or geographical elements. Dyslexic individuals may struggle with symbol recognition and interpretation, leading to difficulties in understanding the information conveyed by the map.

Despite the numerous challenges that dyslexic adults face in the workplace, it is important to recognise that with the right support and accommodations, they can overcome these obstacles and prosper. By acknowledging and meeting the unique requirements of dyslexic adults, organisations can tap into their creativity, problem-solving skills, and unique perspectives, contributing to a diverse and inclusive workforce. Although these researches are not done in India, the challenges and strategies discussed here can be generalised to the Indian population of dyslexic adults who are at great risk of ignorance. In the following sections, we will explore several recommendations and strategies aimed at mitigating the employment challenges faced by dyslexic adults and facilitating their professional success.

Sensitisation Programmes

In a study conducted by Wissel, S., et al, 2022, major recommendations were stated such as dyslexia awareness training was needed at both team and leadership levels, participants during the research thought there should be a better understanding of dyslexia in the workplace, including the positive and negative aspects of individuals with dyslexia and ways to reduce the stigma and discrimination that dyslexic employees may face. Participants indicated that even with limited workplace policies and procedures in place, those with dyslexia could thrive if their employers and managers are flexible, compassionate, and trained to work with them. Participants also stated that it would be desirable if issues surrounding disclosure and workplace adjustments could be discussed and acknowledged atboth the individual and organisational levels.

Creating awareness and sensitising colleagues

Certain accommodations need to be done in the organisation like introducing a buddy system which will help dyslexic adults to enhance their relationship with their peers and informal one-on-one frequent meeting to provide them support. Giving them precise instructions will offer them the freedom to execute their work with greater frequency. Open communication should be promoted within the organisation and on-going verbal feedback should also be provided.

Self-acceptance and awareness

According to a study conducted by Burns, E. et al, (2010), students with dyslexia or other learning difficulties should be supported in becoming aware of their abilities and shortcomings as learners and as potential employees. Educational institutions can offer particularly well-suited employment contexts for individuals with inclusiveness.

Organising work

- Before starting any written work, dyslexic individuals can benefit from creating an outline or a structured plan. Outlines help establish a clear structure for the piece, ensuring that ideas are organised logically.
- Dyslexic individuals often have strong visual thinking abilities. They can leverage this strength by using visual aids such as mind maps or concept diagrams. These visual representations help to connect and organise ideas visually, making it easier to see relationships between different elements of the written work.
- Large writing projects can be intimidating, resulting in confusion and procrastination. Dyslexic people can divide the process down into smaller, more manageable chunks. This aids in maintaining focus, tracking progress, and ensuring that all aspects of the work are addressed efficiently.
- Dyslexic individuals can employ colour coding and highlighting techniques to visually organize their written work. They can assign different colours to specific categories or themes, making it easier to identify and locate information quickly.
- Editing and revising written work is essential for organisation and coherence. Dyslexic individuals can develop a systematic approach to reviewing their work. This may involve reading aloud, using spell-checkers, or seeking the assistance of a trusted proof reader to ensure accuracy and clarity.

Creating inclusive environment

- Extensive organisational training programme should be organised especially for managers and supervisors which would assist them to create a more conducive and inclusive work environment for employees with learning disabilities. This could involve making space for peer assistance, fostering a psychologically secure setting for disability disclosure, and continuing to include persons with disabilities. Such training can minimise the negative effects of job expectations, reduce job stress, and increase workplace devotion.
- In a report submitted by DOSH Ltd., it recommended the development of improved guidance for bank staff, training, accessible information and guidance for people with a learning disability and their supporters. In addition, they should also teach everyone about what a learning disability is and the ways it might affect people's banking. Training for banking staff on

the guidance, the bank's policies, good practice in support and understanding of disabilities should be provided.

Employment Policies

- As a signatory to the UNCRPD, particularly Article 27, India has a responsibility to aggressively raise awareness, reduce prejudice, and protect the rights of persons with dyslexia. As a signatory, India must comply with the UNCRPD since we have established goals and targets to achieve, a process that is tracked and updated on a four-yearly basis. Employing more people with disabilities and employing more neuro-diverse individuals will reduce stereotypical views of people around
- The RPWD Act mandates a reservation of not less than 4% of vacancies in identified posts for PWDs in government establishments, including public sector undertakings. The government also identifies the posts based on the nature of work and disability. Reservation in promotions in government jobs is also provided. Relaxation of certain standards for PWDs during recruitment is also mentioned. The act establishes special employment exchanges for PWDs at the national, state, and district levels. It provides incentives such as tax benefits and higher depreciation rates to private entities that employ a certain percentage of PWDs.

Technological Integration

People involved in the medical profession can use medical apps to check drug names and formulas. Various speech-to-text apps like Google Docs Voice Typing, Microsoft Dictate, Apple Dictation, Windows Speech Recognition etc. are available and can be used to convert spoken words into text without typing. Internet spellchecking methods like Grammarly, Ginger, Hemingway Editor etc. can be used to avoid spelling errors.

Relevant Job Resources

A comprehensive review of workplace policies and methods is required to ensure that hiring procedures are just, equitable, and clear in terms of the types of resources available for employees with learning disabilities and that employees are made aware of all resources available to help them achieve their work goals.

Conclusion

The findings from this literature review shed light on the significant employment challenges encountered by dyslexic adults. Through a comprehensive synthesis of multiple research studies, it is evident that dyslexic adults face various obstacles in the workplace, including difficulties in recruitment processes, limited access to suitable accommodations, and the impact of societal stigma. However, the analysis also underscores the potential for dyslexic adults to thrive in their careers with the implementation of appropriate support systems and interventions. Employers, policymakers, and educators play crucial roles in fostering inclusive environments that value the unique strengths and capabilities of dyslexic individuals. By adopting tailored accommodations, promoting awareness, and understanding, implementing supportive workplace policies, and offering targeted training programmes, organisations can unlock the full potential of dyslexic adults and enhance their professional success. Continued research is needed to explore the long-term effects of interventions and to identify additional strategies that can address the specific needs of dyslexic adults in various occupational settings. Ultimately, by addressing the employment challenges faced by dyslexic adults, we can promote a more equitable and inclusive workforce that embraces the diverse contributions of individuals, regardless of their learning differences. In India there is a real dearth of researches that need to address the concerns related to dyslexic adults who are highly ignored till now. When talking about learning disabilities the focus is only on school going population only but what happens when these people get into adulthood or what about those people who do not receive proper diagnosis in childhood but are now into adulthood. There is a series of question about where are they now? what are they doing? In which sector are they working? How resilient they have become? Etc. Conducting researches on dyslexic adults are the need of the hour in India.

References

de Beer, J.; Engels, J.; Heerkens, Y.; van Der Klink, J. (2014). Factors influencing work participation of adults with developmental dyslexia: A systematic review. BMC Public Health, 14, 77.

G. Stoker, K. Drummond, C. Massengale, C. Bahr, S. Lin, and S. Vaughn, "Dyslexia and Related Disorders Reporting Study," American Institutes for Research, Austin, Texas, 2019.

Glazzard, J.; Dale, K. (2013). Trainee teachers with dyslexia: Personal narratives of resilience. J. Res. Spec. Educ. Needs, 13, 26–37.

Illingworth, K. (2005). The effects of dyslexia on the work of nurses and healthcare assistants. Nurs. Stand, 19, 41–48.

Joseph JK, Devu BK. Prevalence and pattern of learning disability in India: A systematic review and meta-analysis. Indian J Psy Nsg [serial online] 2022 [cited 2023 May 29];19:152-62. Available from: https://www.ijpn.in/text.asp?2022/19/2/152/365472

Leather, C., Hogh, H., Seiss, E., & Everatt, J. (2011). Cognitive functioning and work success in adults with dyslexia. Dyslexia, 17, 327e338.

Locke, R.; Alexander, G.; Mann, R.; Kibble, S.; Scallan, S. (2017) Doctors with dyslexia: Strategies and support. Clin. Teach., 14, 355–359.

Mayo Clinic, "Diseases & Conditions - Dyslexia," mayoclinic.org, 22 July, 2017. Retrieved from: www.mayoclinic.org/diseases-conditions/dyslexia/symptomscauses/syc-20353552.

Morris, D.; Turnbull, P. (2007). A survey-based exploration of the impact of dyslexia on career progression of UK registered nurses. J. Nurs. Manag. 2007, 15, 97–106.

Savolainen, H., Ahonen, T., Aro, M., Tolvanen, A., & Holopainen, L. (2008). Reading comprehension, word reading and spelling as predictors of school achievement and choice of secondary education. Learning and Instruction, 18, 201e210.

Siegel, L., & Smythe, I. (2004). Dyslexia and English as an additional language (EAL): Towards a greater understanding. In G. Reid & A. Fawcett (Eds.), Dyslexia in context : Research, policy, and practice (pp. 132-146). UK: Whurr Publishers.

Stein, D. S., Blum, N. J., & Barbaresi, W. J. (2011). Developmental and behavioural disorders through the life span. Pediatrics, 128(2), 364e373.

Taylor, K. (2017). A Social Constructionist Inquiry Study on the Lived Experiences of Educators with Dyslexia Overcoming Workplace Barriers and Increasing Their Capacity for Success. Ph.D. Thesis, Brandman University, Irvine, CA, USA.

Vogel, S. A., Murray, C., Wren, C., & Adelman, P. B. (2007). An exploratory analysis of the employment related experiences of educators with learning disabilities. Educational Considerations, 34(2), 15e20.

Wissell, S.; Karimi, L.; Serry, T.; Furlong, L.; Hudson, J. (2022). Leading Diverse Workforces: Perspectives from Managers and Employers about Dyslexic Employees in Australian Workplaces. Int. J. Environ. Res. Public Health, 19, 11991. https:// doi. org/10.3390/ijerph191911991

Wissell, S.; Karimi, L.; Serry, T.; Furlong, L.; Hudson, J.(2022). "You Don't Look Dyslexic": Using the Job Demands—Resource Model of Burnout to Explore Employment Experiences of Australian Adults with Dyslexia. Int. J. Environ. Res. Public Health, 19, 10719. https://doi.org/10.3390/ ijerph191710719

World Health Organization, World Report on Disability, Malta: WHO Press, 2011, p. 309

https://www.sciencedirect.com/science/article/abs/pii/S0742051X13000747

https://www.odi.govt.nz/assets/Guidance-and-Resources-files/Employers-Research.pdf

https://www.dosh.org/

17

Impact of Communal Violence on the Dropout Rates

A Case Study of Victim Children in Muzaffarnagar Riots

Shahla Khanam
Md Abu Tarique

Introduction

Education is a fundamental right in the Indian democratic legislative system, and with the 86th amendment (RTE 2010), it has become compulsory for all children up to the age of 14. Through this amendment, every child has been assured the "Right to Education" to contribute to the progress and prosperity of humanity and the nation. 'Every child has the right to education based on equal opportunity (Constitution of India)'. "No child can be excluded from or discriminated against in education on grounds of race, colour, sex, language, religion, political, or another opinion, national, ethnic or social origin, disability, birth, poverty or other status." So, every child should have the right to an education. The Right to Education is a commendable legislation of the Indian Parliament, but the very landmark contribution is smashed during communal violence. However, some children are deprived of this inclusive right due to some circumstances or events. Children are not able to get an education because they are affected by issues- socio-political politico-religious or economic (e.g. War, conflict, and violence).

Furthermore, communal violence has a long-term impact on our society and remains etched in the minds and memories of all people, be it children, men, or women, for the longest time. Children may be seen as the most vulnerable and affected by such violence because they depend on their parents and are not physically and emotionally mature, and their education is also affected. Education is a fundamental right, so we should pay attention to it even in the abnormal circumstances created by events of communal violence. Furthermore, The National Education Policy (1986) emphasises establishing a national education system and institutions to support national integration and several constitutional provisions (Bunker, U., & Patel, K. 2016). Additionally, every child has been assured the right to education. The national child protection policy suggests that "All children deserve a happy childhood and the opportunity to lead a dignified life safe from violence, exploitation, neglect, deprivation, and discrimination". The United Nations Convention on the Rights of the Child (UNCRC-1989) has also supported a robust legal framework to protect from violence (article 19), and every child has the right to education (Article 28). But here, author examines how it affects children's education during communal violence. Due to communal violence, children are deprived of these rights, including education. Deprivation of education is violence. Just as we know that an individual survives rather than needs basic needs –food, clothing, and shelter- we must add that Education is essential for children's growth and all-round development. Education is the most affected weapon of our society. It has maintained moral values, social fabric, and democratic values and helps maintain communal harmony. According to The Ministry of Home Affairs Issues a Guideline (2008**),** "The maintenance of communal harmony, and the prevention/ avoidance of communal disturbances/riots and, in the event of any such disturbances occurring, action to control the same and measures to provide protection and relief to the affected persons, is a prime responsibility of the State Governments**.**" So, we must pay attention to children's education and keep them safe from communal violence. Thus, education is the most powerful tool by which you can change the world, and a well-educated and enlightened mind would make a prosperous country live within.

The Study

Objective

The objectives of the study are as follows:

- To analyse the state of drop-out of children who are victims of communal violence.
- To study the effect of communal violence on the drop-out rates in terms of male and female enrolment.

Methodology

The population sample of the present study constitutes all the 100 children between the age group of 6-14 years from District Muzaffarnagar who were affected by communal violence in 2013.. The sampling technique is purposive sampling. The data was collected based on a field survey of riot-affected villages.

The investigator used self-designed closed-ended questionnaire for the data collection. To increase the scope and reliability of the study, the questionnaire was translated into Hindi language as the main language spoken in the region is Hindi.

The data is analysed with the help of frequency and percentage distribution in Microsoft Excel. The frequency of responses provided by respondents for a particular statement was calculated. Based on the scoring key available, the responses were converted into percentages and then analysed. Afterwards, findings and interpretations were derived based on the results.

Results

The drop-out-related findings are given below:

1. *Withdrawal year of children who are victims of communal violence:* Following the data on the withdrawal year of the school of children who are victims of communal violence in 2013, the field survey gathered information about dropped-out children who are victims of communal violence.

Table 1: Percentage distribution of withdrawal year

S. No.	*Withdrawal Year*	*Percentage (%)*
1	2013	70
2	2014-2016	7
3	2017-2019	20
4	2020-2022	3

The data given in table (1) indicated that the withdrawal year of children who are victims of communal violence, 70% were in 2013 years, 7% were in 2014-16 years, 20% were in 2017-19 years and 3% were in 2020-22 years. This shows that 70% of children who were victims of communal violence in 2013 dropped out.

2. *Age at which he/she dropped out:* A count of 51% children who are victims of communal violence were under the age group of 5-10 years, 32% were under the age group of 11 -15 years, 14% were under the age group of 16-20 years, and 3% were under the age group of 20-25 years. This shows that most children who are victims of communal violence that constituted the sample were under the age group of 5-10 years.

Table 2: Percentage distribution of Age

S. No.	*Age*	*Percentage (%)*
1	5-10 yr	51
2	11-15 yr	32
3	16-20 yr	14
4	20-25 yr	3

3. *Gender of dropped-out children:* The data in Table (3) showed that of the samples 64% were female and 36% were male. Among the dropped-out children victims of communal violence, a higher proportion of females than males were found.

Table 3: Percentage distribution of Gender of dropped out children

S. No.	*Gender*	*Percentage (%)*
1	Male	36
2	Female	64

4. Class of dropped-out children:
The data in the table (4) revealed that in the class of dropped-out children who are victims of communal violence, 45% were in 7-9th standard, 34% were in 4-6th standard, 23% were in 1-3rd standard, 4% were in 10-12th standard, and 0% was in UG. These data indicate that most victim children (45%) are in the 7-9th standard.

Table 4: Percentage Distribution of Class of Dropped Out Children

S. No.	*Class*	*Percentage (%)*
1	1-3rd standard	22
2	4-6th standard	34
3	7-9th standard	45
4	10-12th standard	4
5	UG	0

Discussions

The study revealed that 70% of children who were victims of communal violence dropped out in 2013. Therefore, we found that due to communal violence, there is a loss in the education of the children. According to an official report by *Business Standard* (2013), more than 60,000 children could not attend their schools due to communal violence. During communal violence, along with the education of the children, their rights are also being denied. They are victims of brutal violence, psychological degradation (trauma) and destruction of their homes and schools due to the ideological nature of communal violence.

The study revealed that 62% of the samples were women, so we found that most of the girls dropped out of school due to communal violence—a higher proportion of women than men were found to drop out of school. Gender inequality in education reflects the unequal position of girls and women in general. According to the Ministry of Education, data on dropout rate by gender related to children in district Muzaffarnagar revealed that girls 8.99% and boys 10.61% at the Elementary level, so that data clearly shows that historically, there has been a gap in male and female literacy rates in India. However, education is essential to change individuals' social and economic status.

Conclusion

When there is communal violence, a systematic process is underway to destroy the social structure, and a distinct gap is being created between communities. During communal violence, children's rights are deprived. They suffer brutal violence due to the ideological nature of communal violence and experience psychological degradation (trauma) and destruction of their homes, schools, and places of worship. Due to this reason, children not only lose education but are also brought face to face with severe physical and psychological exploitation like trafficking, sexual abuse and child labour. Asghar Ali Engineer commented that "communal violence is not only the weakest aspect of the Indian polity but also of Indian scholarship. Its growing frequency and intensity defy the riot controlling state agencies as well as the analytical tools of social scientists. A secular Constitution framed based on a long liberal and tolerant Indian tradition, humanitarian instincts of the common man, committed peace activists, concerned intellectuals, not to speak of powerful state machinery and numerically far larger following of the self-proclaimed secular parties have failed to build up defense against the rising tide of communal violence." All communities are affected by violence. Violence has a lasting effect and remains for a longer time in the minds of humans.

It is observed that educational damage occurs and most of the girls had to drop out of school due to communal violence. Higher proportion of women noted to be school dropouts than men. Article 28 of the UNCRC-1989 emphasises on encouraging regular attendance to reduce the dropout rate of children. In the context of girl child education in India, the condition of the girl child in terms of access to education is very poor because of some rigid norms (Kumari, 2020) and some social issues like communal violence and this is the basic reality of the society, the Indian government has to take serious steps in the education system. Because a good education serves as the foundation of a successful life, and is a sign of social progress; and provides the foundation for a great country.

References

Balraj Puri, (1991). *"Religion, Communal Identities and Communal Violence"* Reviewed Work(s): Communalism and Communal Violence in India by Asghar Ali. Source: URL: http://www.jstor.org/stable/41498468

Bunker, U. & Patel, K. (2016). *Education and Communal Harmony*

Engineer, A. A. (1995). *Lifting The Veil Communal Violence And Communal Harmony In Contemporary India.* Hyderabad: Sangam book.

Kumar, r. (2016). Communal Harmony – The Greatest Challenge for India. *International Journal in Management and Social Science*, 14.

Kumari, N. (2022). *Rights of the girl child in India.* New Delhi: Sage Publication India Pvt Ltd.

Websites

https://mha.gov.in/sites/default/files/ComHor141008_2.pdf accessed on 25-8-2023

https://www.business-standard.com/article/current-affairs/muzaffarnagar-riots-children-elude-schools-113100800410_1.html accessed on 5-10-2023 .

https://dsel.education.gov.in/accessed on 25-8-2023 .

https://www.ohchr.org/en/instruments-mechanisms/instruments/convention-rights-child accessed on 25-8-2023

https://www.education.gov.in/sites/upload_files/mhrd/files/upload_document/rte.pdf

18

Role of Gender in Education of Socio-economically Disadvantaged Groups

Sheikh Mohammed Farhan
Sarika Tomar

Introduction

India is a diverse society that has various cultures, traditions, and identities co-exist in the same society. However, this poses a unique set of challenges where there exist socio-economic disparities among different groups. They are further compounded by the historical inequalities which exist among different groups. In such a scenario, education acts as a ray of hope for disadvantaged communities. It allows for social mobility and is a major tool for addressing the discrepancies which exist in society. In such a socio-economic landscape, a key role is played by gender in shaping educational outcomes, particularly among disadvantaged socio-economic groups.

The intersectionality of gender combined with socioeconomic factors make the challenges faced by the women of disadvantaged communities even more complex. Even after making a lot of strides in enhancing educational access, the prevalence of socio-economic disparities and gender-based inequities still makes educational access for women difficult. The research analyses the complex interplay between gender, discrimination against women, and socio-economic status in the context of education within India. (Desai, n.d.)

It is important to discover the underlying factors which contribute to such disparities. The study further explores how women, groups, and NGOs have contributed to removing the barriers to women's education. The role of the National Education Policy 2020 in improving access to girls and SEDGs has also been explored. The paper seeks to analyse the situation while focussing on initiatives taken in this space to contribute valuable insights. They can be critical in ensuring better policies, interventions and making the educational landscape more inclusive and equitable.

Literature Review

The research is substantiated through the study of relevant literature from governmental, scholarly, and other sources. The article 'Educational Disparities in India' by Jenna Cook (Cook, 2020) describes how there is a great disparity in the educational system of India. The rate of female literacy in India is only 62.3% which is much behind the global rate of 79.9%. The issue of education is not only a financial one as discussed by Sushrut Desai in her article 'Gender Disparity in Primary Education: The Experience in India'. (Desai, n.d.) Societal pressures and family obligations often force girls to drop out of school early. The lack of sensitivity to the needs of female students like the lack of access to menstrual hygiene products, lack of washrooms, and other eventualities leads to added difficulty in the continuation of education. The lack of education for mothers, also has an adverse impact on the education of the family, as educational disparities become an intergenerational issue.

The National Education Policy 2020 has special provisions for Socially and Economically Disadvantaged Groups (SEDGs). (Ministry of Human Resource Development, 2020) It specifically includes girls as a disadvantaged group and has several provisions for ensuring that they have access to education. It has been made after a comprehensive analysis of data over the years which showed that girls face additional barriers to education due to gender. It includes initiatives like free education, gender sensitisation of teachers, construction of schools in remote areas, female washrooms, and more. The policy forms an important standpoint for the study of the future of the education of women, particularly those from disadvantaged communities, as it will form the basis of related policies formulated by the Government in the coming years.

Gender and Socio-economic Disparities

The disparities become particularly pronounced when viewed through the lens of gender. The inequalities are exacerbated when gender is also added to the socio-economic disparities faced by disadvantaged social groups. This limits the access of women and girls to education and economic opportunities. There exists a lack of infrastructure, institutions and educators which become roadblocks for women seeking educational advancement. Moreover, gender-based norms are deeply entrenched in our society which restrict the agency of women. Their role is often defined by their gender and limited to a role in domestic households. (Desai, n.d.)

This is evidenced by lower rates of enrolment in educational institutes, high dropout rates, and limited access to family support for seeking higher education. Therefore, in most cases, women of such communities are left to fend for themselves with their self-acquired knowledge and no opportunity to hone their skills further. This condemns them to the mercy of the male members of the household and makes it difficult for them to get an opportunity to escape the shackles of poverty. This is furthered by a system that often neglects the needs of women and leads to the perpetuation of a cycle of disadvantage. (Cook, 2020)

Contributing Factors

A. *Child Marriage*: One of the primary causes of Indian girls' disproportionately low access to education is child marriage. 102 million of India's 223 million child brides were married before the age of 15, making the country the world leader in child marriages in 2016. In contrast, by the age of 18, only 4% of Indian men were married. (UNICEF, 2019)

Owing to poverty, patriarchal ideals, and cultural customs, families frequently place a higher priority on a daughter's marriage than her education. Many girls are married off before completing their schooling because marriage is viewed as a more pressing priority. (Babones & Chase-Dunn, 2012). In India, girls are sometimes referred to as "paraya dhan," a phrase that reflects the societal belief that daughters are a liability.

The word paraya, which means "not one's own," and the word dhan, which means "property and wealth," both allude to the cultural notion that girls should be given up by their father's ownership of them when they marry. Since they are usually the ones who handle most household duties, wives frequently have to drop out of school. Even though females have the choice to pursue their education after marriage, early pregnancies, rigid gender norms, poverty, and the necessity of having domestic help at home make it uncommon for them to do so. (Khan, 2012)

B. *Lack of Menstrual Hygiene:* Ineffective management of menstrual hygiene is frequently a contributing cause to girls' inability to attend school. A lack of accessibility combined with poverty makes it difficult for some girls to get the necessary period supplies. Furthermore, a lot of females don't know why they get their period every month, what happens during their menstrual cycle, or how to preserve their health. In addition, females frequently report remaining at home to avoid shame because of the likelihood that their menstrual blood will stain or leak through their clothing. Over 23 million Indian girls drop out of school each year as a result of inadequate supplies and inadequate knowledge about personal hygiene. (Sivakami, Eijk, Thakur, Kakade, & Patil, 2019)

One in five girls reported missing school because of their menstruation in a study on girls' attendance at schools in rural India. Furthermore, of the females who did go to school, 45% claimed that they had trouble focusing because of their period, and 36% said that they were afraid of losing the pad or cloth in school or that it would smell. More than 80 percent of the girls in the poll were cloth-wearing and did not have access to tampons or sanitary pads. (Bhattacharya, 2019)

C. *Child Labour:* One of the main causes of girls' insufficient education is child labour. They lose out on prospects for success and experience emotional, social, or physical development problems as a result of child labour. Child labour specifically hinders a child's capacity to attend and actively participate in school. Generally speaking, there are two types of child labour: domestic child labour, which is when a child works at home, and child labour that engages children in particular companies for financial gain. With 10.1 million child labourers recorded in India, it has one of the highest rates of child labourers worldwide. (UNICEF, n.d.)

It is harder for the government to keep an eye on homes than it is on factories and corporations. This results in a huge population of domestic workers, the most of whom being young girls. These females may struggle to keep up with their coursework or miss school, which occasionally leads to their dropout. Even if they are able to go to school and do their assignments, they frequently miss out on extracurricular activities and other advantageous possibilities. (Srivastava, 2019)

Role of Women beyond the Domestic Sphere

In the intricate tapestry of socioeconomically challenged communities in India, the multifaceted role of women as educators and mentors within the familial framework emerges as a critical nexus for examination within the broader context of this research paper. Beyond the stereotypes that are attached to them, women in these communities are transforming agents who have a significant impact on the educational paths that their families take. This thorough analysis explores the many aspects of a woman's role, focusing especially on her dual role as mentor and educator. In her role as a teacher, she not only transfers academic knowledge but also acts as a guardian of cultural values, ethical precepts, and a strong passion for education within the family. (Pandey & Pandey, 2020)

Furthermore, her role as a mentor extends well beyond the academic realm, encompassing a spectrum of guidance on life choices, career paths, and personal growth. In the rich sociocultural landscape of disadvantaged communities, these women become architects of holistic development, shaping the moral compass and aspirations of their family members. Their transformative role as educators and mentors expands to address broader societal dimensions, encompassing health, community engagement, and resilience-building.

Women play an important role as guardians of the culture of the community. They are able to instil not only a love for learning but also impart crucial knowledge about the health and well-being of the families. They provide essential information. Once educated, women play an important role in disseminating health-related awareness, contributing to the overall well-being of their families, especially in communities where access to formal healthcare is limited. Their mentoring involves building communal relationships, supporting group projects, and developing fortitude in the face of social and economic hardships. Due to this complex role, women are positioned to play a major part in shaping not just the advancement of education but also the fabric of society as a whole and well-rounded advancement in settings where socioeconomic conditions are difficult.

National Education Policy 2020 and Gender Inclusivity

Categorization of Girls Under NEP

The National Education Policy (NEP), 2020, explicitly classifies female and transgender people as members of Socio-Economically Disadvantaged Groups (SEDGs) according to their gender identities. In addition, socio-cultural identities, geographic identities, and socioeconomic circumstances are among its other classifications. These comprise victims of human trafficking, their offspring, residents of isolated places, and more. (NCERT, 2020)

The NEP's primary goal is to promote "Equitable and Inclusive Education." This aims to guarantee that every child, regardless of background or gender identity, has equal access to educational opportunities. It is attempted to address the issues of youngsters who identify as female or transgender. To support this, the policy further stipulates that in order to guarantee that students in these categories receive an equal and high-quality education, a Gender Inclusion Fund (GIF) must be established. (Ministry of Education, 2023)

Samagra Shiksha 2.0 and Other Initiatives Under NEP for Girls

For the girl children, the objectives are being met through the dedicated provisions under Samagra Shiksha 2.0 which provides specific resources for the SEDGs. The initiatives under the scheme include, opening schools in neighbourhoods to make educational access easier for girls. It further seeks to provide free uniforms and text-books to girls up to the 8th class. This is done to take away the financial burden of educating girls, which had often been a major roadblock for their education. Moreover, to counter the lack of teachers, there has been the appointment of additional teachers and construction of residential quarters for teachers in remote and hilly areas to ensure the spread of education. (Ministry of Education, 2020)

A stipend will also be provided to girls in Classes I through XII who belong to the Children with Special Needs (CWSN) to support their continued education. Creating a welcoming and encouraging learning environment in the classroom requires several actions, including the installation of separate restrooms for girls, the creation of gender-sensitive teaching and learning materials, such as textbooks, and educational programs like teacher sensitisation programmes (Ministry of Education, 2020)

The provision of gender-specific restrooms caters to the unique requirements of female students, guaranteeing their comfort and fostering a positive learning environment. Programmes for teacher sensitization are essential in helping educators become more conscious of and understanding gender issues, which in turn motivates them to implement gender-inclusive teaching methods. Furthermore, gender-sensitive textbooks and other teaching and learning resources work to dispel misconceptions and advance fair representation of both genders in the curriculum. These all-encompassing initiatives support equitable opportunities and girls' involvement in the educational process, which helps to create a more inclusive educational system.

Analysis of the NEP and its Role in Addressing Gender Disparity

The NEP deserves praise for its efforts towards achieving gender parity. Still, there are a number of areas that may need improvement. Enhancing females' access to education is the primary objective of the NEP's gender equality plan. The underlying gender disparities in the educational system have not been fully addressed, despite the fact that this is an important step in the battle for gender equality. Examining the ways in which gender stereotypes impact the content found in textbooks and the teaching techniques applied in the classroom is crucial.

The NEP's focus on skill development and vocational education could perpetuate gendered roles and norms. For example, vocational programmes that are typically associated with women, including cooking, sewing, and beauty culture, may limit the professional options available to women and reinforce gender stereotypes. This could also limit their career opportunities. (Mandal, 2023)

The intersectional nature of gender discrimination has not fully been taken into account. Policies aimed at promoting gender equality frequently ignore the various forms of discrimination that women from marginalised communities face such as Dalit, tribal, and disabled women.

The NEP's emphasis on commercialising and privatising education may have a disproportionately negative effect on women and girls from low-income families. The rising expense of education combined with the focus on skills relevant to the market may make it more difficult for women and girls from low-income families to receive high-quality education. (Payyanandan, 2020)

This suggests that while tackling gender gaps in the education system requires a more sophisticated and interdisciplinary approach, the NEP's emphasis on gender equality is praiseworthy. This would entail addressing the intersectional nature of gender, looking at how gender stereotypes affect instructional methods, and making sure that regulations don't perpetuate pre-existing gendered norms and roles.

Power of Advocacy: Women Championing Grassroots and Policy Change for Disadvantaged Populations

Grassroots Advocacy

The women who belong to disadvantaged communities understand the core issues faced by their population in a better way. They are able to address these challenges effectively. This is achieved by directly working with the affected communities to find solutions and build resilience. The process of grassroots advocacy involves:

- *Mobilising communities*: Women leaders can bring people together, raise awareness about local issues, and empower them to act for positive change.
- *Developing and implementing community-based solutions: Women* often have firsthand knowledge of the resources and needs within their communities. This allows them to develop and implement targeted solutions that are culturally appropriate and sustainable.
- *Building networks and partnerships:* Connecting with other advocates, NGOs, and government agencies can amplify the voices of disadvantaged communities and secure resources for their initiatives.

Policy Advocacy

Women are increasingly recognising the importance of influencing policy decisions that impact their communities. This involves:

- *Lobbying and campaigning:* Women's groups can advocate for policies that address the specific needs of disadvantaged populations, such as access to education, healthcare, or economic opportunities.
- *Holding governments accountable:* Women can monitor and evaluate government policies to ensure they are effective and reach those who need them most.
- *Participating in policymaking processes*: Women's meaningful inclusion in decision-making bodies can ensure that policies are informed by their lived experiences and perspectives.

By combining their grassroots work with policy advocacy, women have created a powerful force for change. They have attempted to bridge the gap between local needs and national policies, ensuring that resources and support reach those who need it most. This approach is crucial for achieving sustainable development and creating a more just and equitable society.

The Study

Statement of Problem

The socio-economic and educational disparities faced by women in disadvantaged communities are further compounded by gender-related challenges. It hinders the holistic development of the women in the community. Women have been taking an active role in various capacities to break the cycle of poverty and overcome these challenges. They play multiple roles as an educator, mentor, community mobilisers, and activists. However, despite their best efforts, there are still several roadblocks faced by them which need to be addressed compellingly.

Research Questions

- What are the current gender disparities in the Indian education system?
- What is the role of women beyond their domestic duties in the promotion of educational and societal values?
- What is the impact of advocacy on women's empowerment?
- How does the New Education Policy, 2020 in India address gender issues, and what are its implications for promoting gender equality in education?
- Can case studies of successful initiatives offer insights into effective strategies for women's empowerment, and what common factors contribute to their success?
- How can research findings on gender disparities and empowerment initiatives be structured to provide actionable suggestions for policymakers, educators, and advocates?

Objectives

- To understand the existing gender-based disparities in the Indian education system.
- To elaborate on the role played by women beyond the domestic sphere.
- To understand the power of advocacy in women's empowerment.
- To analyse the New Education Policy, 2020 through the lens of gender.
- To undertake case studies on how some initiatives have been successful in the empowerment of women.
- To present the findings in a structured manner with actionable suggestions.

Theoretical Framework

The exploration of the role of gender in the education of socio-economically disadvantaged groups involves the application of various theoretical frameworks to understand the complexities and nuances of this intersectional phenomenon. Several theoretical perspectives offer valuable insights into the intricate dynamics at play. Here are some key theoretical frameworks that can inform the analysis in the paper:

Feminist Theories

Liberal Feminism: Focuses on achieving gender equality through legal and policy reforms. In the context of education, liberal feminist perspectives may examine discriminatory practices and advocate for policy changes to ensure equal opportunities for all genders.

Radical Feminism: Explores the root causes of gender inequality, addressing issues such as patriarchal structures within education that perpetuate discrimination. This perspective may highlight the need for transformative changes in societal attitudes and structures.

Intersectionality

Kimberlé Crenshaw's Intersectionality: Recognises that individuals hold multiple intersecting identities, and these intersections create unique experiences of oppression and privilege. Applying an intersectional lens helps in understanding how gender and socio-economic status converge to shape educational outcomes.

Research Methodology

A secondary research methodology has been applied to conduct the research. This involves an extensive review of scholarly literature, academic articles, reports, and case studies to examine women's roles as educators and mentors in socioeconomically challenged communities in India. It also aims to shed light on the existing condition of such women and the challenges that are yet to be addressed to remedy the situation.

The research methodology involves a systematic approach to gather, analyse, and interpret data. Given the conceptual nature of the paper, the methodology will focus on literature review, theoretical analysis, and the synthesis of existing knowledge. Here's an outline of the research methodology.

Literature Review: Conduct a comprehensive review of existing literature on the intersection of gender and socio-economic disadvantage in education. This involves synthesising relevant studies, theoretical frameworks, and empirical research.

Identify key themes, patterns, and gaps in the literature to provide a foundation for the conceptual analysis.

Theoretical Framework: Clearly articulate and justify the theoretical frameworks that will guide the conceptual analysis. This may include feminist theories, intersectionality, social reproduction theory, and others identified in the theoretical framework section.

Apply these theories to critically analyse and interpret the existing literature, offering insights into the dynamics of gender within socio-economically disadvantaged educational contexts.

Conceptual Analysis: Use the selected theoretical frameworks to unpack the complexities of gender and socio-economic disadvantage in education. This involves synthesising information from the literature review and critically examining how gender intersects with socio-economic factors to shape educational experiences.

Explore historical perspectives, cultural influences, and institutional structures that contribute to educational disparities within socio-economically disadvantaged groups.

Case Studies: If relevant, consider incorporating case studies or illustrative examples to provide concrete instances of the conceptual ideas discussed. Case studies can add depth and specificity to the analysis, highlighting real-world applications of the theoretical frameworks.

Policy Analysis: Examine existing policies related to education and socio-economic development, particularly those addressing gender disparities. Evaluate the effectiveness of current policies in mitigating or exacerbating educational inequalities within socio-economically disadvantaged groups.

Case Studies

Educate Girls: It is an organisation that promotes the education of girls in India. They achieve this by employing female students currently pursuing primary or secondary education to go on a door-to-door campaign to impart information to families in the rural parts of India. They encourage them to send their daughters to school by telling them about the benefit of education for girls. Moreover, they also provide training programmes for teachers to ensure that girls stay in school and the quality of education improves.

They have shown a considerable degree of success with reports stating that they have successfully aided over 550,000 girls in rural areas to gain access to education all over India. They have involved over 4,500 volunteers with most of their members being women from local villages. Further, the volunteers are females who realise the importance of their education while doing the work.

Days for Girls: It is an organisation that provides reusable menstrual hygiene kits for girls. These kits include reusable pads and soap for washing the pads afterwards. They are donated to the girls in need and last up to two years. Instead of directly promoting the education of girls, they have taken this initiative to ensure that the menstrual hygiene of the girls is maintained. This is achieved by their volunteers who assemble the kits and the donations of fabrics by major companies. Moreover, they also provide education and training about menstruation through seminars and open discussions. This helps to dispel taboos surrounding menstruation and also helps girls to regularly attend school during periods. They also undertake the job of providing discussions on sex education whenever appropriate.

Findings and Discussions

Gender Disparities in Indian Education System: The study found that gender disparities persist in the Indian education system, with lower rates of female literacy and societal pressures leading to early dropout rates for girls. Factors such as child marriage, lack of menstrual hygiene facilities, and child labour contribute significantly to hindering girls' access to education.

Role of Women Beyond Domestic Duties: Women in socioeconomically challenged communities play multifaceted roles as educators and mentors within their families. Their influence extends beyond academic guidance, encompassing cultural transmission, health advocacy, and community resilience building.

The Power of Advocacy: Grassroots advocacy by women involves community mobilisation, implementing community-based solutions, and building networks for positive change. Policy advocacy includes lobbying for inclusive policies, holding governments accountable, and actively participating in policymaking processes.

National Education Policy, 2020 (NEP) and Gender Inclusivity: Gender inequality is acknowledged by the NEP, which places females and transgender people under the Socio-Economically Disadvantaged Groups (SEDGs). NEP-funded projects like Samagra Shiksha 2.0 are designed to provide females with special resources and assistance, such as free textbooks, uniforms, and stipends for children with special needs (CWSN). The NEP places a strong emphasis on skill development and vocational education, but there are concerns that this could reinforce gender stereotypes.

Case Studies: Self-Help Groups have demonstrated efficacy in promoting entrepreneurship, empowering women economically, and aiding in community development. Successful initiatives addressing the unique issues encountered by girls in education are highlighted by organisations like "Educate Girls" and "Days for Girls." These projects include door-to-door campaigns, teacher training, and raising awareness of menstrual hygiene.

Discussion

The findings show the interplay between socio-economic disparity and gender concerning access to education for women. This shows that an intervention is necessary. Through their many positions, women address various impediments to community development, education, and health, making them significant change agents. The grassroots activism of women for their rights is essential to addressing systemic disparities and fostering inclusive, long-lasting learning environments. While the NEP demonstrates positive progress, intersectionality, gender stereotypes, and other socioeconomic issues resulting from commercialised education require a more nuanced approach. Case studies demonstrate practical strategies for empowering women and girls and emphasise the value of tailored, community-based initiatives.

Conclusion

The research shows that the empowerment of women living in socioeconomically disadvantaged communities is crucial to bridge the gap in their education which is caused due by the intersectional disadvantage they face based on their gender and the community to which they belong. The role played by women in these communities is multifaceted, as it is important for individual growth and removing obstacles to eradicate poverty. Women are harbingers of change who encourage resilience and when provided with education, they further promote educational opportunities in these communities. The efforts of women need to be acknowledged and supported by governmental policies. Non-governmental actors such as activists, NGOs, and Self-Help Groups play an important role in uplifting women of such communities. The complex interactions between gender and socio-economic issues should be acknowledged by policymakers, educators, and practitioners so that the gaps can be addressed in an effective manner. By prioritising education as a driving force behind social transformation and advancement, it is possible to create constructive paths that result in the overall growth of women and their communities. There is a need for a coordinated efforts for education of women through empowering women to ensure that education is not denied to them based on gender irrespective of the social group to which they belong.

References

Babones, S., & Chase-Dunn, C. (2012). *Routledge Handbook of World-Systems Analysis.* London: Routledge International.

Bhattacharya, A. (2019, February 6). *What are the causes of gender inequality in India?* Retrieved from World Economic Forum: https://www.weforum.org/agenda/2019/02/causes-gender-inequality-india/

Cook, J. (2020). *Educational Disparities Among Girls in India.* Retrieved from Ballard Brief: https://ballardbrief.byu.edu/issue-briefs/educational-disparities-among-girls-in-india#:~:text=The%20average%20female%20literacy%20rate,societal%20pressures%20or%20early%20pregnancies.

Desai, S. (n.d.). *Gender Disparity in Primary Education: The Experience in India.* Retrieved from UN Chronicle: https://www.un.org/en/chronicle/article/gender-disparity-primary-education-experience-india

Khan, G. (2012). *Child marriage in India.* Routledge.

Mandal, A. A. (2023). A Critical Analysis of the National Education Policy 2020: Implications and Challenges. *International Journal of Research Publication and Reviews.* Retrieved from https://ijrpr.com/uploads/V4ISSUE7/IJRPR15493.pdf

Ministry of Education. (2020). *Major Features - Samagra Shiksha.* Retrieved from Ministry of Education: https://samagra.education.gov.in/features.html

Ministry of Education. (2023). *National Education Policy, 2020 provides for setting up a Gender Inclusion Fund (GIF) especially for girls and transgender students to provide them equitable quality education.* Retrieved from PIB: https://pib.gov.in/PressReleaseIframePage.aspx?PRID=1944287

Ministry of Human Resource Development. (2020). *National Education Policy 2020.* Retrieved from Education Government: https://www.education.gov.in/sites/upload_files/mhrd/files/NEP_Final_English_0.pdf

NCERT. (2020). *Equitable and Inclusion: Learning for All.* Retrieved from NCERT: https://www.education.gov.in/shikshakparv/docs/Inclusive_Education.pdf

Pandey, M., & Pandey, A. (2020). Indian Woman: A Gandhian Perspective. *International Journal of Multidisciplinary Educational Research, 12.* Retrieved from https://s3-ap-southeast-1.amazonaws.com/ijmer/pdf/volume9/volume9-issue12(6)/8.pdf

Payyanandan, G. (2020). *When Capitalism Meets Patriarchy: How Privatisation In Educations Hurts Women And Girls.* Retrieved from Youth Ki Awaaz.

Sivakami, M., Eijk, A. M., Thakur, H., Kakade, N., & Patil, C. (2019). Effect of menstruation on girls and their schooling, and facilitators of menstrual hygiene management in schools: surveys in government schools in three states in India, 2015. *Journal of Global Health.* doi:https://doi.org/10.7189/jogh.09.010408

Srivastava, R. (2019, August). *Children at Work, Child Labor and Modern Slavery in India: An Overview.* Retrieved from National Library of Medicine: https://pubmed.ncbi.nlm.nih.gov/31477640/

UNICEF. (2019). *Ending Child Marriage: A profile of progress in India.* Retrieved from UNICEF: https://www.unicef.org/india/media/1176/file/Ending-Child-Marriage.pdf

UNICEF. (n.d.). *Child labour and exploitation.* Retrieved from UNICEF: https://www.unicef.org/india/what-we-do/child-labour-exploitation#:~:text=Child%20labour%20deprives%20children%20of,reinforces%20intergenerational%20cycles%20of%20poverty.&text=According%20to%20data%20from%20Census,and%204.5%20million%20are%20girls.

Editors and Contributors

Editors

Dr Jasim Ahmad, Ph.D. (Edu), M.Ed., M.Sc. (Zoology), UGC-NET (Edu), is a Professor at the Institute of Advanced Studies in Education, Jamia Millia Islamia. He also holds the position of Honorary Director of Centre for Distance and Online Education (CDOE) of JMI. Prof. Ahmad has a teaching and research experience of around 25 years; his areas of interests include Science Education, Educational Psychology, Research Methodology and Teacher Education. He has published eleven books and has to his credit around 70 research papers and articles published in journals, around 50 research papers in conferences, 15 chapters in edited books and 16 SLM units, more than 100 invited talks, around 80 workshops, and coordinated several training programmes. 14 Ph.D. degrees and around 50 PG. dissertations have been awarded under his guidance. He has been awarded with the 'Proud Indian Eminent Professor Award 2022' in Teacher Education by IMRF, Andhra Pradesh on the occasion of India's 73rd Republic Day.

Dr Aerum Khan, MSc Botany, B.Ed, MA Education, MA Sociology, DCA, Ph.D. (Botany), Ph.D. (Education) is Associate Professor, Science Education at Dept of TT & NFE (IASE), F/o Education, JMI, New Delhi. She has done courses on *Qualitative Research Methods* from University of Amsterdam, *Feminism and Social Justice* from University of California, Santa Cruz, *Introduction to Philosophy* from The University of Edinburgh, *Psychological First Aid* from Johns Hopkins University, *The Science of Well-being* from Yale University, and *Gender and Sexuality: Diversity and Inclusion in the Workplace* from University of Pittsburgh. She has worked with NCERT, New Delhi, SCERT Delhi. She has been a Visiting Faculty for SOL-Delhi University, IGNOU (continued) and NIOS, and has been Academic Consultant for the British Council. Got published more than 70 articles, chapters and research papers in Botany and Education in National and International journals. She has delivered more than 350 invited talks in different programs. She was the core member of the development team of NCERT for MOOCs for school education on SWAYAM. She has been the Academic Coordinator for the UGC funded project e-PG Pathshala for the subject of Education, joint venture of CIET-NCERT and University of Allahabad. The first online PG level MOOC in Education created by her and team was launched by UGC on the SWAYAM platform on 1 August 2017. She received the MoE sponsored training for SWAYAM Course Coordinators at Chennai, jointly conducted by IIT Bombay, IIM Bangalore, NIEPA Delhi and NITTTR Chennai on the nomination of UGC. In March 2020 she was invited by IIT Madras and JNU, New Delhi to develop video lectures for UG level for National telecast through Swayam Prabha Channels of MoE-GoI, under which she developed 168 video lectures in 5 phases. She is the recipient of the 'Inspiring Woman Awards 2021' from 'Fourth Screen Education' for outstanding and remarkable services in the field of Education.

Dr Ansar Ahmad, Ph.D. (Education), M.Phil., M.Ed., M.A. (Geography), PGD in Disaster Management, Certificate in "Remote Sensing & GIS Technology and Application for UT & Government Officials" from ISRO, Indian Institute of Remote Sensing, Dehradun, is Assistant Professor at the Department of Teacher Training & Non-Formal Education (IASE), Faculty of Education, Jamia Millia Islamia, New Delhi. Earlier he worked as Assistant Professor of Education at Miranda House and Shyama Prasad Mukherjee College, University of Delhi. He has 12 years of Teaching and Research Experience; his area of interests includes Social Science Education (with super specialization of Geography Education), Educational Administration and Measurement & Evaluation. He is a recipient of the International Teacher's Pride Award 2021. Dr. Ahmad is founding editor of a peer reviewed multidisciplinary research journal 'Council for Teacher Education Foundation (CTEF).' He is credited to have published many Research Papers and Articles in various National and International Journals, 5 Books/Chapters and 4 Units/Blocks of SLM. He has delivered 75 Invited Lectures/Talks and attended 50 Workshops and Training programmes. He has been Co-Convener and Organizing Secretary of National and International Conferences, successfully coordinated various Workshops, In-Service Training Programme and Refresher Course for College and University Professors and School Teachers at UGC-Human Resource Development Centre.

Contributors

Dr Anil Manjhi, Assistant Professor, Department of English, Govt. J. Yoganandam Chhattisgarh College, Raipur
E-mail: manjhi.anil3@gmail.com

Ali Asgar, Staff Training and Research Institute of Distance Education Indira Gandhi National Open University, New Delhi
E-mail: aliasgar@ignou.ac.in

Dr Eram Nasir, Assistant Professor, Department of TT & NFE (IASE), Jamia Millia Islamia, New Delhi
Email: eramnasir.jmi@gmail.com

Fariha Siddiqui, PhD Scholar, Department of Educational Studies, Jamia Millia Islamia, New Delhi
E-mail: farihasiddiq22@gmail.com

Gagana Bihari Suar, Lecturer in Education, Bhadrak Autonomous College, Bhadrak
Email: gagan.suar@gmail.com

Jamshed Ahmad, Research Scholar, National Institute of Educational Planning and Administration (NIEPA)
E-mail: jamshed@niepa.ac.in

Prof. Lalbiakdiki Hnamte, Professor, Department of Education, Mizoram University

Lalrochami Ralte, Research Scholar, Department of Education, Mizoram University
Email: scarletchami@gmail.com

Dr Madhu Singh, Professor, St. Xavier's College of Education (Autonomous), Digha Ghat, Patna, Bihar
Emails: madhu408singh@gmail.com

Mahvish Bano, Research Scholar, Department of Education, Ewing Christian College, University of Allahabad, Prayag Raj
Email: banomahvish1997@gmail.com

Dr Mohd Faijullah Khan, Associate Professor, Department of TT & NFE (IASE), Jamia Millia Islamia, New Delhi
E-mail: mkhan44@jmi.ac.in

Mohd Farhan, M.A (Education) student, Department of TT & NFE (IASE), Jamia Millia Islamia, New Delhi
Email: mohammadfarhan064@gmail.com

Mohammad Haider Raza, Research Scholar, Department of TT & NFE (IASE), Jamia Millia Islamia, New Delhi
E-mail: gg9799@myamu.ac.in

Mohd Zuber, Research Scholar and Assistant Professor, Department of TT & NFE (IASE), Jamia Millia Islamia, New Delhi
Email: mzuber@jmi.ac.in

Nayab Parveen, Research Scholar, Ph.D., National Institute of Educational Planning and Administration, New Delhi
Email: nayab@niepa.ac.in

Parvesh Kumari, Staff Training and Research Institute of Distance Education, Indira Gandhi National Open University, New Delhi

Rahul Tiwari, Ph.D. Research Scholar (Law), Govt. J. Yoganandam Chhattisgarh College, Raipur
E-mail: rahuljitc78@gmail.com

Dr Sajjad Ahmad, Assistant Professor, Department of Educational Studies, Jamia Millia Islamia, New Delhi
E-mail: sahmad34@jmi.ac.in

Dr Sarika Tomar, Assistant Professor, Department of Social Work, Jamia Millia Islamia, New Delhi

Sana Fatima, Research Scholar, St. Xavier's College of Education (Autonomous), Digha Ghat, Patna, Bihar
Email: sana.fatima2812@gmail.com

Sana Mukhtar Khan, Research Scholar, Department of TT & NFE (IASE), Jamia Millia Islamia, New Delhi
E-mail: sana.gibbroni@gmail.com

Shabir Ahmed Wani, Staff Training and Research Institute of Distance Education, Indira Gandhi National Open University, New Delhi
E-mail: shabir.94@rediffmail.com

Shahla Khanam, Research Scholar, Department of TT & NFE (IASE), Jamia Millia Islamia, New Delhi
E-mail: shahlajmi123@gmail.com

Sheikh Mohammed Farhan, Ph.D. Scholar, Department of Social Work, Jamia Millia Islamia, New Delhi
Email: smfarhan3366@gmail.com

Dr Shiney Vashisht, Assistant Professor, Delhi Teachers University
E-mail: shiney.vashisht89@gmail.com

Tanvi Pahwa, Research Scholar, Department of TT & NFE (IASE), Jamia Millia Islamia, New Delhi
E-mail: 1tanvipahwa4@gmail.com

Dr Vidyapati, Professor, Department of Education, Ewing Christian College, University of Allahabad, Prayag Raj